Rooting in a Useless Land

Rooting in a Useless Land

ANCIENT FARMERS, CELEBRITY CHEFS, AND
ENVIRONMENTAL JUSTICE IN YUCATÁN

Chelsea Fisher

UNIVERSITY OF CALIFORNIA PRESS

University of California Press
Oakland, California

© 2023 by Chelsea Fisher

Cataloging-in-Publication Data is on file at the Library of Congress.

ISBN 978-0-520-39586-2 (cloth)
ISBN 978-0-520-39587-9 (pbk.)
ISBN 978-0-520-39588-6 (ebook)

32 31 30 29 28 27 26 25 24 23
10 9 8 7 6 5 4 3 2 1

CONTENTS

ACKNOWLEDGMENTS

Many people helped me write this book, and I've been looking forward to thanking them in this way for a long time. My thanks extend back first to formative years at the University of Michigan, where I was enrolled in the graduate program in anthropology from 2011 to 2019. I thank my professors in the Museum of Anthropological Archaeology and the Department of Anthropology: Joyce Marcus and Kent Flannery for stories and cupcakes around the seminar table; Henry Wright and the late Jeff Parsons for rambling conversations in High Civ; John Mitani, Andrew Shryock, and Bruce Mannheim for breaking down subfield borders; Lisa Young for many warming conversations in the coffee range; Jason De León for expanding my awareness of what archaeology can conspire to be; and all the faculty whose classes and guidance got me through. Thank you, too, to the researchers at Michigan and beyond who took me with them on their projects, with special thanks to Chuck Spencer and Elsa Redmond of the American Museum of Natural History for my time in Oaxaca. This book grew out of research I began during my doctoral thesis work, and so I thank my committee members—Joyce Marcus, Kent Flannery, Rob Beck, and Rebecca Scott—for helping these ideas to germinate.

There are traces interwoven throughout this book of the dear friends I made at Michigan, and I thank especially Maire Malone, Chris Sargent, Aaron Sandel, Anna Antoniou, Travis Williams, Bree Doering, Marcela Benítez, Jess Beck, Rachna Reddy, Laura Yakas, V Koski-Karell, Alex Sklyar, Alli Caine, Nama Khalil, Iride Tomažič, Tim Everhart, and the many other grad students who made Ann Arbor my home. Thanks, too, to my dear friend Katie Kinkopf, for sharing her brilliance, for appreciating medieval animals and monks, and for releasing me from the obligation to keep kayaking that day.

The other seedbed for this book is of course Yaxunah, where I spent time as a member of PIPCY, the Proyecto de Interacción Política del Centro de Yucatán. PIPCY has had four codirectors, and I'm grateful to each. Thanks to Travis Stanton for first taking a chance on me in 2013 and for supporting my research in Yaxunah ever since; to Traci Ardren for being a leader down the rabbit hole of the weird and fascinating world of celebrity chefs in Yaxunah; to Aline Magnoni for showing me how to be a careful and community-engaged researcher; and to Scott Hutson for so generously sharing his early work at Tzacauil with me.

I feel strong gratitude for all the members of PIPCY over the years who helped the raw materials of this book come together in ways direct and indirect. Thank you to all PIPCY members and especially those who helped with the fieldwork that contributed to this book: Ashuni Romero Butrón, Roger Sierra, Agustín Calderón, Kadwin Pérez López, Juan Pablo Sanchez-Williams, Anna Bishop, Patrick Rohrer, Vania Carrillo Bosch, Jessica Wheeler, and Carmen Sarjeant. I am especially grateful to the PIPCY members who were with me on multiple seasons of the project and continue to be some of my dearest friends. Thanks to Nelda Issa Marengo Camacho for teaching me about meaningful community engagement, for taking me to the doctor all those times, and for the many vegetarian options; to Gustavo Novelo Rincón, Siki, for revealing the powerful magic of *corte* drawings and for so generously sharing his excavation knowledge with a beginner; to Harper Dine for setting up grids, directing excavations, drawing, and for all our cumbia-infused conversations to, from, and in Tzacauil; to Tanya Cariño Anaya for her wonderful work in the field and her ability to counter existential angst with flagging tape; to César Torres Ochoa for the Tzacauil Acropolis test pit and for making me laugh harder than anyone; to Ryan Collins for being there through events strange and wonderful alike, from glyphs shimmering on the walls to modern caches; to Steph Miller for being the kind of magical person who makes every day in the field feel like a gift; to Julie Wesp for the contractual agreement to open a restaurant with me, for bringing the Yaxubanda together, and for countless laughs in the *comedor*; to Carolina Bendaña for helping me navigate the politics of returnable Coke bottles; and to Dan Griffin for sharing his spirit of adventure during that wonderful surface collection season, for his ability to talk to anyone, and for taking us all to Calakmul. These were the people with whom I learned to approach each day *con corazón abierto, ganas de aprender y actitud*.

I was fortunate to work with researchers at the Universidad Autónoma de Yucatán (UADY) in Mérida who helped me gain new insights into the artifacts and samples collected from Tzacauil. Thanks to Mario Zimmermann for teaching me so much about soil chemistry and residue analysis during the holiday season of 2017, and for becoming a dear friend in the process. I appreciate the support of Lilia Fernández Souza, who mentored me as an undergraduate when I was at the UADY for a semester in 2010 and seven years later welcomed me into her lab as a doctoral student. Thanks to Iliana Ancona Aragón for analyzing the ceramic materials that came out of the Tzacauil excavations, and to all the other folks at the UADY Facultad de Antropología for making me feel welcome during my time there.

I don't think I would have recognized the connections between my work at Tzacauil and a larger story of land sovereignty and environmental justice if it weren't for my time as a faculty member in the Environmental Studies Program at Washington and Lee University, starting in 2019. I'm especially grateful to Robert Humston for trusting me to follow my curiosity both in research and teaching (even when it repeatedly brings me back to strange places like Biosphere 2 and nuclear waste markers) and for supporting me at every step along the way. Thanks to Debra Frein for all our talks, for supporting the Environmental Studies Program in so many ways, and for Tucker basement solidarity. I owe so much, too, to the many environmental studies students whose eagerness to learn encouraged me to keep learning, especially those students who dedicated their time at W&L and in my classes to learning more about environmental justice, including Clara Albacete, Allie Stankewich, Bri Mondesir, Mayahuel Hernandez, Justin Littlejohn, Judy Park, Sarah Hollen, Ella Powers, and Christopher Watt.

My time in Lexington has been so much richer because of my friendship with Marisa Charley, who, in addition to being a treasured friend, has also taught me so much about community building. I'm grateful to Jessica Wager, both for being a dear friend and for being so generous with her knowledge of Indigenous culture, education, and technology. Jess was instrumental in getting me involved with W&L's Native American and Indigenous Cohort, which has been a gift for both my work and for my relationship with this place where I live. I'm thankful to the cohort members, especially Jess, Kelly Fujiwara, Lynn Rainville, Harvey Markowitz, Victoria P. Ferguson, and Tom Camden for welcoming me into their community and their collective work.

Many institutions also made this book possible. My thanks to the Instituto Nacional de Antropología e Historia for granting the permits that allowed our archaeological investigations to happen. Thanks, too, to the local authorities and governing bodies of Yaxunah for granting their permission to conduct this research in their *ejido* lands, and for their cooperation in carrying it all out successfully. This research was funded by generous support from several funding agencies: the National Science Foundation's Graduate Research Fellowship Program and Doctoral Dissertation Improvement Award; the Wenner-Gren Foundation Dissertation Fieldwork Grant; the US Department of Education Fulbright-Hays Program Doctoral Dissertation Research Abroad Fellowship. And from the University of Michigan, the Rackham Merit Fellowship, the Rackham Graduate Student Research Grant, Rackham International Research Award, and Rackham Dissertation Fellowship; from the University of Michigan Department of Anthropology, the Titiev Fellowship and the Department Summer Research Grant; from the University of Michigan Museum of Anthropological Archaeology, the Richard I. Ford Award for Anthropological Research on Humans and the Environment and the James B. Griffin Scholarship; and the Tinker Foundation Field Research Grant through the University of Michigan Center for Latin American and Caribbean Studies. I also benefited from the Lenfest Summer Research Grant Program from Washington and Lee University, the Washington and Lee University Environmental Studies Program, and the Proyecto de Interacción Política del Centro de Yucatán.

While writing this book, I was glad to have opportunities to learn with and from my colleagues in archaeology. Thanks to Amanda Logan for modeling how archaeology can connect to modern food sovereignty and for generously offering comments on an earlier draft of this book. Her work has been tremendously influential for me, and I appreciate all the ways she made this book stronger. Christian Wells was also a reader for an earlier draft, and I'm deeply grateful to have had the feedback of someone as engaged in applied environmental anthropology as Christian. He reminded me to remember the sacred in farming, and for that, as for all the support he's given me since I was just learning my Munsell colors, I thank him.

Thanks to everyone who participated in the 2019 Society for American Archaeology (SAA) session I chaired, "Advancing Public Perceptions of Sustainability through Archaeology," for engaging in thoughtful conversation about a topic so important to me, and especially Anna Antoniou, Arlen Chase, Carole Crumley, Colin Quinn, Christopher T. Fisher, Anabel Ford, Verónica Pérez Rodríguez, Eric Proebsting, Cynthia Robin, Vernon

Scarborough, Joseph Tainter, and Mario Zimmermann. For many productive conversations, thanks to the organizers and participants in other key conference gatherings that cross-pollinated this work: to Anna Antoniou, Elspeth Geiger, and the participants of the 2022 SAA session "Decolonizing Diet: Supporting Indigenous Food Sovereignty through Archaeology"; to Amanda Logan, Sophie Reilly, and the participants of the 2021 Theoretical Archaeology Group Annual Meeting session "Archaeology for Food Justice: From Inequality to Food Sovereignty"; and to Céline Lamb and the participants of the 2018 SAA session "Reconceptualizing Rurality: Current Research in the Ancient Maya Hinterlands." Thanks to my co-editor, Arlen Chase, and to all the contributors to our 2021 *Heritage* special issue on Maya archaeology, for sharing so many effective examples of community-engaged and collaborative research. I was grateful to have opportunities to work through my thoughts about archaeology and food sovereignty at the Maya at the Playa Conference in 2021 and the Tulane Maya Symposium in 2020. Along the way, I'm glad to have encountered brilliant and creative scholars whose work inspires my own, including Miguel Cuj, Daniel Vallejo-Cáliz, Tiffany C. Fryer, and Keitlyn Alcantara.

The year that passed between finishing the first draft of this text and writing these acknowledgments was also a year of emerging from isolation. Looking back I feel profoundly grateful for the reunions and new encounters that, I now recognize, lent their texture and energy to the pages that follow. I thank Maire Malone and Rachna Reddy for our time together in Boston, Julie Wesp for hosting me in Raleigh, and my brother Daniel Fisher for revisiting the Rainforest Café in the Menlo Park Mall with me. I'm grateful to Sister María Gonzalo, OCSO, and the community at Our Lady of the Angels Monastery in Crozet, Virginia, for offering me their openness, hospitality, and guidance. Thanks to Alejandra Campos, who came into my life at the end of my work at Tzacauil and back into it near the end of writing this book, for her wonderful mind and her support.

In late summer 2022, I attended the Colby Summer Institute in Environmental Humanities in Waterville, Maine, for a few golden days of workshops, talks, lake swimming, pool playing, bell pepper breaking, and skygazing. Thanks so much to the organizers and participants of the Summer Institute for the creative catalyst: Chris Walker, Kerill O'Neill, Mel Chen, Elizabeth DeLoughrey, Sunil Amrith, Kathryn Yusoff, Justine Bakker, Tom Doran, Christiana Zenner, and the many other brilliant folks I met there. Thanks, too, to V Koski-Karell for sharing their brilliance with me, and for sharing the many cave-and-mine-related explorations that accompanied me through the late stages of this book.

I thank my editor at the University of California Press, Kate Marshall, for being an advocate for this project and making it all come together. Thanks to the many other UC Press folks who assisted with getting this book published, especially editorial assistant Chad Attenborough, production editor Jeff Anderson, and author marketing communications manager Teresa Iafolla. Thanks to Beth Chapple for carefully copyediting and proofreading the text, and to Emily LeGrand for indexing it. For an earlier draft of this book, I was grateful to have the constructive feedback of reviewers—thank you. I also thank Kathryn Killackey for lending her gifts as an artist to bring Tzacauil alive through illustrations. My gratitude goes to everyone whose behind-the-scenes work made this book a book, and to the trees that made the pages.

I give deep thanks to my family, especially to my parents Roseanne and Jeff Fisher, for their support and love, for bringing me to museums, for letting me repeatedly attempt to bake ancient Egyptian bread in the toaster (using a recipe that also doubled for making paste), and for encouraging me to try to make papyrus from Palm Sunday reeds. My parents gave me what I needed to locate my endless fascination with ancient worlds, and they supported me so that I could make it my career. Thank you.

I can only try to convey the gratitude I feel for Joyce Marcus, my dear teacher and mentor. I met Joyce when I picked her up from the Cleveland airport on October 19, 2009 (she is a hieroglyph expert, so specific dates matter), when she came to my college to give a talk about Maya royalty. The following year she took me on as her graduate student, and she has been generously pouring out her support for me ever since. I think of her every time I have the opportunity to support one of my own students. Joyce taught me that in a world of uncertainties, writing is always available and can provide a sense of feeling grounded again. I've been grateful for that lesson and for the ground I found in writing this book.

This book was written in the homelands of the Yesa and their descendants, among them the Monacan (Lexington and Rockbridge County, Virginia), and in the homelands of the Pawtucket and Agawam (Rockport, Massachusetts). It is built on the education I received while living in the homelands of the Anishinaabeg, the Three Fire Confederacy of the Ojibwe, Odawa, and Potawatomi Nations, and of the Wyandot Nation (Ann Arbor, Michigan). It is based on research I carried out while living in the lands of the community of Yaxunah, located in the homelands of the Yucatec Maya. I am grateful to the Indigenous people who stewarded these lands and waters, who lived and continue to live in mutual relationship with the places most important to me.

And finally, my most heartfelt thanks and deepest gratitude to the community members and families of Yaxunah, who invited me to learn on their land, who contributed their labor to this work, and who sustained me with their friendship and with their food. Thank you all.

Rooting in a Useless Land

SIXTY-SIX MILLION YEARS AGO, an asteroid pierced the surface of a shallow sea and buried itself in the ocean floor, just north of the karst that was to rise from the water to become the Yucatán Peninsula. The force of this asteroid ruptured the Earth's rhythms so greatly that an impact winter immediately descended, a churning of the climate so intense that three-quarters of the planet's species—many of them dinosaurs—died out.[1] The asteroid left a void under the sea, a crater. In the time of humans, the crater will be called Chicxulub, named for a nearby fishing village on the flat plain of the limestone coast. I find Chicxulub listed in a Yucatec Maya glossary. It tells me Chicxulub means "the devil's flea."[2]

Sixty-six million years after the asteroid hits, it's spring of 2022 and a new theme park is opening in Chicxulub. The theme park is called Sendero Jurásico, Jurassic Trail. Tourists come to see the dinosaurs: a fiberglass triceratops perched on a pedestal of limestone rubble, a fiberglass brachiosaur standing alone in a swampy lagoon, the front half of an animatronic velociraptor bursting out from a wall of vegetation. For decades, tourism in the peninsula has hinged on ancient Maya civilization and archaeology, but Sendero Jurásico reaches beyond the pyramids to beckon tourist dollars towards a different past. "Chicxulub is the place where it all happened," says a local politician in a speech at the park's opening celebrations. "It's the place where the course of life on the planet changed forever."[3] Tourists at Sendero Jurásico can commemorate the Cretaceous-Paleogene (K-Pg) mass extinction with hot dogs and dinosaur-shaped pizzas.

At the theme park's grand opening, the politician takes care to remind his audience, with a touch of pride, "We started, not with zero, from nothing, we started with a dump." He's speaking literally: the patch of coastline where

FIGURE 1. Wind turbines on the road to Chicxulub. Photo by the author.

animatronic dinosaurs now roam was previously a *basurero clandestino*, an unauthorized dump. Press releases praise private investors for removing more than five hundred tons of garbage to clean the ground for the dinosaurs, while the people who actually moved the waste—almost certainly from local Indigenous Maya communities—are neatly erased from the narrative.[4] So, too, disappear the five hundred tons of garbage; where did it all go? These questions appear to be not only unanswered but also unasked. The official story of Sendero Jurásico is that it has converted useless land into useful land.[5] The theme park, the public is told, will bolster sustainable tourism in Yucatán.

These shores are no strangers to sustainability stories. On another day, I drive out to Chicxulub from the city of Mérida, passing through the newest strata of urban sprawl creeping towards the coast. The highway cuts across the almost lunar rockiness of the northern peninsula, and in the near distance stand the white metal trees of an alien forest. They are turbines, and this is a wind farm (fig. 1). So many clean energy projects, like this wind farm, enable private companies, many of them foreign, to proclaim net zero emissions. Yet the land required for wind farms, solar parks, nature preserves, and biofuel plantations does not start from zero, from nothing. In a troubling number of cases, these projects occupy lands bought for cheap or downright stolen from Indigenous communities.[6] Not far from this highway, development plans for a Chicxulub wind farm are on pause after local Maya landowners protested that five thousand hectares of their agricultural landhold-ing had been sold without their consent or even their knowledge.[7] Such on-the-ground realities quickly complicate the glossy sustainability stories handed to us in corporate branding.

These stories are haunted by a tension that takes many forms. I sense that tension in a theme park built on the ghost of a clandestine dump, and I sense it in wind farms built on ground where generations of forests and farmers previously lived together. This tension has been unfolding now for hundreds of years, and its messiness makes me hesitate to pin it down with words. But if I were to try, I'd say this tension is a conflict between different ways of being with land. It's a conflict between extractive land relations and mutual land relations. By extractive land relations, I'm talking about actions and beliefs that prioritize economically profitable ways of being with land while dismissing or, often, dismantling most other ways of being with land as use-less, inefficient, and wasteful. This extractive reckoning is predicated on a calculated categorization of useful versus useless.

Mutual land relations situate the value of land not in terms of use or use-less but instead in deeply rooted relationships of reciprocity, symbiosis, and care.[8] Mutual land relations are far older than their extractive counterparts, and mutual reciprocity continues to be the beating heart of Indigenous eco-logical paradigms around the world. Humans on every inhabitable continent learned, over thousands of years and through the teachings of good times and hard times, to practice restraint and reciprocity in their engagements with land. Sometimes that learning came through the experience of environmen-tal degradation, through erosion, extirpation, salinization, and other human-crafted ecological imbalances. This element of learning matters: mutual land relations are not somehow innate or intrinsic—they are collectively learned, cared for, and passed along through culture and across generations of rela-tionship among particular people and places.[9]

Extractive land relations are younger and they, too, have been learned. They have been incubated and refined only over the last five hundred years on plantations, in missions, in mines, in factories, and in company towns. Extraction sits at the core of colonialism and its current manifestations under late capitalism.[10] It is the driving force of global climate change and environ-mental injustice. The doctrines of extraction insist it can continue forever, but by its very definition, it cannot. As Indigenous communities and other advocates for mutual land relations have been telling us for a long time now, a return to reciprocal relationship with land offers possibilities for restoration, for healing some of the damage wrought by extraction.[11] But the struggle to unlearn extraction goes on.

The archives of this struggle between mutual land relations and extractive land relations are stored in the land and seas of virtually every place on the planet. It's why Indigenous Maya lands in northern Yucatán were transformed into cattle ranches, then into henequen (a species of agave once used for producing much of the industrial world's twine) plantations, then back to subsistence farmland and forest, then into wind farms or dumps or dinosaur theme parks. Under the logic of extraction, useless lands have value only when they are converted to useful lands; the practices that accomplish that conversion—deforestation, damming, pollution, plantations—tend to render most other kinds of land relations impossible. Potawatomi environmental philosopher Kyle Powys Whyte writes that settler-colonial land relations "systematically erase certain socioecological contexts, or horizons, that are vital for members of another society to experience themselves in the world as having responsibilities to other humans, nonhumans, and the environment."[12] In Whyte's understanding, environmental justice conflicts involve "one society robbing another society of its capacities to experience the world as a place of collective life that its members feel responsible for maintaining into the future."[13] Extractive land relations uproot possibilities for mutual land relations. Yet even as extractive logic asserts its supremacy, mutual land relations continue—preserved, nurtured, and passed on in pockets of resistance.

Sendero Jurásico feels like an omen, and I study the Yucatecan tourism industry's tentative pivot from ancient Maya tourism to dinosaur tourism with great interest. For a while now it has seemed that when ancient Maya civilization is invoked in popular media, it's been for climate change collapse parables. Unsustainable farming, unsustainable forestry, severe drought, severe violence, political upheaval, societal breakdown—what can we learn?[14] But perhaps, here and now, people have become exhausted with this kind of story. Maybe the market researchers think that people are still hungry for apocalypse but for one that carries with it no lessons to be learned because it is utterly unstoppable. Maybe they think people crave the absolution of an asteroid.

I am trying to offer a different sort of story. Instead of abandoning the lands discarded as useless by extractive land relations, what if there were a collective rooting in those lands? Useless lands are lands stripped of their history; to transform land into a commodity, the deep connections among beings (human and nonhuman) and land have to be uprooted first. Environmental justice conflicts—pipelines, strip mines, water and air pollution, toxic waste dumping, biopiracy, deforestation, land grabs—all rely on the uprooting of history to turn land into a fungible, usable resource. What could happen if history, deep history that roots into the ways past people lived with land for long centuries before colonial logic rendered land useless, were restored to these lands? Rather than the desolation of an apocalypse or yet another sustainability parable, the restoration of history in useless lands offers possibilities for a different future, for a patchy and granular restoration of mutual land relations.

That restoration will be patchy and granular because particular histories matter: these are precise entanglements.[15] Though similar systems and structures may be at play, deep histories of land cannot be universalized. The precise entanglement I engage here takes place deep inland from the coasts of the Chicxulub crater, in an Indigenous Yucatec Maya community called Yaxunah and its collective agricultural landholding, or *ejido*. Between 2015 and 2017, I worked as an archaeologist with Yaxunah community members at the site of an ancient Maya farming village, Tzacauil, in the forested edge lands of the Yaxunah ejido (map 1). Private developers periodically try to acquire that land. Yaxunah landowners have so far rejected these offers, deciding that the long-term erosion of food sovereignty and community access to firewood, building materials, game animals, honey, agricultural land, and clean water outweighs any promise of a brief burst of cash.[16]

At the same time, the calculus of that decision is in flux for a surprising reason: a cadre of world-famous celebrity chefs, along with several sustainable development initiatives, have made Yaxunah a global destination for culinary tourism. These interventions, combined with the increasing vulnerability of subsistence farming, are together—I believe unintentionally—reshaping land relations in Yaxunah. The "useless land" narrative is slowly spreading in the ejido edge lands, bringing with it the growing likelihood that these lands will be sold, or otherwise taken, for conversion into more useful ground.

What would it mean to restore deep histories to these edge lands, instead of transforming them into nature reserves, ecotourism attractions, wind farms, dumps, or dinosaur theme parks? What would it mean to root in useless lands?

ʰ℘   ʰ℘   ʰ℘

I drove by Sendero Jurásico on my way to the beach a few months ago and looked at it with curiosity but no real intention of going in. I can resist a

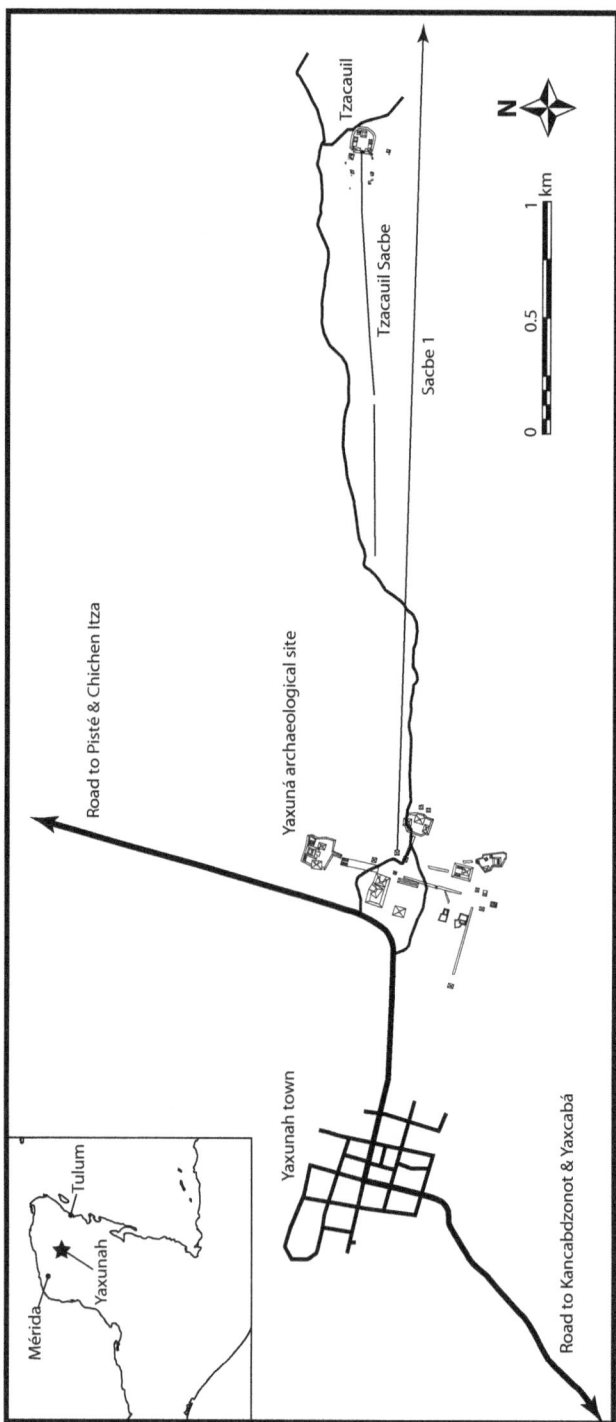

MAP 1. The eastern lands of the Yaxunah ejido, showing the modern town of Yaxunah, the Yaxuná archaeological site, and the Tzacauil archaeological site. The inset map shows Yaxunah's location in the central interior of Mexico's Yucatán Peninsula, as well as the locations of Tulum and Mérida.

half-finished dinosaur theme park, but I can't resist historical echoes. Like this one: in 1978, geologists scouting sites for oil drilling in the Gulf of Mexico were surprised to detect strong magnetic anomalies off the north coast of the Yucatán Peninsula. These anomalies, found during the insatiable hunt for fossil fuels, were the first clue in recognizing Chicxulub as the long looked-for site of the impact crater responsible for the K-Pg mass extinction.[17]

Also in 1978, trucks began secretly dumping liquid contaminated with toxic polychlorinated biphenyls (PCBs) alongside miles of rural highways in North Carolina. State authorities handled the illegal dumping by building a landfill to bury the contaminated waste. The community response to this particular toxic landfill started the modern environmental justice movement.[18]

Environmental justice conflicts have deep roots in histories of colonial and capitalist extraction, but the environmental justice movement is still quite young, an offshoot from the American civil rights movement.[19] The sixty thousand tons of PCB-laced waste dumped by the North Carolina government in rural Warren County would have gone quietly into the ground—and into the water table—if Black community organizers had not taken action, pointing out that the waste posed a direct threat to public health. Environmental sociologist Robert Bullard compiled data from Warren County and other polluted regions to demonstrate, decisively, that environmental benefits and risks are not distributed evenly in the United States: the benefits go disproportionately to white communities, while the risks go disproportionately to Black communities and communities of color.[20] Bullard's first systematic documentation of environmental racism soon grew to include the wider concept of environmental justice, which considers not only the racialized dynamics of how environmental risks and benefits are assigned but also how class, gender, ethnicity, immigrant status, and disability impact those decisions.[21]

Though the modern environmental justice movement is only a few decades old, the origins of environmental justice conflicts themselves reach many centuries back. Most of these conflicts originate, in some way, in the extractive land relations of colonialism.[22] Max Liboiron, a Michif researcher of plastic pollution, is careful to emphasize that colonial land relations insist on their own exclusive dominance: "Colonization is not just about having access—it is also about eliminating other types of relations that might threaten that access."[23] The colonial roots of contemporary environmental justice conflicts are readily apparent as soon as you start to look.[24]

When Energy Transfer Partners asserted access to land to build the Dakota Access Pipeline (DAPL) even though the pipeline posed real threats to the drinking water, land, and sacred places of the Standing Rock Sioux Tribe, their assertion and its assumptions were reproducing deeply historical extractive land relations of the American frontier. Kyle Powys Whyte has written of this conflict, "US settler colonialism viciously imposed harm and risks on the ancestors of the Standing Rock Sioux Tribe that have continued through the DAPL ordeal. It is precisely this social process of settler colonialism that explains why it is no accident that Energy Transfer sought to build a key segment of DAPL through tribally significant lands and water systems."[25]

When the public sanitation needs of rural Black communities in Lowndes County, Alabama, were ignored by the (predominantly white) local government to the point that many Black families were living among open pools of worm-ridden human waste, that systemic neglect was reproducing the extractive land relations and racialized violence of slavery. Environmental justice activist Catherine Coleman Flowers, who brought national attention to the Lowndes County waste crisis,[26] called it "the final monument to the Confederacy."[27]

Land grabbing is a very particular kind of modern environmental justice conflict with deep historical connections to colonialism and imperialism, and it's the one at the heart of the story I'm telling here.[28] Colonialism has always been about taking land. Modern land grabbing both reproduces colonial land relations and enacts new kinds of land relations shaped by late capitalism.

There was a sharp increase in global food prices in the first decade of the twenty-first century. Feeling pressure to shore up agricultural production, agents for powerful countries and corporations rushed to acquire large tracts of land for farming, as well as for growing biofuels.[29] Yet available land was scarce within the political borders of many of these land-hungry nations, and so much of the land being sold in those years was in other countries. Often the sale of lands happened with limited or no consultation with local communities, and with little transparency.[30] Millions (and potentially hundreds of millions) of hectares have been sold in this way.[31] Most land grabbing has been concentrated in Africa, but significant amounts happen in Asia and Latin America as well.

There is no one kind of land grab. There are transnational and domestic land grabs, there are land grabs of huge areas and land grabs of relatively restricted areas, and there are land grabs of varying degrees of legality and fraudulence. Some are clear-cut in their environmental destruction, but there are also green grabs, the troubling phenomenon of land acquisition for ostensibly pro-environmental purposes like photovoltaic power stations for solar power and lithium mines for electric vehicle batteries; well-intentioned or not, these acquisitions reproduce colonial land relations.[32]

Two patterns cut across land grabbing's many shapes and form the core for how I engage with it as an environmental justice conflict. The first pattern is the systemic exclusion of local (often Indigenous) communities from full participation in the decision-making process of land ownership and its transfer. This exclusion can occur as discrepancies between official paperwork and on-the-ground realities of land use, cursory consultation meetings (often without translators for Indigenous language speakers), propaganda campaigns designed to whip up local support (or the illusion of local support) for land deals, or the outright forging of community members' signatures on documents authorizing land sales. All these exclusions have happened in Yucatán.[33]

The second pattern I call the useless land narrative. The process of separating economically productive lands from all other lands has long been a tool of colonial land relations; words like *wilderness* and *wasteland* become weapons by which land is cast as useless or unused and therefore available for dispossession and development.[34] Deployment of the legal principle of *terra nullius*, Latin for "nobody's land," is one of the most overt ways that the useless land narrative has been mobilized to assume ownership over land.[35] Reflecting on the exchanging, selling, and stealing of land, the scholars Eve Tuck and Marcia McKenzie wrote: "The most important aim in recasting land as property is to make it ahistorical in order to hack away the narratives that invoke prior claims and thus reaffirm the myth of terra nullius."[36]

Useless land narratives depend on and emerge from the rendering of land as empty spaces without history. Practices that reaffirm land *with* history, then, create anticolonial possibilities for undoing useless land narratives.[37]

❧   ❧   ❧

The erasure of history impacts land, and it also impacts people.

Let's look at fossils for a moment. Not the plastic fossils next to the dino-pizza stand at Sendero Jurásico, not actual fossils in rock, but living fossils. In evolutionary biology, living fossils are extant species that look very much like extinct species from the far distant past that are known only from the fossil record. Echidnas and crocodiles, ginkgoes and ferns, sharks and coelacanths and aardvarks—living fossils appeared to nineteenth-century biologists as frozen in time, or removed from it all together. Contrary to the initial impressions of these early scientists, advances in genetic research reveal that like any other species alive today, living fossil species have been evolving all along. They are not frozen in time or out of time altogether. Their similarities to extinct species are only cosmetic.[38]

I think of living fossils a lot in the superfoods sections of "healthy" (code for expensive) grocery stores. The branding used to sell packages of quinoa, chia seeds, cacao powder, and a whole host of other allegedly ancient products tends to play pretty recklessly with history: the marketing collapses ancient farmers of the past and Indigenous farmers of the present together into a single ahistorical category.[39] The past is uprooted and appropriated for legitimacy, leveraged into sustainability narratives designed to sell various ancient grains to my precise demographic of white, educated millennials.[40] In many sustainability stories for sale, present-day Indigenous farming communities are cast as living fossils of ancient farmers, frozen in time or out of time altogether.

As with living fossils, the resemblance is superficial. It's true that Indigenous and traditional communities around the world have indeed preserved many farming and foraging practices that originated hundreds or thousands of years ago, along with all sorts of foodways, recipes, preservation techniques, and nutritional knowledge. Many key leaders in the food justice movement, like Leah Penniman of Soul Fire Farm, culinary historian Michael Twitty, and the Indigenous chefs and activists of the food sovereignty group I-Collective, emphasize the importance of ancestral knowledge in creating more just food systems.[41] Reclaiming ancestral foodways is important work happening in communities that have been historically disenfranchised, but that work gets complicated when corporations appropriate ancestral foodways as a brand.

Too often, when Indigenous farmers and foodways show up in greenwashed sustainability stories, the suggestion is that they are somehow preserved from ancient times, unchanged as if fossilized in resin or rock. But ancestral practices and traditions have been changing all along. This has been especially true during the past several centuries of colonialism, capitalism, and planetary climate change.[42] To cast Indigenous and traditional ecological knowledge[43] as fossilized or frozen in time is to erase not only these historical forces but also the legacies of resistance and community survival that enabled that knowledge to be here today. Indigenous ecological practices are more political and more historically contingent than most sustainability narratives will admit.

The same is true for ancient farmers. Archaeological research is coalescing to show that farming communities of the past were incredibly dynamic. Farmers were sensitive to environmental and political shifts, and they sometimes drove those shifts themselves. As we learn more about these past societies, implications for our current time and for our modern food webs distill into clarity.[44]

Here are some examples of what archaeologists are learning. Research projects in the sprawling urban-agricultural landscapes of Angkor in Cambodia[45] and Caracol in Belize[46] are both showing how investment in centralized infrastructure—hydraulic systems and terraces, respectively—initially enable cities to thrive, but over time can become rigid and increasingly vulnerable to breakdown.[47] Elsewhere in the world, patterns are solidifying to show that grassroots agricultural sustainability, developed within communities over generations, can be dismantled by imperial interventions in just a few short years; this pattern holds whether in the Roman Empire's interventions in Turkey,[48] the Aztec Empire's interventions in the Lake Xaltocan region,[49] or the colonial British Empire's interventions in Ghana.[50] Contexts as geographically distant as the Ancestral Puebloan desert societies of the American Southwest and Norse colonies in the circumpolar North Atlantic alike reveal that doubling down on precarious subsistence practices during episodes of climate change can be disastrous, but embracing flexible and decentralized practices can enable community survival.[51] The past makes clear that sustainability is never an ahistorical or apolitical stasis.

And yet most of the sustainability stories floating around us, in ads and in stump speeches, on social media and in corporate social responsibility reports, are comfortably ahistorical and apolitical. I'm certainly not the first to notice how diluted the term *sustainability* has become, and I'm not sure if it's salvageable.[52] If sustainability is to be salvaged, it must be complicated first.

That complication starts with recognizing the deep historical tensions between extractive land relations and mutual land relations. Complication also begins with resisting the pressure to universalize.[53] Specific histories and particular relationships matter. For the specifics and particulars of the stories I work through in the chapters ahead, complicating sustainability means challenging claims about sustainable food and agriculture, even when—especially when—those claims are well-intentioned.

ﻉﻭ   ﻉﻭ   ﻉﻭ

Yaxunah hosts a complex ecosystem of celebrity chefs, and I think pretty much all of them have good intentions. Some celebrity chefs go to Yaxunah to film, some to participate in elaborate cooking demos. Some attend regional culinary festivals that feature excursions to Yaxunah. Some cook with Yaxunah ingredients. Some cook with Yaxunah cooks. Depending on how much food media you consume, the names of these celebrity chefs might mean nothing to you, or they might mean a lot: René Redzepi, Daniela Soto-Innes, Roberto Solís, Rick Bayless, Vladimir Mukhin, Ben Shewry, Christian Francesco Puglisi, Rosio Sanchez, David Kinch, Ricardo Muñoz Zurita, Blaine Wetzel, Ana Roš, Mike Bagale, David Chang, Virgilio Martínez, Helena Rizzo. Those are just the names I recognized enough to include; there are others.[54]

Why do these celebrity chefs come to Yaxunah? A central reason is that the government of Yucatán and a string of nonprofits selected Yaxunah for sustainable development interventions in the 1990s.[55] The first decade of interventions cleared the way for an eventual agreement between Yaxunah community members and a sustainable development nonprofit known as Fundación Haciendas del Mundo Maya (FHMM, Maya World Haciendas Foundation). FHMM facilitates celebrity chef engagement with Yaxunah. The highest profile engagement that organization has brokered to date was in 2017, when Danish celebrity chef René Redzepi worked with Yaxunah cooks and farmers to launch his limited run pop-up restaurant, Noma Mexico, in the coastal resort town of Tulum.[56]

Yaxunah's specific landrace[57] maize is integral to this celebrity chef ecosystem. Before Noma Mexico opened, René Redzepi and his team proclaimed Yaxunah tortillas—made from Yaxunah maize—the best they had tasted throughout their journeys around the peninsula.[58] The pop-up went on to feature those tortillas made by Yaxunah women in full view of the diners. One of these tortilla makers, Rosalía Chay Chuc, was later singled out for an episode of Netflix's prestige food series *Chef's Table*, and now tourists flock to Yaxunah eager to eat her famous tortillas. FHMM opened a boutique tortilla mill in an elegant colonial building in downtown Mérida to sell Yaxunah maize tortillas—mainly, as far as I can tell, to hipster foodies. This maize makes money.

But even as Yaxunah maize is celebrated internationally, the on-the-ground reality for Yaxunah maize farmers is precarious.

Indigenous Maya farmers in Yucatán have, for centuries now, practiced a form of swidden maize farming known as *milpa*. The Maya milpa is deeply entangled with mutual land relations and cosmologies that understand land, water, soil, air, animals, and plants as interrelated persons. The work of a milpa farmer, or *milpero*, is reciprocal: in return for the conditions desired for a successful harvest, the milpero fulfills obligations to these nonhuman persons through sacred practices and offerings at each step of the milpa cycle.[59]

The milpa cycle replicates and depends on the ecological relationship between forest fires and biodiversity. The milpero selects an area of mature forest, and with permission from that land's nonhuman guardians, chops the vegetation, lets it dry, and then carefully burns it. Then, after offering gifts, the milpero plants the burned land with a biodiverse assemblage of maize, beans, squash, and sometimes additional crops, too. Usually a single area of land will be planted for two years in this way, and then the milpero will continue the cycle elsewhere in the forest. The forest actively reintegrates the harvested field back into itself; the succession of new wild plant and animal life that moves into the field forms another important part in the cycle, in forest biodiversity, and in Indigenous Maya foodways. As originally developed over centuries of sustained human-land interactions, the Maya milpa is ecologically balanced because its practitioners emulate and cooperate with the life cycles of the forest.[60]

Contrary to how extractive land relations would cast the milpa, it can't be understood just by looking at a freeze-frame of active fields ("useful" land). Viewed through mutual land relations, the milpa is a dynamic agroforestry system, designed to be practiced on the scale of entire forest landscapes (including many ostensibly "unused" and "useless" lands not under active cultivation) and across multiple generations of farmer-forest reciprocity.[61] These kinds of practices, however, depend on Indigenous Maya land sovereignty: if farming communities lack secure access to forested land, milpa agriculture can become precarious.

Centuries of land grabbing, from colonial dispossession to late capitalist privatization, have had precisely this undermining effect on Maya milpa agriculture. The most recent waves of land precarity trace to neoliberal agrarian reforms of the nineties.[62] Like other Mexican towns, Yaxunah maintains a collective agricultural landholding, or ejido. Mexico's ejido system was originally conceived to ensure community access to collective landholdings indefinitely. But in just the last few decades, the Mexican government legalized the privatization of ejido lands. This change opened the door to all sorts of shady land deals and outright land grabbing as private buyers raced to acquire ejido lands for development. Though Yaxunah has not privatized its ejido lands as I write this, there have been interested buyers and even a few offers made.

Aside from land precarity, Yaxunah milpa farmers face other challenges. Beginning in 1994, the North American Free Trade Agreement (NAFTA) inundated Mexican markets with cheap, US-grown corn (a term I will use along with *maize* to describe *Zea mays*), and filled convenience store shelves with ultra-processed foods. Severe hurricanes and droughts increasingly disrupt the seasonal rhythms of milpa agriculture and can wipe out entire harvests.[63] For many Yaxunah families, these shifts mean that it has become much less risky to pursue cash-earning employment and buy industrial maize from stores than it is to grow their own landrace maize crop.[64] Yaxunah community members who continue to farm understandably want to buffer against these risks, so they try to maximize yields by buying commercial maize varieties and spraying crops with chemical herbicides and pesticides.

But of course, *that* kind of maize is not what celebrity chefs and hipster foodies come to Yaxunah looking to eat. So a few years ago, FHMM moved to ensure a supply of landrace, certified organic, Yaxunah maize by partnering with another sustainable development nonprofit, the International Maize and Wheat Improvement Center, known by its Spanish acronym CIMMYT. CIMMYT works with Yaxunah farmers (and farmers in other Indigenous Maya communities) to run the "Sustainable Milpa Project," a model for sustainable maize agriculture, at least according to FHMM and CIMMYT promotional materials.[65]

CIMMYT has its own sustainability story: the organization claims that Indigenous Maya milpa practices—specifically the periodic burns used in preparing new fields—are responsible for a wide range of environmental degradation, including deforestation, increased carbon emissions, and biodiversity loss.[66] CIMMYT is not alone in this campaign. Several sustainable development initiatives in Yucatán promote "no-burn" milpas as sustainable, on the claim that Indigenous Maya milpa practices use more land than necessary and harm forest ecosystems.[67] In a report commissioned by the Nature Conservancy and the Mexico REDD+ (Reducing Emissions from Deforestation and Degradation) Alliance, the objective of "sustainable Mayan milpa" is to combine "the traditional technique with some improved techniques; such as achieving a sedentary milpa instead of a migrating one, elimination of burning, and incorporation of organic fertilizers."[68]

CIMMYT's Sustainable Milpa Project claims to solve these perceived problems through intensification. Rather than farmers shifting their fields from forest patch to forest patch over generations, CIMMYT's no-burn intensive milpa "allows farmers to farm the same land for many years without resorting to deforestation or burning."[69] A CIMMYT blog post reporting on the project in June 2019 pairs a prominent photograph of a smiling Yaxunah elder standing in a milpa with this text: "These efforts led [the elder] ... to adopt conservation agriculture concepts in his milpa and to stop burning soil residues since 2016. As a result, his maize yield grew by 70% from 430 to 730 kg per hectare, and his income increased by 300 dollars. 15 farmers sharing property rights over communal land have followed his example since."[70] That might sound good, but less publicized is that the maize grown through these methods isn't usually destined for Yaxunah tables. In 2017, when Redzepi was collecting ingredients for Noma Mexico, FHMM and CIMMYT arranged for him to source "sustainable corn," grown and certified organic in the intensive model milpas of Yaxunah, for the pop-up.[71] That sustainable corn did not stay in the Yaxunah community, but journeyed to Tulum, where diners paid $750 each, after service charges and taxes, for the privilege of eating it.

Sustainable development projects that condemn Indigenous Maya milpa agriculture as environmentally destructive deracinate history from the land. The controlled burns of Indigenous Maya milpa agriculture emulate the restorative role of forest fires.[72] Controlled burns form the foundation of milpa's capacity for long-term stability and resilience—I could say, its sustainability—but only when farming communities are empowered with secure land sovereignty.[73] Controlled burns only work as intended when Indigenous Maya farming communities sustain multigenerational access to forests. The perceived environmental threat detected by sustainable development projects is not resolved by adding "some improved techniques" to traditional milpa farming—it's resolved by restoring deep historical connections between Indigenous Maya communities and their lands.

No-burn milpas, like those advocated by the Sustainable Milpa Project, might be becoming one of the only economically viable ways to practice farming in Yaxunah—not because the technique is inherently more sustainable but because the maize grown in these plots meets the standards of celebrity chefs and foodie tourists. Meanwhile, the edge lands of the Yaxunah ejido, forested places further from town where milpa agriculture fed the community since the early twentieth century, are rarely now, if ever, farmed. Whether intended or not (and I think not), the partnership among celebrity chefs and sustainable development projects in Yaxunah has helped to strip the history from the edge lands of the ejido. It shouldn't come as a surprise, then, that these edge lands have attracted the most attention from private developers interested in parceling up and purchasing Yaxunah lands; the useless land narrative permeates the forest and starts to settle in.

Land near the eastern boundary of the Yaxunah ejido stirs particular interest among private developers. I've heard they think it has good ecotourism potential. There's water, wildlife, forest thick enough to be marketed as "jungle," and a road to get out there. There are also ruins.

ᕒᕀ   ᕒᕀ   ᕒᕀ

The ruins are why I'm part of any of this. I told you about the ecosystem of celebrity chefs; it's time to talk about the ecosystem of archaeologists.

Yaxunah's ejido lands are textured with the stone, soil, plaster, and clay remains of past communities, starting with ancient Maya settlements from nearly three thousand years ago and continuing up until 1844, when Indigenous Maya uprisings known as the Maya Social War (or Caste War) caused the desertion of the colonial town of Yaxunah and a couple of nearby plantations. The contemporary town of Yaxunah was founded on the site of the abandoned colonial town in the early twentieth century by Maya families who had been displaced from their homes during the war. Most Yaxunah community members today descend from these families.

Ancient Maya mounds and ceramics are visible on the ground surface, no digging necessary, throughout the town of Yaxunah and the surrounding ejido lands. The mounds are stone and rubble platforms. They usually just look like piles of rocks, and they're almost always covered in thick vegetation. Centuries ago, the mounds supported buildings made of wood and thatch, all of which have long since decayed or burned. The Yaxunah ejido has hundreds, probably thousands, of mounds.[74] Most were foundations for houses, but several formed the bases of massive pyramids.

By the time Yaxunah's ejido gained legal recognition in 1934, foreign archaeologists had already been coming around to take measurements of the largest pyramids—and to take artifacts—for at least seven years. The first large-scale archaeological project based at Yaxunah began in 1986 and built on these earlier forays, ultimately running for a decade under a constellation of academic archaeologist directors from the United States and Mexico.[75] When that first project ended, Mexican government archaeologists continued research in Yaxunah for a few years. After a pause, another project, again under foreign direction, restarted archaeological research in the Yaxunah ejido in 2007. This project was called PIPCY,[76] and a couple of its codirectors had worked at Yaxunah as graduate students in the nineties. PIPCY incorporated a wide range of smaller projects managed by experienced archaeology students from Mexico and the United States. These smaller projects enabled student members of the project to collect data for theses and dissertations. That was why I joined PIPCY and came to Yaxunah as a graduate student for five field seasons between 2013 and 2017.[77]

Most archaeological research that's happened in the Yaxunah ejido has been in the ejido's largest archaeological site, an ancient city officially known, a little confusingly, as Yaxuná. Modern Yaxunah sits on the western fringes of ancient Yaxuná, and the camp where the archaeologists stay (a former ecolodge, more on that later) is located right between them.

Yaxuná was the capital of the central Yucatán region during early periods of ancient Maya history.[78] In later periods, Yaxuná's royal leaders became embroiled in political conflicts with rival cities like Coba and Chichen Itza.[79] A lot of the archaeology that's been done in Yaxuná has tried to understand these political shifts through the stuff ancient noble people and royals left behind, usually by excavating the biggest and oldest buildings. For decades now, the pyramids, monumental plazas, longest roads, and elaborate palaces of Yaxuná have drawn archaeologists, who in turn have pulled in grant money, which in turn has been used to employ Yaxunah community members on the project every field season as excavators, screeners, drawing assistants, surveyors, brush clearers, cooks, cleaners, stonemasons, renovators, and artifact washers.[80]

Yaxuná has become useful land. Decades of archaeological interest in the site have made the site a reliable source of income for the Yaxunah community. It is open to the public, and while the site lacks the tourism infrastructure of nearby Chichen Itza (restrooms, ATMs, snack bars, gift shops, ticket booths), the presence of a few reconstructed buildings, walking trails, and roads connecting to Yucatán's highway system all mean that Yaxuná balances a feeling of being "off the beaten path" with the accessibility necessary to get there pretty easily (fig. 2). This balance seems to appeal to a slightly more adventurous set of tourists than the experiences offered by commercialized archaeological sites like Chichen Itza or Tulum do. And more of these

FIGURE 2. Yaxunah community members walking through the Yaxuná archaeological site. The mounds of stone rubble are the remains of ancient buildings. Photo by the author.

tourists keep coming, as the Yaxuná ruins inevitably show up, either in drone footage B-roll or in sweeping slow-motion montages, in nearly all the celebrity chef shows and foodie YouTube videos filmed in Yaxunah.[81]

In the logic of extraction, Yaxuná's perceived *usefulness* exacerbates the perceived *uselessness* of much of the ejido beyond the central core of Yaxuná-Yaxunah, especially in the edge lands. Yet Yaxuná is not the only archaeological site in the Yaxunah ejido. The remains of ancient farming villages abound in the landholding, in wooded places once cultivated by Yaxunah community members' fathers and grandfathers but that now are rarely, if ever, farmed. These edge lands are the kinds of places that get stripped of history in service to the useless land narrative. And these are the kinds of places potentially capable of countering it.

Tzacauil is the site where I worked most of my time as a grad student in the Yaxunah ejido (map 2).[82] It's a small archaeological site right near the eastern edge of the landholding, an area that periodically attracts private developers, as I mentioned before, for its ecotourism potential. To get to the edge lands of the eastern ejido is not easy; for me and my team, working at Tzacauil meant a daily drive of about half an hour over the rolling

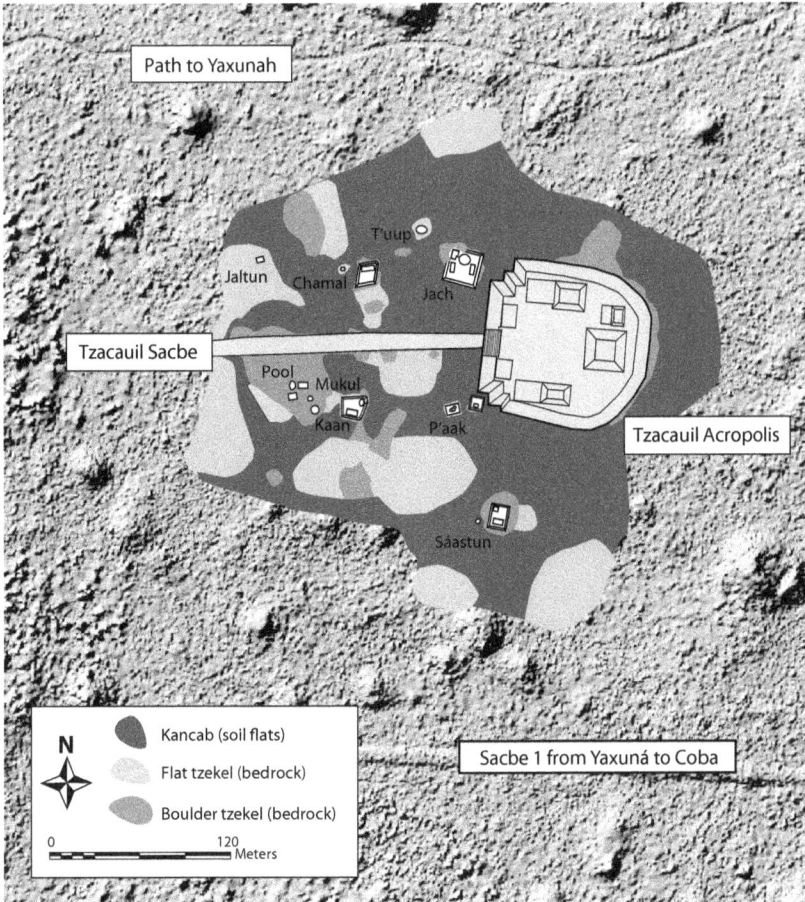

Path to Yaxunah

T'uup

Jaltun Chamal Jach

Tzacauil Sacbe

Pool Mukul

Kaan P'aak

Tzacauil Acropolis

Sáastun

N

Kancab (soil flats)

Flat tzekel (bedrock)

Boulder tzekel (bedrock)

Sacbe 1 from Yaxuná to Coba

0   120
                        Meters

MAP 2. The Tzacauil archaeological site. This map integrates lidar data with findings from a traditional ecological knowledge–based walking survey to depict the site's patchwork terrain of soil flats and exposed bedrock. Major monumental architectural features are indicated, as are the nine homesites discussed in the text. Architectural features have been redrawn and modified from mapping data originally published in Stanton, Hutson, and Magnoni, "PIPCY, primera temporada del campo," and are represented according to the stylized conventions ("malerization") typical of archaeological maps of Maya sites.

and rocky terrain of an overgrown dirt road in a rented pickup (fig. 3). Few Yaxunah community members find it useful to journey out to these edge lands on their own anymore, and in this matrix of perceived uselessness sprouts the possibility of privatization. The edge lands are contested ground, but places like Tzacauil hold the histories of ongoing farmer-forest relationships in their stone and soil archives quietly. Those histories

FIGURE 3. Members of the Tzacauil excavation team stop near an active milpa in the Yaxuná archaeological site, preparing for the drive out to the eastern edge lands of the Yaxunah ejido. Photo by the author.

complicate, challenge, and counter the assumptions of the useless land narrative.

This countervalence is what makes a small and seemingly insignificant archaeological site like Tzacauil worth careful consideration. Taken out of that context, Tzacauil is much like the hundreds of other sites found sown throughout the forest. The site is most noticeable for its large pyramid, the Tzacauil Acropolis. The acropolis is a monumental stone and rubble platform, collapsing and covered with trees, and on top there's a cluster of smaller platforms that would have supported buildings. The acropolis was built when Maya people in this region began to dedicate their communities fully to agriculture, about twenty-two hundred to eighteen hundred years ago. Archaeologists don't fully understand the role these acropolis groups held in early farming communities, but many agree they were related to the political and religious practices of emerging kings and other institutionalized leaders.[83] Just east of the acropolis, the bedrock terrain is punctured in two places, creating natural openings down to the water table. These two permanent water sources, known locally today as Xauil and El Manantial, made life possible for ancient farmers in these edge lands.[84]

From the base of the Tzacauil Acropolis, a raised road made of limestone radiates out and runs west back towards the city center of ancient Yaxuná, 3.2 kilometers away.[85] These causeways are known among Maya speakers and archaeologists as *sacbes*, a Yucatec Maya word meaning white road. This sacbe, the Tzacauil Sacbe, heads directly for Yaxuná but stops short about halfway there.[86] The team of archaeologists that first mapped Tzacauil suggested that for its time, the road may have been the longest in the Maya region. The longest road in the precolonial Maya world, period, happens to pass just south of Tzacauil. Known as Sacbe 1, this road spans just over 100 kilometers and connects Yaxuná with the ancient city of Coba, now a heavily trafficked archaeological site in Quintana Roo.[87] Sacbe 1 was built centuries after the Tzacauil Sacbe, when both the road and the acropolis were already in ruins.

On the ground, there are several smaller stone platforms scattered around the Tzacauil Acropolis, on either side of the Tzacauil Sacbe. These platforms were foundations for houses made of wood and thatch, and they are the clearest remains of the ancient farming communities that lived at Tzacauil over about a dozen centuries. From archaeological investigations in these house foundations, as well as the open areas around them, my team and I were able to gather a sense of the deep history of Yaxunah's edge lands as understood through Tzacauil. The land itself is an archive of more than twenty centuries of changing land relations: the foragers who first experimented with farming, the thriving early farming village that practiced a nascent form of urban agriculture, the later mobile farming communities whose flexibility enabled them to live through the political and climate upheavals known popularly as the Maya collapse, and the colonial conversion of forests into commodities.

"Landscapes are not backdrops for historical action: they are themselves active," says the anthropologist Anna Tsing of human-disturbed forests. "Watching landscapes in formation shows humans joining other living beings in shaping worlds."[88] Extractive land relations are predicated on making land a static backdrop by first rendering land ahistorical. Yet counternarratives are archived in the land itself. Archaeology, when practiced in collaboration with communities, makes possible the recovery of deep histories of land from the land itself. Land with history resists conversion into fungible resource. Specific histories and particular relationships matter to this work.

᛭   ᛭   ᛭

Specific histories and particular relationships matter, and it's time I bring my own into clearer focus. I was born in 1988 from a bundle of European settler lineages that landed in the present-day United States between the 1600s and 1921, and I grew up in New Jersey. I knew I wanted to be an archaeologist at eleven years old; I had been out of school for months with Lyme disease at the time and coped by becoming infatuated with ancient Egypt, and that was pretty much that. (The ancient Maya came soon after.) There are childhood threads with food, too. My dad worked as a chef at a restaurant in town and my mom would take me and my brothers to visit him some afternoons in the alley behind the kitchen. I loved it: we got to eat hot fries out of white paper bags, though once I made the terrible mistake of playing in what I believed to be a pile of snow but turned out to be a pile of fishy ice next to a dumpster. Years later, my first jobs would be just around the block from that alley, first at an Italian deli and then across the street scooping ice cream. Food and archaeology have always been entangled for me: I got the Lyme disease that led me to archaeology from a tick that found me playing in the overgrown grapevines and apple trees of my late great-grandfather's garden.

Years later, I entered the doctoral program in anthropology at the University of Michigan. By that point, it was 2011 and I had already been studying archaeology for four years, at college in Ohio as well as at a Mexican university in Yucatán for a semester, and I had completed two archaeology field schools in Honduras and Arizona. Now as a graduate student at Michigan, I would spend another eight years learning to be an anthropological archaeologist. The university sent me to excavate on projects in Belize, Oaxaca, Veracruz, Texas, and Romania, but with encouragement from my adviser, I knew I wanted to complete my doctoral research on early Maya farming societies in Yucatán. At that time my motivations were pretty simple: I could see a "gap in the research" and I wanted to fill it, and plus I liked Yucatecan food. I became a part of PIPCY, the archaeological project based in Yaxunah, because PIPCY's director said yes when my adviser sent out a volley of emails looking for excavations that would take me on in 2013.

The first two summers I was part of PIPCY I worked in the Yaxuná site, assisting with excavations in huge monumental complexes and then collecting surface ceramic samples from house mounds. By my third season, in 2015, I was allowed to direct my first excavations at a pair of Yaxuná houses. I had hoped the houses dated to the early farming period, but midway through the season one of the project directors glanced at the ceramics coming out of the excavation and announced they were later—too late to be of use for my doctoral thesis. Within a few days, the project shut down those excavations and I transferred everything out to Tzacauil, a half hour's drive away, where I was assured by the project directors that I was more likely to find the early stuff I was seeking. I went on to dedicate a total of nine months between 2015 and 2017 to investigating Tzacauil, and for several of those months, I was the only archaeologist around. It was particularly during those months that my ideas about archaeology crumbled and then reformed.

By the time I first went to work at Tzacauil in 2015, I had been coming to Yaxunah long enough that community members began to open up more with me, and I with them. Out in the edge lands of Tzacauil, Yaxunah men and I began spending a lot more time talking, usually while eating together, and I finally started to hear what was actually going on in the community—not just the bits that felt relevant to my questions about life two thousand years ago. I listened to stories about hurricanes, about diabetes, about the price of herbicides, about land deals gone wrong in neighboring towns, about offers to buy the very land we were eating breakfast on. That was the same summer the celebrity chef Rick Bayless came to film an episode of his TV show in Yaxunah. Even as I continued with my excavation plans and set myself to making sense of Tzacauil's ancient history from my drawings and field notes, I started to appreciate that something important was unfolding in Indigenous Maya land relations, food, and agriculture right now.

I shifted my research so that I could connect what I was finding in the ground to what was actually happening in the Yaxunah ejido. Back in Michigan, I started paying close attention to the ways chefs were engaging with ancient foodways and techniques, and I started visiting urban farms in Detroit. I later took an intensive urban agriculture training in Atlanta to learn more about the relationship between environmental justice, food sovereignty, and history. When I received a grant to live in Yucatán for a year, I rented a house in the capital city, Mérida. I began talking to vendors at farmers markets and connecting with the urban farming scene there, too.

By my final season as a grad student in 2017, Yaxunah women were traveling to Tulum to make tortillas at Noma Mexico, and Noma Mexico line cooks were partying in Yaxunah on the town's patron saint day. Talk of potential offers to buy ejido land, of the prices Noma was paying for eggs and corn, and of anxieties about rain saturated our conversations during the final months of work at Tzacauil. And I could begin to envision how the history of the edge lands, what our team of community members and archaeologists were finding at Tzacauil, was somehow entangled with those conversations.

It took a few more years to trace out those tangles. Most of the ideas I share here emerged during my time teaching about environmental justice, food sovereignty, and archaeology as an environmental studies college professor in Virginia, where I've been since finishing my PhD in 2019. I finished writing this book in late 2022, after returning to Yaxunah for the first time in years that summer. I went back for a month to reconnect with community members and to start the work of establishing an ongoing collaborative archaeological program in the ejido. As long as the Yaxunah community wants me working with them and in their land, I hope to be there, a guest with roots.

ෑ෨   ෑ෨   ෑ෨

The chapters ahead are my attempt to restore roots to a land cast as useless.

Chapter 1 begins in the present to explore how and why celebrity chefs, sustainable development programs, and useless land narratives converge in Yaxunah. Chapter 2 takes the story to the forests of the Yaxunah ejido, to situate the edge lands within Indigenous frameworks of mutual land relations and within the experience of collaborative traditional ecological knowledge surveys at Tzacauil.

The next chapters jump back in time to offer a deep history of Yaxunah edge lands as gathered through archaeology at Tzacauil. In chapter 3, I write about the first farmers in the ejido edge lands and their transition from foraging to planting permanent homesites in soil-rich patches of Tzacauil. I connect the intensive, homesite-localized agricultural practices of this first farming community (ca. 250 BC—AD 250) to the emergence of urban agriculture in later Maya cities. Then, in chapter 4, I continue this history by carrying Tzacauil into the era of the controversial Classic Maya collapse, to consider how flexible innovations in agriculture enabled later farmers of the edge lands to live through political instability and climate change (ca. AD 550–1100). The dynamic history outlined in these chapters undermines any static conception of Yaxunah ejido edge lands as useless.

I contend with the tensions between Indigenous Maya land relations and colonial land relations in chapter 5, where I pull together sixteenth-to-nineteenth-century documentary history to consider how those tensions manifested in these edge lands. Chapter 6 bundles everything together by reflecting on the entangled ways that use and efficiency manifest both in archaeology and in land grabs, and how practices of engaged archaeology can create possibilities for restoring history and mutual land relations to contested ground.[89]

Specific histories and particular relationships matter. I keep saying this, and I repeat it here to make clear that I speak as an outsider, a provisional guest in the Yaxunah community who has been invited to grow provisional roots. Yaxunah landowners might decide to sell their ejido lands, or they might not—ultimately, that isn't my business. I'm not interested in pushing against communities who do decide to privatize land, but I am interested in pushing against the systems that force those difficult decisions. Neither should what I share here be understood as *the* history of Yaxunah edge lands, it's one history, from one outsider, and there is room—and need—for many others. Restoring history to land, this practice of rooting in precisely the places discarded as useless lands, empty lands, and wastelands is a move towards countering extractive land relations, but it is not the last move, nor can it be a move made alone. I hope that what I share here makes you want to seek out ways to root in the useless lands that matter to you.

Sixty-six million years ago, when the asteroid hit, a force so powerful roared out from the Chicxulub crater that it ripped open the bedrock of the Yucatán Peninsula. Those rips in the rock created portals to subterranean waters; they became cenotes, the main and often only source of permanent freshwater on the peninsula. From far away in space, if you mapped out the locations of Yucatán's cenotes—including the handful in the Yaxunah ejido—you would see that they form rings, rippling lesions in the land, each opening a scar marking that day of disaster. But on the ground, a different kind of encounter becomes possible. You find the stone remains of ancient homes gathered around the cenotes. You notice metal and plastic buckets waiting, ready, gathered there too, and you hear birds singing and feel the coolness coming off the water. You see that the edges of cenotes are curtained with the roots of trees, plunging down deep to drink from underground rivers. You find life rooting in the wounds of an old apocalypse. May more roots grow.

———

ONE

The Celebrity Chef Lands in Yaxunah

THE TOWN OF YAXUNAH is rooted in the center of the Yucatán Peninsula. A world away, on the eastern edge of the peninsula, a glittering white band separates the green of the forest from the blue of the Caribbean: this is Tulum. Businesses crowd the beach. They beckon to tourists with names that promise enlightenment and release, sweat lodges and nightclubs, green juice and mezcal. The trees along the main strip are lush, but this is no jungle; patches of overcast sky pierce through the leaves and the gash of the road splits the canopy.

On this shoreside strip there is a ruin dating to AD 2017. The ruin was a restaurant. Only residues remain. A small palapa sits neglected with dead leaves nesting in the thatch. Ornate sculptures made of woven wooden switches hang abandoned in the trees, and a white concrete wall hunches under the shaggy fringe of desiccated grass bundles. Anyone passing by can peer beyond the wall into the inner courtyard, where the ashen sediment of the road gives way to a fine white powder of platonic Caribbean sand. Black plastic garbage bags lie bloated, full of dead leaves, and strewn about the ground. This is Noma Mexico, and all stray tourists typing the address into their phones will be met with an epitaph: permanently closed.[1]

The original Noma—the parent of Noma Mexico, permanently closed—is in Copenhagen.[2] The restaurant is helmed by chef René Redzepi, a celebrity and household name in his own right, or at least if you happen to count foodies or lovers of cooking shows in your household, that is. Among folks who take seriously the task of ranking restaurants, Noma has held the top place in the world for years.[3] Redzepi and the Noma team have scattered short-lived offspring—temporary restaurants known as pop-ups—across continents. Pop-ups in Australia and Japan preceded the one that briefly blossomed here on this now-neglected patch of Tulum. The launch of each pop-up was widely hyped in culinary circles, and the fleetingly brief existence of each catalyzed a finite and FOMO-inducing number of write-ups and social media posts. Years after their posting, I study these fragments of online detritus like they were ancient texts.

I think I'm compelled to keep returning to the ephemera surrounding Noma Mexico because I see in the pop-up a brazen and playful and troubling story about one of the slipperiest ideas of late capitalism: sustainability. Sustainability has saturated our food landscape, not because we are eating in sustainable ways necessarily, but because corporations (and celebrity chefs) have repurposed sustainability as a brand. It wasn't always this way. As originally envisioned in a dry and practical 1987 UN document called the *Brundtland Report*, sustainable agriculture meant producing food using practices that would let future generations keep on with it, and maybe ideally conserve and enhance the environment.[4] But with the rise of green capitalism in the past couple of decades, sustainability has become a marketing strategy that capitalizes on environmental anxiety. There's a growing market share of wealthy consumers seeking to alleviate a vague sense of ecological guilt (for carbon emissions, for palm oil plantations, for sad sea turtles with bellyfuls of plastic) through products and experiences that promise sustainability and environmental justice. Whether those promises are kept is of little concern for most consumers—and often, they aren't.[5]

Noma Mexico played at ephemerality, but it also capitalized on a fantasy of sustainable food and authentic food targeted at the wealthy.[6] That fantasy—that sustainable food is a meal sourced hyperlocally, adapted by foreign hands, consumed in the breath between round-trip flights (often intercontinental), and through a cool transaction of $750 USD, after tax, per meal—is one whose legacies live far longer than the pop-up itself.

Yaxunah is one place where those legacies are still unfolding. The town and its people, located a couple hours' drive inland from Tulum, became deeply entangled with Noma Mexico and Redzepi. But Redzepi is not the first or only celebrity chef to capitalize on Yaxunah as a vehicle to meet outsider (wealthy, often white) expectations for sustainable and authentic Yucatecan food from Indigenous Maya fields, kitchens, and tables.

Celebrity chefs landed in Yaxunah not by accident but by way of the historical tangles of extractive land relations. To explain how this happened, I have to tell you about sustainable development initiatives, and especially the ways that well-meaning plans to promote sustainable agriculture tend to deracinate histories of mutual land relations from land and communities. I believe that chefs and sustainable developers have good intentions. But I also believe they are inadvertently helping to seed useless land narratives in the edge lands of the Yaxunah ejido and in other forgotten forests, in this way indirectly contributing to the on-the-ground realities of land grabbing in Yucatán. The construction of useless land relies on the uprooting of history, so here I try to restore it—beginning with the history of celebrity chefs in Yaxunah and their complicated attraction to Yucatecan food.

ə⁊ ə⁊ ə⁊

Yucatecan food is an archive—a complex, edible, delicious archive. Eating it is one thing, trying to define it is another. The Yucatecan culinary anthropologist Steffan Igor Ayora-Diaz tracks Yucatecan food's distinct aromas, flavors, and textures back to a few foundational patterns. You won't find much dairy or beef, but you will find pork, fowl, and eggs; you'll find tamales and meat cooked in banana leaves, not corn husks; you'll taste citrus-based marinades and the heat of chile garnishes; and the spices you'll encounter will be Middle Eastern by way of the Caribbean.[7] There will be red and white onions, tomatoes, beans, squash, avocados, chayote, garlic, cabbage, potatoes, radish, plantains, *chaya* (a leafy green known also as tree spinach), oregano, cilantro, epazote, parsley, thyme, *hoja santa* (an aromatic shrub), and several kinds of chiles, maybe most famously the habanero. There will be corn tortillas, but also French baguettes and white rice. Pork lard will lend its smooth richness to almost everything, and you'll cut its luster with the bright acid of lime and pink pickled onions.[8]

Yucatecan food is decidedly not like the cheesy, beefy, flour-tortilla-enfolded Mexican food I grew up eating as a white child in suburban New Jersey. But to be clear, according to Ayora-Diaz Yucatecan food is not Mexican food at all. "There is a prevailing and complex opposition between a territorializing, national Mexican cuisine and a deterritorializing, regional Yucatecan cuisine," he says.[9] Food, like land, is an archive of historical relationships, and in Yucatán's food, Ayora-Diaz reads a series of cultural and culinary entanglements born from Yucatecan resistance to Mexican nation-building projects.

Yucatán was an independent republic for brief bursts in the first half of the nineteenth century, before it was reabsorbed back into Mexico in 1848. During their struggle for autonomy, powerful Yucateco[10] families turned away from Mexico and established strong cultural and economic ties with the Caribbean, Europe, and United States. Yucatán's emerging cosmopolitan identity was shaped, too, by influential immigrant communities from Lebanon and Syria, as well as by laborer communities of Korean, Chinese, and African descent. These diverse cultural influences (and their recipes, cooking techniques, and foods) became integrated with local ingredients and Indigenous Maya culinary traditions, and then codified by cooks and eaters into a set of canonical dishes to create what today is recognized as Yucatecan gastronomy.[11]

Yucatecan food is rebel food. It's cosmopolitan food. I think it's clear that a lot of celebrity chefs like to think of themselves as cosmopolitan rebels. It makes sense to me that celebrity chefs drawn to Yucatecan food would want to locate the most authentic expression of that culinary spirit. And for reasons I'll explain, it makes sense to me that they would feel they found it in Yaxunah.

But it's important to note, as Ayora-Diaz does, that lots of Yucatecans— and certainly lots of foreigners who eat and cook Yucatecan food—aren't aware of the complex historical entanglements at work in Yucatecan cuisine. "Contemporary Yucatecans perceive their taste preferences as a 'natural' disposition that emerges from the climate, the local culture and values, and the cultural temperament of local people," Ayora-Diaz says.[12] When people do think about the origins of Yucatecan food, they tend to assume it's a simple equation of Spanish cuisine plus Maya cuisine. But, he writes, "this imagination endorses the concealment of the historical process whereby the practices, values and preferences of subordinate people, including immigrants and local indigenous groups, have become integrated into a single and shared Yucatecan taste."[13] Specific histories and particular relationships matter, and their erasure is almost always going to be, in some way, extractive.

೩> ೩> ೩>

Away from screens, I have had but one corporeal encounter with the celebrity chef in Yucatán.

I recognized Rick Bayless the instant he walked into the restaurant. For the staff of Apoala, a high-end eatery serving Oaxacan-style food in downtown Mérida, it took about twenty minutes. It was late on a Sunday evening in July of 2015, and the restaurant was nearly empty. Rick, his wife (Deann; I recognized her from Rick's TV show), and his overexcited observer (me, silent and trying desperately hard to appear nonchalant at a table across the room) were the only patrons in the place.

Somewhere in my own uphill process of convincing myself that I totally was capable of a quick, non-awkward breezy tableside chat with Rick, someone on staff realized that the white guy quietly sampling the table salsas was in fact regarded widely as the (or at least, a) leading expert on Mexican cuisine in the United States. I knew the Rick Bayless brand included multiple Mexican restaurants, a line of "authentic" salsas, seasonings, and taco kits (which he sold to corporate food giant ConAgra in 2016), and a TV show called *Mexico: One Plate at a Time* (*MOPAT*).[14] I had been an enthusiastic consumer of all.

I could tell Rick had been recognized when the restaurant suddenly started to mobilize. The sign on the door was flipped to the "CERRADO" side: Apoala was now closed. A new waiter appeared at my table, politely but pointedly asking if I was ready for my check. I claimed to still be eating, but we both knew that was a lie. For the last ten minutes I had been shredding straw wrappers in nervous excitement, and from the disdainful glance the waiter gave the pile of paper shreds on the table, he knew that, too. The head waiter, who before Rick's recognition had spent the past hour in the nearly empty restaurant decanting bottled water into my glass after every two sips, had abandoned my table, rallied his staff, and descended on the Bayless party.

I watched, slowly dragging a fork around the residues of mole on my plate in what I hoped was a convincing pantomime of still eating, as the waiters pushed several tables up to join the Bayless' four-top. Now Rick sat at the head of the long table. As if on cue, in began to filter more people—mostly young, mostly from the States, and a few Mexicans, I guessed—cheerful and relaxed and hungry. They joined the Baylesses at the banquet and were soon lifting shots of mezcal, making toasts. I noticed the high per capita rate of forearms sleeved with colorful tattoos of knives and vegetables; they were all chefs, I realized. Later I would learn that Rick often took his Chicago-based restaurant staff on these kinds of educational trips to different regions of Mexico. After a few mezcal shots, the restaurant rose into an excited hum as the young chefs laughed and urged each other to taste the moles and *chapulines* (toasted grasshoppers) now flowing from the kitchen to their table.

Over in the corner, my stressed new waiter asked me again if I was ready for the check. The door was locked, and I was the only barrier standing between the staff's undivided attention and their VIP table. I reluctantly admitted I was finished, and he dropped the check immediately. I pretended to study the bill closely, but I was really just buying time to work up my nerve.

You see, I felt like I had to say something to Rick. Parasocial relationships are a tricky thing (for one, I keep slipping into a first-name basis writing about him, something I'd never do for any of the other chefs I discuss here). I had "met" Rick five years earlier, during winter break of my junior year of college. I was home killing time before I left for a semester in Mérida, for what would be my first time in Mexico, and spending a lot of time watching long stretches of daytime public television in my parents' basement. And there was Rick, with his reliable brand of nerdy wholesomeness on his show *MOPAT.*

Rick didn't just cook on his show. He ate with gusto at market stalls in Mexico City, hung out with fishermen in a tiny coastal village near Puerto Vallarta, tasted tequila with agave farmers in Jalisco. And, in my favorite episodes, he strolled archaeological ruins while he invited me to imagine the culinary past of these ancient landscapes. I was hooked.

Later, when I started studying in the anthropology graduate program at the University of Michigan, I was starstruck to learn that Rick had been in the same program. He had been working on his PhD in linguistic anthropology when he dropped out to start his first restaurant. I sat dazzled at a seminar table as Kent and Joyce, two professors who'd spent much of their careers working in Mexico, told me about having him in class before he left for his linguistic fieldwork. He ended up never completing the course requirements. Years after Rick dropped out of the program, he invited the two professors to come to Chicago to eat at his restaurant Frontera, which at that point had become wildly successful. When Rick came out to visit their table, Kent and Joyce ceremonially ripped up his "incomplete" for their class and they all had a good laugh.

Now here's a part of the story I feel weird about: I had been at Apoala that night because I suspected Rick might be there. I was in Mexico doing my own grad school fieldwork in Yaxunah, and I had just started working out at the edge lands of the Yaxunah ejido in Tzacauil. My fellow project members and I had come to Mérida that weekend for a Fourth of July party, and when we got to our hotel and all got online, I saw a Facebook post from Rick saying that he was going to be *in Yaxunah* that very weekend filming an episode of *MOPAT.* We were going to miss him.

I swallowed my disappointment and enjoyed the parties, but towards the end of the raucous weekend I slipped out for a late dinner on my own. I considered the restaurants in the touristy Centro district, most of which served Yucatecan food. I calculated that if Rick and crew had been in Yaxunah all weekend, they might be back in Mérida this evening. And if they had been eating Yucatecan food all weekend, they might want to eat something different tonight. So I went to the lone Oaxacan restaurant in Centro and was shocked when my experiment with celebrity chef channeling actually worked.

I did stop at Rick's table before I left Apoala, swerving at least one protective waiter to do so. Of course it was awkward. Rick looked tired and had been scrolling on his phone when I approached already babbling, and I wasted no time in playing my only two cards to mitigate his clear (and justified) annoyance at the interruption: I told him I was an archaeologist working at Yaxunah, and I name-dropped Kent and Joyce, our professors in common. It salvaged enough of his good humor to shake my hand. Feeling grateful for this clear signal that the interaction was over, I said goodbye and with an apologetic shrug to the waitstaff I bolted out the door into the night.

A year later, the episode Rick had been filming in Yaxunah that weekend aired. By the time I watched it, my feelings about Rick had veered away from the adulation I had felt for him that night at Apoala. Critical conversations about cultural appropriation were starting to gain more attention in the United States, and the status of folks like Rick Bayless—a white, non-Latinx chef from Oklahoma hailed as the national expert on Mexican food—came under question. I'd listened, pained with embarrassment, as Rick fumbled an interview on the National Public Radio podcast *The Sporkful* in a series called "Other People's Food."[15] When the host asked about the role race and privilege may have played in his success, Rick got defensive and hinted pretty strongly that pointing out his whiteness was irrelevant and approaching reverse racism. Rick is divisive. Critics cast his restaurant and grocery empire as cultural appropriation, while supporters offer counterexamples of the many ways Rick has demonstrated deep respect for and a willingness to learn about Mexican history and culture through food. Regardless of how you feel about Rick, I think all can agree that the rising influence of more Mexican and Mexican American chefs—chefs like Daniela Soto-Innes, Wes Avila, and Enrique Olvera—has been a good thing for Mexican cuisine in the United States.

The Yaxunah episode of Rick's show, titled "Pit Cooking, Sacred and Smoky," came near the end of the show's eleventh season, a multiepisode exploration of Yucatecan cuisine.[16] Just as I've studied breathless Instagram posts from Noma Mexico diners, I've studied this episode, trying to understand why Yaxunah so strongly allures celebrity chefs and the foodies who follow them.

In the episode, Rick partners with Miriam Peraza, a respected chef from Mérida, as his cultural liaison. They meet up in Yaxunah and are joined by members of Lool K'uum, a small cooking collective, though the collective isn't acknowledged. (The episode seems to suggest that this is just what's happening in Yaxunah on any given day.) Miriam and Rick look on as Yaxunah men, dressed in the immaculate white shirts, pants, and straw hats that make up the traditional Maya "look"—at least the look that's donned performatively in tourist settings—shovel out a cooking pit in a backyard garden. The men build a fire in the pit and stack chunks of limestone on top.

Meanwhile, Yaxunah women make tortillas, "by *hand* over an open fire," as Rick's reverent voice-over tells me. Rick goes on, narrating, "Miriam helped direct the preparation of the suckling pig," and we see Peraza and two Yaxunah women—wearing the feminine version of the traditional look, brightly embroidered dresses known as *huipiles*—wash the pig, juice sour oranges, and rub achiote paste onto the raw meat. The women cover the pan of marinating pork with banana leaves and pass it off to the men. The men lower the pan into the pit, rest it on top of the smoldering coals and hot rocks, cover it with more banana leaves, and then shovel earth back into the pit to cover the cache. Through the magic of editing, the scene jumps forward four hours into the future, and the men excavate the pan back out of the earth.

The scene cuts again, and now I see Rick and Miriam Peraza alone under a thatch-roofed *palapa*, beholding the slow-cooked, steaming pig—the famed Yucatecan dish known as *cochinita pibil*. With tortillas, they pinch off tender pieces of pork. "Miriam offered me the unique opportunity to taste that pork right when it came out of the pit with some of those beautiful, fresh-made corn tortillas," Rick says in the voice-over. "This is a unique flavor, unique to this place, cooked with this unique method from local ingredients. It's a perfect expression of this community, its history, and its geography." As they bite into their tacos, the men and women of Yaxunah are nowhere to be seen.

ॐ   ॐ   ॐ

Neither Bayless nor Redzepi, nor any of the other celebrity chefs who have come to Yaxunah to cook, stumbled upon the town accidentally; their course was charted for them decades ago and is inextricable from the larger course of global sustainable development, late capitalism, and extractive land relations.

Sustainability was still a fresh new idea when the presidents of Mexico and the United States signed the North American Free Trade Agreement (NAFTA) in 1992.[17] With their signatures, they catalyzed sweeping agrarian and economic reforms that continue to shape the food landscape of the continent decades later. Cheap US-grown corn, much of it transgenic, flooded Mexico along with all manner of industrially manufactured food and drink. The imported corn outcompeted native landraces and drove countless small-scale Mexican maize farmers out of agriculture, and increasingly, out of Mexico. The influx of corn syrup and white flour meant that calories were rarely scarce, but nutrient-dense and locally produced traditional foods became harder for rural Mexicans to obtain.

As the anthropologist Alyshia Gálvez has said, NAFTA replaced *food sovereignty*, in which rural Mexicans were empowered to grow and eat their culturally preferred foods, with *food security*, in which there was an abundance of cheap but nutritionally poor and industrially processed foods.[18] This is both a public health and environmental justice problem. Handmade landrace maize tortillas have become a food accessible mainly to wealthy outsiders, while the rural Mexicans whose ancestors domesticated maize and invented tortillas are left to live more and more on white bread, noodles, and Coke.

The early nineties were also high season for sustainable development projects. The same year NAFTA was signed, business leaders and academics in Yucatán chartered an initiative backed by the state to improve the livelihoods of rural communities.[19] They called their nonprofit the Fundación Cultural Yucatán (FCY, Yucatán Cultural Foundation). FCY materialized the tensions of NAFTA's food security for food sovereignty swap: the organization professed commitments to education, cultural diversity, ecological stewardship, and economic development—all while harboring folks like Fernando Ponce García, an executive from Coca-Cola México, on its advisory board. FCY moved to pilot three major development projects across Yucatán. One was at Izamal, a picturesque colonial city with distinctive yellow buildings, where FCY launched a mix of education and microcredit programs. A second was at Tabi, an abandoned hacienda (plantation) complex; there the foundation fund-raised for architectural preservation to transform the ruins into an interpretive center. The third project was at Yaxunah.

The FCY advisory board saw that Yaxunah had potential as a tourist destination. The nearby archaeological zone of Chichen Itza had been declared a UNESCO World Heritage Site just a few years earlier and was attracting visitors from around the world. Soon a new paved road would be built connecting Yaxunah to Pisté, the hub for Chichen Itza tourism. The FCY board reckoned that if even a slice of Chichen Itza's tourists added a visit to Yaxunah onto their day trips, it would mean major economic opportunities for the Yaxunah community.

Taking advantage of those opportunities, FCY figured, would be a simple manner of preparing Yaxunah community members with some infrastructure and the know-how to create marketable heritage. Starting in 1994, the foundation established cooperatives at Yaxunah dedicated to hospitality, artisanal crafts, and traditional agricultural practices. Working with FCY, Yaxunah community members learned to carve wooden masks and other souvenirs. They started a poultry farm. They planned an ecotourism trail in the eastern ejido lands to bring visitors out on bikes to archaeological sites and cenotes. They built an ecolodge to host and feed guests. Yaxunah was going to be a place where the adventurous tourists among the masses would journey for an alternative sort of experience: this was going to be a place for backpackers, a place to buy authentic handmade souvenirs directly from artisans, a place to eat traditional Yucatecan foods grown locally, cooked locally, and served by local Maya people.

But nearly all these sustainable development ventures quickly proved unsustainable. Elías Alcocer Puerto, an anthropologist who has lived and worked in Yaxunah for decades, has written that internal fissures and a lack of community leadership undermined the long-term viability of these projects.[20] Like other sustainable development projects before and after, the motivations came from the experiences and expectations of outsiders, rather than a clearly expressed community need and community-controlled response. One initiative that survived was artisanal wood carving. Today many Yaxunah families continue to produce wooden souvenirs, which eventually end up for sale on the vendor tables scattered throughout Chichen Itza, as a less risky alternative to farming.[21]

The Yaxunah community decided to lease the defunct ecolodge, a cluster of thatched-roof huts and a spacious dining and common area, to archaeological projects for use as a field camp in the nineties. By then the first major archaeological project (mostly involving archaeologists from the States) had already been working at the Yaxuná ruins for a few years and its members were happy to move into the old ecolodge. Yaxunah families ran hospitality at the camp the way they had when it was a hotel. At first the cooking was handled by a Yaxunah man, Nazario, whose credentials included running a hot dog cart at Chichen Itza; his experience cooking for foreigners was at this point still a rarity in Yaxunah.[22] Nazario's hot dog era didn't last long, and over time Yaxunah community members shifted camp cooking duties to a group of local women.

Calamity came in September 2002, when Hurricane Isidore swept across the peninsula. The damages were staggering; across southeastern Mexico the storm destroyed tens of thousands of houses and left hundreds of thousands homeless. Trees were ripped out of the ground and maize fields were torn apart. Livestock, beehives, and poultry perished. Isidore upended rural communities all over Yucatán. Even though by this time the FCY nonprofit had dissolved, the path had been cleared for more sustainable development projects—and now the need was urgent.

Just weeks after Isidore, a group of Mexican entrepreneurs founded a new nonprofit organization to provide aid to impacted Indigenous Maya communities. They called their organization the Fundación Haciendas del Mundo Maya (FHMM, Maya World Haciendas Foundation).[23] Previously, this group of entrepreneurs had focused on restoring old haciendas (plantations) and transforming them into boutique hotels. The idea was that the hotels would then create what the entrepreneurs called sustainable tourism, basically amounting to economic opportunities for Maya communities living near the restored haciendas.

When FHMM incorporated as a nonprofit, they expanded beyond high-end hotels to development initiatives across the Yucatán Peninsula: adult education, heritage botanical gardens, cultural events and workshops, libraries, housing, and community infrastructure. But as with FCY, the roster involved with FHMM raises questions about potential conflicts of interest. The nonprofit's founder, Roberto Hernández, is a billionaire businessman and former CEO of Banamex, Mexico's second largest bank. A quick look through FHMM's website at the time of my writing reveals that nearly every member of its advisory board has close ties to Banamex, and resumés marbled with powerful connections—chairman of the Aeroméxico airline, director of the Mexican branch of McKinsey & Co. consulting—to the corporate world. The history of sustainable development projects in Yucatán cannot be untangled from capitalism.

It took FHMM a few years to reach Yaxunah. Meanwhile, Hurricane Isidore had not spared the community, and many Yaxunah families sought new ways to support themselves in its wake. The group of Yaxunah women who had worked together cooking for foreigners at the archaeological camp decided that feeding tourists seemed to promise a more reliable livelihood than farming alone. So the women mobilized. They partnered with the Yaxunah cultural center, one of the few surviving ecotourism ventures seeded in the nineties that had managed to hang on thanks to local buy-in. In 2005, with the assistance of the cultural center and its advisory board, ten Yaxunah women founded a culinary tourism cooperative. They called themselves the Lool K'uum (Squash Blossom) collective.[24]

In her article tracing out the history of Lool K'uum's founding, anthropologist Traci Ardren describes how the women pooled their money to get trained in cooking techniques for foreign tourists, who were coming in greater numbers to Yaxunah.[25] The typical tourist in the first decade of the 2000s who ventured to Yaxunah usually came seeking a more "authentic" experience than the Disneyish, polished version of Yucatán packaged by the cruise lines. Yaxunah, at a twenty-five-minute drive from Chichen Itza, was just far enough off the beaten path to give adventurous travelers a sense of remoteness—while still being close enough to said beaten path to get everyone back to the all-inclusive resort by dinnertime. But even the most allegedly adventurous of these foreigners had certain expectations (and prejudices) about eating in rural Mexican towns. The Lool K'uum collective set out to master recipes that would prove palatable to this kind of tourist. They adopted scrupulous sanitation practices and adjusted the spice and flavor of their dishes for non-Yucatecan palates. Foreigners came expecting to see their own definition of authenticity, and the Lool K'uum cooks learned to meet that expectation too: instead of the shorts, skirts, and T-shirts they'd usually wear while cooking, the women would wear immaculate embroidered huipiles and tuck flowers into their hair. They embraced the performativity of their role.[26]

Lool K'uum and FHMM were moving on parallel paths through the landscape of culinary tourism. While Lool K'uum was getting off the ground, FHMM was stepping into a new venture: marketing artisanal products, like sea salt and honey, made in Maya communities. They launched a gourmet food brand, Traspatio Maya, as a channel for selling maize and produce grown by Maya communities to upscale restaurants in Mérida, Cancún, and luxury resorts. To FHMM, the prospect of partnering with the Lool K'uum collective—a grassroots team of Indigenous Maya women cooks who already knew how to prepare food that met foreign expectations of authenticity—must have been irresistible. FHMM and the Lool K'uum collective formally partnered in 2013.

છે   છે   છે

Like its precursors, FHMM brought to Yaxunah sustainable development programs that championed social entrepreneurship, environmental education, public health, and infrastructure improvements. But I think the critical FHMM project in Yaxunah—the one that made the village a pilgrimage destination for celebrity chefs—had to do with agriculture.

FHMM partnered with a Mexican agricultural research nonprofit, an organization with deep ties to Rockefeller money and the Mexican government known as the Centro Internacional de Mejoramiento de Maíz y Trigo (CIMMYT, International Maize and Wheat Improvement Center). (I promise this is the last acronym I'll ask you to remember in this chapter.) The alliance of FHMM, CIMMYT, Banamex, universities, and other agencies set about disrupting the traditional milpa practices of Yaxunah and a handful of other Yucatecan towns through an initiative called, naturally, the Sustainable Milpa Project.

The Sustainable Milpa Project advocates for no-burn, intensive milpas as a sustainable alternative to traditional Indigenous milpa practices that rely on controlled burns and shifting fields every couple of years. I believe that the Sustainable Milpa Project has good intentions: it's initiated important conversations with Yucatec Maya farmers about climate resilience, even as those initiatives have been executed in ways that casually blame Indigenous subsistence farmers for global climate change. This is messy. Well-meaning interventions can sow unexpected consequences.

Take, for an example, seed saving. Seed saving is a critical practice for building Indigenous food sovereignty and for preserving agricultural practices that can adapt to the extremes of climate change. After NAFTA, the flow of cheap US-grown corn—a lot of it transgenic—pressured Mexican subsistence farmers to start growing industrial corn varieties. Countless landrace maize varieties, the biodiverse heirloom seed stocks that had been adapted over generations to particular places and for diverse growing conditions, were damaged or destroyed by this shift. This biological violence is troubling beyond the extinction of culinary heritage alone: landrace maize varieties contain genetic adaptations for resilient agriculture in a changing climate, with strains of drought-resistant and pest-resistant plants still barely studied by science.[27]

The Sustainable Milpa Project has piloted seed-saving efforts in Yucatán: CIMMYT initiatives include collecting and distributing landrace maize varieties from and to Maya farmers, and maintaining a maize germplasm bank sheltering tens of thousands of heirloom maize varieties. In Yaxunah, farmers partnering with CIMMYT and the Sustainable Milpa Project are encouraged to actively preserve landrace maize varieties. These are native to central Yucatán and materialize the region's particular textures of Indigenous Maya ecological knowledge in every kernel. And through CIMMYT initiatives, Yaxunah farmers get trained in growing landrace maize according to the standards of organic agriculture.

The production of landrace maize in Yaxunah was not going to go unnoticed in a global culinary ecosystem that places a premium on authenticity and hyperlocality, and especially not given FHMM's marketing. To talk about landrace maize is to evoke the kind of granular specificity of place usually reserved for wine aficionados. Like the wine world's concept of *terroir*, landrace maize embodies the taste of a landscape—not just its soil and rainfall but generations of farmers and forests interacting through the centuries. Yaxunah has been able to protect these flavor histories in its maize at a time when farmers across Mexico are being pressured to sow genetically engineered crops and thus enter a cycle of dependency on commercial seeds, pesticides, machinery, and biotechnology. When that placeless industrial corn passes through a factory, the mass-produced tortillas that result are anonymous and ahistorical. But when Yaxunah landrace maize passes through the careful hands of a skilled Yaxunah cook and is finished on a *comal* (griddle) over a wood fire—well, that tortilla is going to be something quite different. That tortilla is going to have roots.

FHMM wagered that wealthy (especially foreign and wealthy) people would pay a lot of money to eat this different tortilla. During their early partnership with Lool K'uum, FHMM marketed Yaxunah's landrace maize under the Traspatio Maya brand. A portion of the landrace maize grown in Yaxunah stayed in the village, where the Lool K'uum cooks used it to make handmade tortillas for tourists during cooking demos and tourism events.

Yaxunah's landrace tortillas became integral as FHMM started to liaison between the community and a new niche of potential customers: celebrity chefs. Famous chefs had existed before, but social media and the Food Network transformed the possibilities for culinary renown in the 2010s. Chefs who knew how to harness digital platforms could suddenly share their food with a huge audience—a much larger clientele than what their restaurants could seat. Chefs competed to showcase their engagement with little-known regional cuisines, feeding into a wider conversation about culinary authenticity unfolding across the internet.[28] FHMM, as an organization equipped with robust international and corporate connections, had already established itself as an intermediary for wealthy seekers of "authentic," "traditional," and "sustainable" culinary experiences among the Maya of Yucatán.

While FHMM stood to benefit by bringing celebrity chefs into Yaxunah, the people of Yaxunah were active participants in these engagements; this wasn't something that just happened to them. Their agency, particularly the agency (and talent) of the cooks, matters. The food itself matters. Yaxunah became a landing place for celebrity chefs because of the long history of sustainable development projects in the community, and also because Yaxunah cooks actively developed a careful fluency of how and when to translate their culture for foreigners, of how and when to deploy the cultural capital of Maya cuisine in contexts that satisfied the desires and expectations of outsiders.[29]

The tortillas made by these cooks captured the landscape itself in corn. They materialized in *masa* not just hundreds of years of Indigenous ecological knowledge but also the interventions of neoliberal reforms and sustainable development programs. First FCY and then FHMM planted the infrastructure for "sustainable tourism" in Yaxunah and brought outside attention to the community. Lool K'uum cooks learned to orient their traditional cuisine towards that outside attention. CIMMYT assisted Yaxunah farmers in growing landrace maize in ways that allowed the maize, and the tortillas, to be marketed as organic. By the mid 2010s, no other tortillas tasted like Yaxunah's because no other town matched its precise mingling of Indigenous knowledge with neoliberal disruption.

ॐ   ॐ   ॐ

René Redzepi tasted one of those tortillas in November 2016 and the impacts are still reverberating in Yaxunah years later. Leading up to that encounter, Redzepi and his Copenhagen restaurant, Noma, had become famous for innovating "New Nordic" cuisine. Noma's New Nordic approach depends on the hyperlocal sourcing of seasonal ingredients. The restaurant usually does an annual round of three menus that change with the seasons: the seafood season from February to May, the vegetables season from June to September, and the game and forest season from October to December. The Noma team complicates modern culinary sensibilities with techniques revived from the past—fermentation, foraging, dehydration—to offer eaters an unequivocal sense of place and time through food.[30] This is the sensibility Redzepi brought to each of his pop-ups, and eventually, to Tulum.

In 2016, Redzepi was looking for a new challenge; I guess winning the title of best restaurant in the world four times over makes one restless. He temporarily shut down the flagship Noma and left Denmark. Then he traveled to Mexico to plan a new pop-up, to be based in Tulum, for a short run of seven weeks. The story of Redzepi's quest to launch Noma Mexico is chronicled in the memoir *Hungry: Eating, Road-Tripping, and Risking It All with the Greatest Chef in the World* by Jeff Gordinier, a food critic for the *New York Times* who hung out a lot with Redzepi during the lead-up to the pop-up.[31] Gordinier refers, only semi-jokingly, to Redzepi as a cult leader. *Hungry* reads like hagiography, and I get the sense that Gordinier counts himself as one of the chef's most ardent disciples. I read his accounts with a hearty grain of (artisanal sea) salt.

Gordinier writes that Redzepi was stressed out and feeling adrift in Yucatán when he found FHMM. Noma Mexico had just lost a million-dollar backer, who dropped out amid the financial anxieties immediately following the 2016 US election. Redzepi was agonized that he'd now have to charge $600 per person, before taxes and service charges, to eat at Noma Mexico "just to break even" and he dreaded the social media backlash he knew would follow.[32]

On the day the *New York Times* would announce Noma Mexico publicly for the first time—November 18, 2016—Redzepi was in Mérida with his squad trying to figure out logistics for the pop-up. Aside from Gordinier, the squad included Redzepi's creative partner Rosio Sanchez, a Mexican American chef with Noma connections who now owned the Copenhagen restaurant Hija de Sanchez, and Roberto Solís, Redzepi's friend and a Mexican chef who owned one of Mérida's highest-profile restaurants, Néctar. Both Sanchez and Solís reside in the realm of celebrity chefs, though not quite at Redzepi's level of influence.

Solís had already collaborated with FHMM by that time, and it's likely that he, as Redzepi's friend and ally with the strongest base in Yucatán, brought Redzepi and FHMM together. Gordinier introduces the organization this way: "Visibly on edge, [Redzepi] and the group pulled into the offices of an organization in Mérida that sought to support and protect Mayan artisans and farmers throughout the Yucatán Peninsula." This "organization" is unnamed in this moment, but based on other passages in Gordinier's memoir, along with Noma blogs and FHMM press materials, it's clear the organization is FHMM.[33] Gordinier continues, "When we walked in, we saw arrayed on a large table examples of their wares: chiles, radishes, herbs, cobs of red and purple and orange corn, pyramids of a local salt called *espuma de sal*, and a dark watery honey, suggestive of vanilla, that the Mayan people used for medicinal purposes."[34]

Redzepi "spoke to the people behind the organization with a warm but forceful directness," saying,

> We've taken over a jungle site near Tulum where we're going to build a restaurant. . . . Actually it's going to be announced in the *New York Times* in about ten minutes. We'll be serving five thousand people in two months. So if we want these ingredients, suddenly we'll need a lot of them . . . so if we want to get these things, can we get a lot? . . . We've actually been to quite a few places in our inspiration journeys. We're trying to find the ingredients and be more inspired about how we cook. We're on the hunt for things like this that would inspire even Mexicans.[35]

The organization's representatives reassured Redzepi that he'd have 350 "Mayan" families working to supply his vision for Noma Mexico—the "jungle site" in one of the most developed areas of the Yucatán Peninsula.[36]

A day or two later, FHMM arranged to show Redzepi and crew the new suppliers for Noma Mexico. Hungover from a stress-induced evening of mezcal shots, Redzepi, Sanchez, Solís, Gordinier, and the rest of the squad piled into a van and drove east out of Mérida. They arrived in Yaxunah just in time to behold the unearthing of cochinita pibil, the same pit-cooked pork dish Rick Bayless had highlighted in his own sojourn to Yaxunah just over a year earlier.

Gordinier describes a scene much like the one filmed for Rick's show: Yaxunah cooks masterfully giving foreigners what they want to see and taste. Yaxunah men dug up the pig, the women of Lool K'uum cooked tortillas, and all were dressed in immaculately white traditional clothing. Whether the foreigners realize these clothes were part of a performance being put on for their benefit, Gordinier does not say.

Redzepi watched, entranced, as the Lool K'uum cooks deftly shaped the tortillas and flipped them on the comal. "We should ask them what they're doing in April and May," Redzepi said.[37] The Noma crew ate the cochinita tacos—slow roasted pork, buttery soft fat and acid from achiote and citrus, wrapped in a handmade landrace maize tortilla, topped with fresh pickled red onions and habanero—and were astonished by the flavors. They decided then and there that they would source all the maize for Noma Mexico from Yaxunah, through FHMM.

Just getting the maize wasn't enough. Gordinier recalls, "it was clear that [Redzepi] now felt as though he had to take things a step further," and so Redzepi hired the women of the Lool K'uum collective on the spot to make tortillas "on full display in between the dining room and the kitchen at the pop-up in Tulum."[38] Looking back on the experience in a later blog post, Redzepi and his creative partner Sanchez remarked: "We chose to source our corn from Yaxunah because it was there that we tasted the best tortillas of our entire trip."[39]

Revived by the hangover-obliterating power of cochinita tacos, Redzepi gathered his disciples to leave Yaxunah for their next stop. "He knew how to inspire his team," Gordinier says. "And so it was that the communion with the cochinita pibil was followed by a trip deeper into the past": they visited Chichen Itza.[40] Yaxunah, of course, has plenty of (unrestored, vegetation-covered) ancient ruins if team Noma had wanted archaeology. But I reckon that a superlative figure like "the greatest chef in the world" would gravitate towards a UNESCO World Heritage Site and wonder-of-the-world-designated (and hypercommercialized) archaeological site like Chichen.

Gordinier recounts the visit, documenting Redzepi's impromptu stint as a tour guide of Maya archaeology. I recognize much of what Redzepi is quoted as saying as the fabricated crowd pleasers most tour guides give to foreigners, and so I presume this wasn't Redzepi's first time there. The culminating moment of the trip happens in the Chichen ball court, a huge rectangular open area flanked by high stone walls. Anyone who has visited the site will recall the incessant sound of clapping and shouting as tour guides tell their charges that the ball court was engineered to transmit sound perfectly.[41] Sure enough, Redzepi soon has his team calling to each other from across the court's vast space. Gordinier again marvels at the chef in the final passage of this chapter: "It was, at that moment, possible to imagine a conversation between the creative dreamers of the present moment and their counterparts centuries earlier."[42] Redzepi, a wealthy European man, is explicitly rendered an heir to ancient knowledge—ancient Indigenous Maya knowledge.

There is a certain vulnerability in what Gordinier's memoir shares about Redzepi's initial encounter with Yaxunah (and overshares: I quote hungover Redzepi, or at least Gordinier's recollection thereof: "In a lot of these Mayan villages—alcohol is forbidden. Because it drives them crazy."[43]). I am glad for this glimpse into the often-obscure machinations of contacts and connections, and yet I am frustrated by Redzepi's single-mindedness in his engagement with Yaxunah, at least as it's portrayed in the memoir. And it matters

FIGURE 4. Whole grilled pumpkin served at Noma Mexico. Photo by T. Tseng. Licensed under CC BY 2.0. https://www.flickr.com /photos/68147320@N02/34285632664/in/photostream/

that the consequential trip to that village is immediately followed by a pilgrimage to the most famous and most visited archaeological site in Yucatán. Gordinier's picture of Redzepi is that of a man positioning himself, his restaurant, and his cuisine in communion with a very selective history, one that connects the ancient past to a performative present and neatly brushes aside the intervening centuries of colonialism, capitalism, and extractive land relations.

Noma Mexico opened in April 2017 and existed for seven weeks. Tickets for the restaurant—$600 USD each, plus an extra $150 for taxes and service fees—went on sale in December 2016 and sold out in three–and-a-half hours. Most people curious about Noma Mexico had to be satisfied with photos posted by food bloggers and reviews from restaurant critics. Even then, to quote the *New York Times* restaurant critic Pete Wells, who wrote a salty nonreview about refusing to review the pop-up, reviews of "a pop-up that sold out months ago" were "spectacularly useless."[44] Most critics just gushed: "the meal of a lifetime" said one,[45] "the most enviable meal of the year," said another.[46]

The women of the Lool K'uum collective are mentioned in nearly all the reviews. Their presence seems as integral to the dining experience as the food itself, which is inventoried in breathless detail: lobes of cacao, banana ceviche, melon clam from the Sea of Cortez, kelp oil, *salbutes* with dried

FIGURE 5. *Cerdo pelón* (pork) tacos served at Noma Mexico. The menu listed the tortillas as being made of "fresh milled corn from Yaxunah." Photo by T. Tseng. Licensed under CC BY 2.0. https://www.flickr.com/photos/68147320@N02/34999424421/in/photostream/

grasshoppers, sapote, starfruit, and mango in *chile de árbol* broth, whole grilled pumpkin (figs. 4, 5, and 6). "The best table may be No. 23, parked front and center amid the greenery and with a view of the kitchen that captures the four local women whose sole job is making tortillas," said Tom Sietsema for the *Washington Post*.[47] From Joshua David Stein for *GQ*: "At the very heart of the restaurant, on the steps of the kitchen, four women in traditional dresses from the Yaxunah community in the Yucatán handmade tortillas during the day as well as through dinner service."[48] Even Pete Wells, curmudgeon author of the "spectacularly useless" viral nonreview, notes succinctly: "Directly in front of the kitchen, four women from a nearby Mayan village make tortillas."[49] The landrace maize, made visible through the Indigenous women making tortillas, became totemic of Noma's commitments to sustainability.[50] A reservation and $750, after taxes, bought diners the privilege of being able to say they had partaken in the landrace communion, in Noma's rite of global sustainability.

ॐ ॐ ॐ

Noma Mexico fed its last diners on May 28, 2017. Then it was over. The Lool K'uum cooks went home to Yaxunah. Redzepi returned to Copenhagen and

FIGURE 6. Yaxunah women preparing handmade tortillas with Yaxunah maize at Noma Mexico. Photo by T. Tseng. Licensed under CC BY 2.0. https://www.flickr.com /photos/68147320@N02/34743903380/in/photostream/

reopened the flagship Noma a few months later, now as its own campus with an urban farm, fermentation lab, and staff sauna. His social media accounts hint at returns to Yaxunah. A post from early 2019 tagged to the town shows a huipil-clad Yaxunah woman flipping tortillas on a comal, while in the background Redzepi cheers her artful maneuvers. A series of posts from February 2020 shows Redzepi and his family traveling around the peninsula on a sabbatical, and it includes a video from a cooking demo at Yaxunah. When I close Instagram and switch over to Google Maps, I locate the site of the former Noma Mexico ("we've taken over a jungle site near Tulum") and study the pixels for hints of what happened here. It's become its own sort of archaeological ruin. Time goes on.

After Noma Mexico, Redzepi and Solís, the celebrity chef of Mérida restaurant Néctar, partnered again—and again with FHMM—to launch a series of gastronomic festivals in Yucatán known as Hokol Vuh. Billed as "an unprecedented sustainable culinary event," Hokol Vuh annually brings in the most revered chefs in the world to immerse themselves in Maya cuisine.[51] The festival is based in Mérida; from there the chefs journey around the peninsula. They cook their way through FHMM's outposts across Yucatán, from luxury hotels in renovated ex-haciendas to the rural communities where food and artisanal goods are produced for FHMM's brands. The chefs immerse themselves in Maya archaeological sites, markets, and milpas. Yaxunah is, of course, among the places they visit.

Hokol Vuh's first edition took place just months after Noma Mexico ended its run in the summer of 2017. Famous chefs like Blaine Wetzel (an American Noma alum and then chef at the Willows Inn on Lummi Island, Washington) and Ana Roš (a Slovenian chef and owner of the two-Michelin-starred restaurant Hiša Franko) participated in the festival, along with the more familiar faces of Redzepi, Solís, and Sanchez.[52] The festival returned in November 2019 for a second edition, this time bringing along even more standouts: Daniela Soto-Innes (then chef at Atla in New York City), Mike Bagale (formerly of Alinea in Chicago), Virgilio Martínez (of Central in Lima), and many more.[53] Promotional materials and social media posts document the growth of Hokol Vuh in glittering detail. An Instagram post from the first edition, tagged to Yaxunah, shows Roš learning to make tortillas alongside Lool K'uum women while the other Hokol Vuh participants look on.[54] Posts from the second edition make vigorous use of the hashtags #sustainablemaya and #agriculturasostenible (sustainable agriculture).[55] Redzepi said he wanted chefs to fall in love with the food and people of Yucatán, as he did.

All of this attention on Yaxunah from the top of the culinary world naturally spread out and down to the level of "foodies"—a term I don't like, even as I begrudgingly accept I might be one, a little bit. Foodies are a hipsterish species of adventurous eater, attentive to the discourse of culinary sustainability and authenticity, and often willing to pay up to participate in it themselves. Foodies (or at least their precursors) had been coming to eat at Yaxunah long before Noma Mexico, as their visits were what motivated the Lool K'uum collective to form in the first place in 2005. But the late 2010s, with Noma Mexico and Hokol Vuh's deeply Instagrammable content tagged to Yaxunah, attracted a new generation of foodies to the community. Social media posts from that time show foodies cooking and eating in Yaxunah, tagged liberally with hashtags like #sustainablemaya. National Geographic offered "expeditions" to visit Yaxunah. Tour agencies sold rural homestay packages, complete with authentic Maya meals. Yaxunah entered the realm of influencer culture.

ॐ   ॐ   ॐ

Then Netflix came, hungry for content. Yaxunah was no stranger to the occasional television show requiring a "Mayan experience" before that time, as the various well-connected organizations involved in the community acted as intermediaries. But the rise of new genres of cooking shows and food docuseries—particularly the emergence of a kind of documentary sometimes called "food porn" for its sensuous, slow-motion shots of food, scored to crescendoing swells of orchestral music—converged just so with the rise of celebrity chef culture to reinvigorate television production at Yaxunah.[56]

In one key example, Chef David Chang (famous for restaurants like Momofuku and the food writing publication *Lucky Peach*) produced a Netflix documentary series, *Ugly Delicious*, featuring an episode dedicated to tacos.[57] While Chang goes on a taco crawl across Los Angeles, a production crew in Mexico visits Noma Mexico chef Rosio Sanchez in Yaxunah to document the cochinita pibil experience. Women of the Lool K'uum collective, prominent in this episode, would have already been familiar to viewers attentive to the Noma expanded universe. One of the women, unnamed in the episode, would soon transform Yaxunah's culinary landscape once again.

Rosalía Chay Chuc grew up in Kancabdzonot, a town neighboring Yaxunah, and moved to Yaxunah when she married her husband Ernesto at age 18. She speaks Spanish and Yucatec Maya (many adults in Yaxunah speak only limited Spanish). Doña Rosalía had long been a member of Lool K'uum.[58] Through the collective, she often cooked for us archaeologists at camp; I remember chatting with her in the kitchen, I remember her smile, and I remember her food. It was delicious, of course—I'd say pretty much all the meals I've eaten that were prepared by Lool K'uum cooks have been delicious. Doña Rosalía had been one of the tortilla makers at Noma Mexico.

To my outsider eyes, the strength of the Lool K'uum collective and its success as an organization resided in collaborative practices of mutual support nurtured by the participants and their families. The dynamic nuances of such a collective are not compatible with the mythos of the individual at the heart of celebrity chef culture. And so it was that Netflix elevated doña Rosalía above her collaborators in an episode of the critically acclaimed documentary series *Chef's Table*.

Chef's Table epitomizes the food porn trend of the late 2010s and early 2020s culinary documentaries. From its first season, the series established a clear template: each episode centers on a celebrity chef, crafting a narrative of his or her (but usually his) trials and triumphs, intoned in reverent voiceovers. Dramatic music underscores the narrative throughout, while slow-motion, exquisitely rendered shots of restaurant kitchens play out on screen. The series uplifts chefs as heroes, as rebels, leaders, geniuses—and beyond all else, as individuals.[59]

Connections between the *Chef's Table* roster and Redzepi's orbit are many, even though Redzepi himself has not appeared in the series; for instance, Hokol Vuh participants Roš and Martínez each had their own episode (in seasons 2 and 3, respectively) and other participants trained with *Chef's Table* subjects, as with Soto-Innes, who got her start working with Enrique Olvera (season 2). In more recent seasons (and in response to critical backlash)[60] the show has increased representation of chefs of color, women chefs, and non-celebrity chefs. Doña Rosalía was not the first non-celebrity chef the show featured, but her episode, part of a limited series dedicated to barbecue cooking, stands out for focusing on the story of an Indigenous woman with no formal culinary education.

Doña Rosalía's episode follows the show's standard tropes, painting her as a lone defender of Maya culture and tradition in a changing world.[61] The episode's central narrative is captured early in this statement by doña Rosalía: "Si no rescatamos la tradición maya, lo que creemos se va a perder" (If we don't rescue Maya tradition, our beliefs will be lost). To me, this narrative reads as one contrived by the show's producers, rather than one driving doña Rosalía herself—especially given the prominent place traditional lifeways hold in Yaxunah and in other Maya communities across Yucatán and the Maya region. I don't engage with this episode as an unfiltered view into a Maya woman's worldview. I read it as an artifact meant to relieve an audience (a relatively wealthy foodie audience) anxious about its culpability in the dynamics of globalization, climate change, and the erosion of Indigenous food sovereignty.

Read in this way, the episode is a rich text. Its plot covers doña Rosalía's early life through her tenure as a tortilla maker at Noma Mexico. In between, we get lots of interviews with Roberto Solís and Ricardo Muñoz Zurita (a Yucatecan chef and author), recounting how they "discovered" doña Rosalía, brought her to Tabasco to co-run a high-profile cooking demo, and eventually connected her with Redzepi. Towards the end the episode begins to feel overtly like marketing: the two male celebrity chefs tell us that Rosalía is willing to serve anybody who wants to come to her table, and the cinematography shifts to scenes of well-dressed outsiders—foodies in the wild—eating in slow-motion taco reverie while Rosalía looks on, shyly smiling, from the corner.

Just as Redzepi was drawn to the archaeology of Yucatán, the *Chef's Table* producers rely on the ancient Maya to heighten the sense that Indigenous traditions are in danger of disappearing. Ruins provide a visual landing for lost ways of life. Doña Rosalía's first voice-over in the episode narrates over lush footage of the Yaxuná archaeological site, just outside town: "Mis abuelos nos contaban que ellos tenían este maíz allá en las ruinas . . . muy antiguas. Ya no existe" (My grandparents used to tell us that they had this maize out in the ruins . . . very ancient maize. It doesn't exist anymore). We see doña Rosalía walking along the ancient mounds, dressed in a huipil. She continues, "Esa tierra es la última conexión de los mayas" (That land is the last connection with the Maya).

Later, towards the close of the episode, doña Rosalía again walks the Yaxuná ruins while her voice-over imagines a future conversation with her daughter. "Porque si vas a un lugar y le piden, ¿quién eres y de dónde vienes? Sabes, siempre tiene su tierra" (Because if you go to some place and they ask you, "Who are you? And where are you from?" You'll know. You'll always have your homeland). The ruins, and Rosalía's solitary vigil among them, materialize a continuity in the landscape, a collapsing of millennia through food and this one woman who cooks it. You, the viewer, can come to her table and eat that food—visit Chef Rosalía's website to book your culinary experience now.

Many people already have. Right after doña Rosalía's *Chef's Table* episode aired, the internet's attention to her and to Yaxunah surged. Google searches for Yaxunah spiked to an all-time high. Social media accounts in Rosalía's name were soon rolled out. While these accounts are clearly managed by someone fluent in English, Spanish, and Instagram (in other words, almost certainly not doña Rosalía herself) they continue unabashedly to lure foodies to Yaxunah to eat in doña Rosalía's "house."[62]

Even with a pandemic raging, Rosalía and her representatives began advertising cooking experiences for guests as early as November 12, 2020. When influencers began arriving to eat at doña Rosalía's table, their posts further pollinated the narrative seeded by *Chef's Table*. "Ate the most authentic Mayan food in Yucatán" a Tulum yoga influencer told her eleven thousand followers beneath a photo of herself grinding corn with Rosalía.[63] A Mexican YouTuber posted footage of herself wandering the Yaxuná ruins before the meal in a video titled *"Conocí a Rosalía! La famosa chef de Netflix"* (I met Rosalía! The famous Netflix chef) for her hundreds of thousands of followers.[64] Over the months since the episode released, doña Rosalía's ghostwritten social media accounts frequently invoke connections to the ancient

Maya—the *Popol Vuh* or Maya creation story, sacbes, pyramids—and, steadily since April 2021, they attach #sustainabletourism to almost every post.

Globalization *does* deracinate and erode Indigenous food sovereignty, but the narrative of Yaxunah marketed in *Chef's Table* is simplified to a fable, one palatable to the kind of person who watches the show in the first place. This is a narrative that essentializes Indigenous communities as fossils of ancient civilizations and positions outsiders—from celebrity chefs to foodies—as uniquely capable of saving those communities through capitalism.

ॐ   ॐ   ॐ

Environmentally anxious consumers, particularly those of us living relatively comfortable lives in wealthy nations, do not want to think about how our avocado toast is fueling cartel violence in Mexico or how our quinoa bowl is destroying biodiversity in the Andes.[65] We pay extra for absolution from these anxieties. Certification labels—the seals promising us that our groceries are "dolphin friendly" or "organic" or part of the "rainforest alliance"—act as "some sort of moral shield, allowing those of us with disposable income to pay extra for our salvation," as the writer Benjamin Lorr puts it.[66] Food media and celebrity chefs likewise promise relief from these anxieties. What we are buying with $750 spent at a Noma pop-up isn't actual restitution for Indigenous communities impacted by globalization and climate change—we are purchasing relief from our fears that we are part of the problem. We are buying a sustainability story.

This story, it seems, may not be itself sustainable. The Noma expanded universe has been under scrutiny lately as Noma-trained American chef Blaine Wetzel (an attendee at Yaxunah cooking demos during Hokol Vuh's launch) was exposed by the *New York Times* for lying about the sourcing of ingredients at his restaurant, the Willows Inn on Lummi Island in Washington.[67] Following the Noma tradition of hyperlocal cuisine, Wetzel's restaurant had presented its ingredients—essentially all of them—as being foraged or grown right on Lummi Island. But the island is only just over nine square miles, and the restaurant was serving twenty-five different plates to as many as forty people for six nights a week—the claim was "mathematically impossible." Whistle-blower former staff at Willows Inn described buying rotisserie chickens from Costco and trimming frozen Alaskan scallops into the shape of local pink singing scallops. "Wild" venison supposed to have been harvested from the island was actually farm-raised and from out of state. This exposé sparked outrage, and, I think more anxiety; this was a look behind the curtain of the sustainability story marketed by brands like Noma, revealing instead an uncomfortable on-the-ground reality of artifice.

Optics matter, and in late 2016 Redzepi knew how it would look when he increased the admission price of Noma Mexico to $600. "Hopefully the public is not going to slaughter us," he worried to Gordinier.[68] To garner goodwill, Redzepi and creative partner Sanchez announced partway through the pop-up that, for the remainder of Noma Mexico's run, 90 percent of the income from the walk-in-only bar menu would go to the "Maya Mundo Foundation" and thus towards "the sustainable social and economic development of Mayan communities in the Yucatan Peninsula." Redzepi and Sanchez name the recipient of their donations "Mundo Maya" in their press release,[69] and this is the name that media outlets picked up on in articles praising the gesture.[70]

At first when I read this coverage I was confused—who was this nebulous Maya World foundation Redzepi and Sanchez had found for their donations? On a closer read I saw that just once do they give the full name of the organization: Fundación Haciendas del Mundo Maya, that familiar FHMM with its familiar connections to banks and multinational corporations.

The omission of haciendas here feels important to me. Haciendas were plantations. On haciendas, Indigenous Maya people, along with immigrants from other lands, were effectively enslaved through debt and forced to grow cash crops, specifically henequen, a fibrous plant that was essential to the development of industrial agriculture in the United States. FHMM's first venture was converting former haciendas into boutique hotels—what they called a sustainable tourism model. While the organization has since branched out, its involvement in luxury hotels based in ex-haciendas continues and remains preserved in the foundation's name.

Celebrity chefs and sustainable development programs claim to be in conversation with the past, but too often they uplift a version of history that neatly jumps from the ancient Maya to the Maya of today. By deftly skipping over the complicated legacies of colonialism and neoliberal reforms, their brands uphold a story of sustainability that doesn't have to examine the deep harms that extractive land relations have done to Indigenous communities. In Redzepi's January 2023 announcement that he would close the flagship Noma for good, he said that the Copenhagen restaurant had become "unsustainable"—not environmentally, but "financially and emotionally."[71] But in that same declaration, he made clear that Noma pop-ups would continue.

Redzepi's quiet implication that the pop-ups *are* sustainable echoes his choice to gloss over the "hacienda" in the announcement of what really amounted to a negligible charitable donation to a sustainable development organization: both actions materialize the deep problems with this sort of sustainability story. This sort of story deracinates history from land. This sort of story renders land useless.

⁎   ⁎   ⁎

People are saying, now, that Tulum is no longer the place to be; the beaches got overcrowded and choked with sargassum seaweed left by a noxious bloom in the warming Caribbean. Then people said the place to be was Hol Box, a tiny gemlike island off the coast of Quintana Roo; Hol Box now overflows with the garbage of tourists and is sinking under the rising sea. Then people said the clear blue waters of Bacalar Lagoon would make it the "next Tulum"; the incoming flood of tourists and their waste have turned the sapphire water an opaque and sickly green. Each of these destinations was promised at some point to be the place where sustainable tourism would thrive. What happens to those places, when the attentions of the wealthy and environmentally anxious flutter off to the next sustainability story? What happens when those lands get cast aside as used up, as useless?

One day during Noma Mexico's run, I am closing an excavation unit at Tzacauil, out at the far edge of the Yaxunah ejido. I'm drawing a quick sketch of some rocks when I notice the T-shirt that Arturo, a Yaxunah community member working on the excavations, is wearing. The shirt is emblazoned with the silhouette of a fish and the words *Mexico: One Plate at a Time with Rick Bayless—Yucatán*. The memory surfaces suddenly: in the Yaxunah episode of Rick's show, Arturo was one of the men who digs up the pig out of the pit. Today he is digging on behalf of a different interloper. As I slip the finished drawing inside my metal clipboard, I ask him, "Where'd you get that shirt, Arturo?" He uses the heel of his hand to push a clod of earth off the trowel's blade. He is silent for a moment, trying to remember, then answers with a shrug. "Some guy. We cooked for him."

TWO

Murderer of the Woodland

ONE OF THE OLD YUCATEC Maya names for the milpa farmer is *aj kiim-saj káax* (*el asesino del monte*, the murderer of the woodland).[1] This is a name that recognizes the life of the forest and the obligations that come with taking life in exchange for the crops of the cleared field. Forest and human lives braid together: generations of milpa farmers live and die and regenerate in entanglement with the forest, as generations of the forest live and die and regenerate in entanglement with milpa farmers. In the woodlands of the Yaxunah ejido, the community's collective landholding, generations of Maya farmers and forests have cultivated together a deep ecological intimacy over millennia; the milpa and the maize grown there are archives of this entanglement, of rooted and mutual land relations.

Yet the Yaxunah edge lands also hold the seeds of narratives that would cast these woodlands as useless. Out at the eastern edge, near the ruins of Tzacauil's ancient farming village, linger the vestiges of a failed ecotourism venture—a bike path out to the ruins and the Xauil cenote just beyond—and the whispers of interested private developers who have come and gone, and may come again. A few Yaxunah community members keep bees out in these edge forests, or come here to hunt, but rarely if ever now are these lands chosen by *aj kiimsaj káax* for the clearing of a new field, the planting of a new milpa. To walk the forest of the ejido edge is to read in the land a tension between the old and ongoing stories of mutual land relations, and the newer, insistent narratives of extraction. To walk the forest of the ejido edge, I think, might also create possibilities for re-rooting and restoring history to useless land—perhaps even if the walking is not for choosing a new cornfield, but for recording residues of ancient farmers in the land.

Walking the forest is an entry into the rhythms of the milpa cycle. The *milpero*, the milpa farmer, walks the woods to identify a plot of the forest that is ready to be cultivated. He cuts down the vegetation on the plot and lets it dry out.[2] Later, he burns the desiccated brush at the apex of the dry season, right before the rains come (fig. 7). Then he sows seeds in the burned parcel and tends the crops that grow there.[3] After the first harvest, he can cultivate the plot one more time and still raise a crop, but after that the cultivated land needs to recover. The milpero walks on to find another patch of forest to start the cycle over again. The forest reclaims the old field and begins its own rhythms of restoration: a succession of wild species fills in the clearing, and young saplings spared during the burn spread new branches to receive the clearing's generous sunlight. The plants and animals involved in the forest's succession are as vital to the milpa cycle as the cultivated crops. When the woodland has matured again—perhaps decades later—a future milpero may walk the land, recognize its readiness, and the cycle will repeat.[4]

But that was kind of mechanical, the way I just described the milpa cycle. Milpa is more than that. Every moment of the cycle is rooted in webs of mutual land relations and mediated by rituals of petition and gratitude.[5] The braiding together of Maya agriculture and cosmology is ancient: the oldest known Maya creation story, the *Popol Vuh*, says that the gods made the first humans, the ancestors of the Quiché lineages, from cornmeal and water.[6] In the sixteenth century, the Spanish friar Diego de Landa wrote about seeing Yucatec Maya farmers practicing rituals to petition ancestors for aid with planting, rains, and good harvests.[7]

Many of these rituals were still being practiced in Yucatán into the twentieth century and continue in the twenty-first. To ask permission before clearing a patch of forest for cultivation, a Yucatec Maya milpero might make a ritual of *hetz lu'um*, or feeding the land; chopping the forest is understood as a risk to the balance of the world (remember "murderer of the woodland") and could incur punishment if the farmer doesn't first petition the land's divine guardians.[8] Farmers offer more prayers to request protection from snakes once the clearing begins.[9] If, after all this, a field is struggling, a milpero might carry out the ritual of *loh*, or curing the land, to turn things around.[10] Milperos leave gifts of food and beverages to placate the *aluxes*, the spirit guardians of the forest and fields, and to convince them not to cause damage to crops.[11] In times of drought, the *ch'a-chaak* ceremony petitions for rain: a *h'men*, or shaman, leads the ritual by offering incense and food on a leafy altar made of saplings and young maize plants, while around the altar

FIGURE 7. Burning a milpa in the mid-twentieth century, as documented during a Carnegie Institution of Washington expedition to the Maya region. Gift of the Carnegie Institution of Washington, 1958. © President and Fellows of Harvard College, Peabody Museum of Archaeology and Ethnology, 58-34-20/58815.

men gather, making the rumbling sounds of thunder, and a chorus of boys croaks like frogs.[12] The ceremonies of the agricultural field affirm reciprocal bonds between farmers and divine guardians of the land, and emplace that reciprocity in the land itself.[13]

The milpa is the universe in microcosm. Before Yucatec Maya milperos begin to cut out new fields from the woodlands, they ritually center the chosen patch of forest by marking the four corners and the middle with piles of stones. Offerings are made at the center point, and by these practices milperos "transform the land from wild forest to cultivated land"[14] in a mirroring of the same cosmic structuring by which the gods first ordered creation.[15] The rituals that imbue the milpa with spiritual power are meant to *wa'akuntik yuntzil*, or "stand up the lords," in the four corners and center of the field, thereby replicating the order of the universe.[16]

These practices root deeply in the land: cache offerings found in the caves of the Yaxunah ejido hold whispers of past agricultural rituals,[17] and cross-shaped etchings—the quincunx structure of the cosmos—were found carved into the plaza floor of the earliest public gathering place in the ancient city of Yaxuná.[18] Tzacauil farmers probably walked the woods of today's ejido edge lands westward to gather in the center of Yaxuná. They came together in the plaza to celebrate the rhythms of the agricultural round on the solstices and equinoxes, and then walked back out to the edge lands to their farms and gardens, their houses and kitchens. Those that rooted their homes at Tzacauil would not have understood the land as useless.

᳏   ᳏   ᳏

Aj kiimsaj káax, murderer of the woodland, carries in its name a certain truth: trees do die to make the milpa possible. Traditional milpa, as developed through Indigenous Maya ecological knowledge and practices, relies on the careful use of controlled burns. The ash left by burning dried vegetation restores nutrients into the soil. But with this loss of life, there is regeneration. The controlled burns of the Maya milpa replicate the restorative power of natural wildfires: they curb pests, suppress disease, foster the growth of forage for animals, replenish soil health, prevent more extreme wildfires, and bolster forest biodiversity.[19] The Maya milpa can be considered sustainable because its practices emulate the ecological relationships found in nature, in mature and healthy forests—but that sustainability is contingent on farmers being able to apply the full range of their ecological knowledge to the management of the forest, and on their being able to pass those practices on to future generations. That ability hinges on secure land sovereignty and access to forested land.

There is a counternarrative that the Maya milpa and other forms of Indigenous swidden farming are unsustainable because they involve burning.[20] This view lumps subsistence milperos together with the corporations and governments responsible for industrial-scale deforestation: the burden of the carbon emissions caused by the large-scale eradication of forests is shunted onto the shoulders of small-scale farmers practicing traditional agriculture. The reality is that many milpa farmers have *not* been empowered to apply a full range of Indigenous traditional ecological knowledge (TEK) to forest management, nor to pass that knowledge on to the future. Proponents of colonialism and capitalism have conspired for centuries to dismantle Indigenous land tenure. Blaming Maya milpa farmers and their TEK for climate change is just one more iteration of a campaign to erode their land tenure and to undercut their intergenerational access to forested lands. The forest-farmer relationship, made visible in the milpa, becomes contested ground in ongoing environmental justice conflicts rooted in questions about land sovereignty.

There's an entire worldview breathing in a term like *aj kiimsaj káax*. That the Indigenous Yucatec Maya language holds in its ecological-lexical trove a term for farmer that translates to "tree killer" resonates with what Robin Wall Kimmerer calls "the grammar of animacy" in her book *Braiding Sweetgrass*.[21] Indigenous cultures often do not draw the same hard lines between life and nonlife that settler cultures impose on the world around them. Scientific borderlines between biotic and abiotic are porous or not there at all in many Indigenous reckonings of ecological relationship. This inclusivity, maybe, is one of the chambers in the beating heart of mutual land relations.

Kimmerer, a botanist and Potawatomi woman, writes of learning for the first time the Ojibwe term *wiikwegama*, which translates as "to be a bay." In noun-heavy English, "to be a bay" feels clunky; languages whose skeletons are verbs and not nouns feel strange and unfamiliar to minds steeped in English. For Kimmerer, after the initial unfamiliarity comes the paradigm shift: "To be a hill, to be a sandy beach, to be a Saturday . . . all are possible as verbs only in a world where everything is alive. Water, land, and even a day. The language is a mirror for seeing the animacy of the world, for the life that pulses through all things, pines and nuthatches and mushrooms. This *is* the language that I hear in the woods, this is the language that lets us speak of what wells up all around us."[22]

In an echo of *wiikwegama*, the Yucatec Maya term *aj kiimsaj káax* acknowledges the real lives and real deaths of tree participants in the milpa cycle. Through Indigenous languages and their grammars of animacy, the speaker honors the gift the woods make in allowing themselves to be felled and burned.

For thousands of years, Maya people in Yucatán have enacted the animacy of mutual land relations through practices of reciprocity with forests, soil, and water.[23] Permission is asked and offerings made before and after animals are hunted. Altars are built in the woods to make gifts of maize, incense, liquor, flowers, and cigars to forest guardians. In subterranean caves and cenotes, underground pilgrims leave offerings and collect holy water, and aboveground in times of drought, ritual practitioners petition for rain while children chant like frogs around the altar. Relationships of mutual obligation constitute the sustainability of the Maya milpa: even as milperos burn parcels of the forest, they spare young saplings by leaving them cut at breast height.[24] The saplings preserved in this way are cut back enough so that they don't block the sun for the crops, but left tall enough so that they will live to lead the forest's restoration when the field has finished its work.

Deforestation, clearcutting, timber harvest—when we speak these words, we are alienated from the loss of life that is viscerally alive in an old term like the woodland murderer, *aj kiimsaj káax*. More than just a question of semantics, the distinction between living and lifeless entities, between nonhuman beings and "natural resources," is at the core of the environmental justice conflicts and deeply entrenched inequalities alive in extractive land relations today.[25]

In that charged vein, the anthropologist Elizabeth A. Povinelli writes that the power structures of late capitalism are formed in geontopower, or the regulation of the distinction between Life and Nonlife that underlies extractive land relations.[26] When a manganese mining company intentionally damages a sacred site known to Indigenous Australians as a living being named Two Women Sitting Down, that is geontopower. "The sovereign people of geontopower are those who abide by the fundamental separation of Life and Nonlife with all the subsequent implications of this separation on intentionality, vulnerability, and ethical implication," Povinelli writes. She wonders, "is it easier to think of the end of capitalism than the intentional subjectivity of Two Women Sitting Down?"[27] There are signs that geontopower can be challenged: Indigenous Māori activists waged a 140-year campaign to recognize the Whanganui River as their ancestor, and in 2017 they won—the government of New Zealand granted the Whanganui River legal personhood.[28]

My own roots in the Americas are settler roots. My fields—anthropology and archaeology—have historical roots tangled in colonialism and extractive land relations. When I walk the forests of the Yaxunah ejido—a provisional guest with provisional roots—I have to make it an active practice to try to decenter the assumptions of the land relations I've inherited. For me it's been useful to walk with anthropologist Anna Tsing's concept of multispecies world making.[29] Recognizing the forest as a multispecies world, cocreated by human and nonhuman beings, is an invitation to recognize the porosity of our own edges and those of the other beings of the forest, while still acknowledging the outsize ecological impacts that human institutions can have on the land.

"Humans have aways been involved in multispecies world making," Tsing says. Writing about the human-disturbed forests of the Pacific Northwest, she goes on: "Humans shape multispecies worlds when our living arrangements make room for other species. This is not just a matter of crops, livestock, and pets. Pines, with their associated fungal partners, often flourish in landscapes burned by humans; pines and fungi work together to take advantage of bright open spaces and exposed mineral soils. Humans, pines, and fungi make living arrangements simultaneously for themselves and for others: multispecies worlds."[30]

In Tsing's reckoning, forests are multispecies worlds cocreated and recreated by gatherings and ungatherings—and it's the encounters, not the envelopes of "self-contained individuals," through which transformations emerge and historical shifts move in land.

The dry scrub woodland of central Yucatán is a forest world far removed from the towering evergreens of the Pacific Northwest, yet there is resonance here. The Maya milpa is an ongoing encounter among farmers, trees, maize, rocks, wind, earth, spores, guardian spirits, fire, rain, insects, birds, microbes, and clouds, among unknown and unknowable participants. The relationships are continuously unfolding and historically contingent: milpa is never practiced in an ahistorical vacuum. It is always in conversation with what has happened before—walking the land, the milpero reads the forest for signs of when it was last cleared, and if it might be ready to be planted again now—and that conversation reaches back into the deep past. The archives of that conversation are written in the landscape. They're there in the stone ruins of ancient farming villages, in a discarded Coke bottle, in subtle shifts in soil chemistry, in the height and girth of trees. And, I guess, that's why I'm there too. As an archaeologist—a member of a group that I might sometimes call an invasive species in these woods—I am drawn to these quiet but tangible records of more than twenty centuries of forest world making in the Yaxunah ejido lands. I am drawn especially to those woodlands of the ejido that have started to be seen as useless, that have attracted the attention of private developers.

Tsing says: "Forests—with their unbounded spaces and diverse ecologies—are everywhere a challenge for privatizers."[31] This has certainly proven true in

Yucatán, where for the past five hundred years, first Spanish settlers, then plantation landowners, and now enactors of neoliberal agrarian reforms have attempted to bundle forests into legally discrete parcels from which to extract wealth. The lines around landholdings are at once imaginary and very real, arbitrary artifacts but practically capable of shaping the realities of forest worlds.

The woodlands of the Yaxunah ejido are co-creators of a multimillennial multispecies forest world, but as a legal entity, Yaxunah's landholding is much younger. Following the uprisings of the Mexican Revolution, agrarian reforms granted communal landholdings, the ejidos, to rural communities across the country.[32] The invisible border that encloses Yaxunah's ejido, today some 4066 hectares including forests, fields, archaeological sites, water, caves, animals, and plants, is less than a century old as I write this. The Yaxunah ejido was officially established in 1934.

Since the late twentieth century, it's been legal for rural communities to sell their ejido lands—a move meant to incentivize economic development that also opened the door to shady land deals and outright land grabbing.[33] The ejido is an imperfect system of land tenure, and there are those who call for its abolition altogether. When I talk about the Yaxunah ejido as a place for restoring history to multispecies forest worlds, I'm doing so not because I think these 4066 hectares hold inherent meaning as a bounded unit, but because arbitrary lines like this one shape the lived realities for nearly all people alive today. A long view of mutual land relations, and of environmental justice, asks us to work within the borders of systems like the ejido, while also digging under, climbing over, and pushing through them.

❧   ❧   ❧

As Noma Mexico's seven-week run was just getting started in the spring of 2017, I was in Yaxunah getting ready for my third season of archaeological fieldwork at Tzacauil, out at the eastern edge of the ejido. It was peak dry season. The forests of the ejido were skeletal and sparse, the ground at its most visible. When the land is thirsting for rain, it's the best time to undertake archaeological survey work. Over the course of one dry week, one of the last before the rains began, a group of six Yaxunah men and women and I walked the woodlands of Tzacauil and the ejido's eastern edge. This walking survey wove conversations about Maya TEK into the documentation of archaeological features: the stone foundations of the homes of ancient Maya farming families and the lands surrounding them.

Gathering the group for the TEK-based survey had taken a couple of weeks. When I first met with Yaxunah's local authorities to ask for their help finding a team of *ejidatarios*, community members who hold collective rights to the ejido, to walk and talk around Tzacauil with me, they suggested four men. All four had experience as milpa farmers, all four were familiar with the eastern ejido forests, and all four had worked with me before in past seasons.

But I also wanted women on the survey. Milpa farming is traditionally the domain of Maya men, but other kinds of agriculture—specifically, the cultivation of gardens and orchards around the home—are traditionally associated with women. Archaeological investigations at other Maya sites were showing that intensive cultivation around ancient residences played an integral role in past Maya food systems.[34] I felt that Yaxunah women might be more attuned to recognize signs of ancient gardening TEK in Tzacauil than Yaxunah men, and certainly more than I am.

When I asked the local authorities about hiring women, they were skeptical at first. Archaeological projects had been running in the ejido since the eighties. In all that time, only men had been hired to do fieldwork. These authorities, a group tasked with all matters concerning the ejido including archaeological sites, told me that women wouldn't be interested and if they were, they'd get too tired; this group of authorities were themselves all men. Yaxunah's other branch of government, the municipal authorities, supported the idea from the start but were limited in their jurisdiction to influence ejido matters beyond the town; this group of authorities was headed by Yaxunah's first woman *comisaria*. Still, the ejido authorities hinted that they might be open to a change, so we agreed to meet a second time.

About half an hour before that second meeting, Nazario, a friend of mine (and the former Chichen Itza hot dog cook I mentioned in chapter 1), dropped in to find me at the archaeologists' camp. Nazario was currently serving as the treasurer of the ejido governing body and would be at the upcoming meeting. He called me out of my hut with a low whistle and motioned me over, then whispered instructions: bring some snacks and some cold Coke to the meeting. Really cold Coke, he specified. Without a further word he wheeled his bike out of camp and rode off.

I followed his orders, swinging by one of Yaxunah's small *tiendas* on my way to the town hall. I arrived with a big sack of chips, a stack of plastic cups, and a huge bottle of really cold Coke. Nazario, already seated with the other authorities when I arrived, gave me an ever-so-slight nod of approval as I

FIGURE 8. The *xíimbal k'áax* survey team walking the forests of the Yaxunah ejido edge lands. Photo by the author.

offered refreshments. The meeting unfolded over salt and cold sweetness, and as usual most of the talk went down in Yucatec Maya. I sat politely, looking from speaker to speaker, gathering up the loose phrases of Spanish mixed in as I tried to follow. The Coke must have been cold enough, because the authorities agreed to another meeting—and this one, they told me, would be open to women *ejidatarias* interested in participating.

At that next meeting, six Yaxunah women, all ejidatarias, came and heard my proposal for the TEK-based survey in the eastern ejido—with more Coke and snacks, of course—and ejido authorities translated between Spanish and Yucatec Maya as needed. We eventually agreed that if any of the women were interested in being hired to participate, they were welcome to show up on Monday morning (May 1, 2017) for one week of, as I fumbled to describe it, walking and talking in the woods. When the sun came up on Monday, I was delighted to see two of the women, along with the four men recruited earlier, waiting outside the camp. This was the survey team.

The seven of us walked, talked, wandered, and wondered our way through Tzacauil and the forests of the eastern ejido over the next week (fig. 8). On the morning of the first day, I stumbled through a longer explanation of what I hoped to learn alongside the six ejidatarios, but as with so many things, we figured it out by getting started.

The Tzacauil site has one large pyramid (the Tzacauil Acropolis), a raised limestone causeway (the Tzacauil Sacbe), and a scatter of lower mounds loosely clustered around the acropolis.[35] All are covered in trees and scrubby vegetation; there hadn't been any burning in this part of the ejido in a long time, because no one had made milpa in this part of the ejido in a long time. The littler mounds are the stone and rubble foundations for long-gone houses made of wood and thatch. These were once the homesites of ancient farming families. The open lands around the littler mounds, I suspected, might have been used by those families for cultivation.

The TEK-based survey team walked the woodlands around each of Tzacauil's ancient homesites in a sort of collective practice of on-foot imagination. At each homesite, we tried to imagine what had drawn ancient farming families to that particular place. We tried to detect signs in the soil and rock that archived how past people collaborated in the cocreation of their patch of the multispecies forest world. We felt out subtle differences in soil, documented reservoirs in bedrock, mapped out ancient walkways, identified plants, looked for water, tracked animals, and studied how the sunlight fell. Mostly we walked and talked, and I logged what I was learning from these six practitioners of forest TEK onto a lidar map of Tzacauil I kept stored in a tablet that hung around my neck.

The TEK-based survey that these six Yaxunah community members and I walked our way through combined the practices of traditional archaeological surveys, where surface features like building foundations and stone piles are recorded on maps, with "walk-in-the-woods" data-collection techniques used by ethnobiologists.[36] This survey surprised me: while much of what we did together was done for my benefit and within the structure of a transaction (I was, after all, paying the community members to walk with me), we finished pretty much everything I had planned for the survey by the second day. The remainder of the week together became slow, open-ended, and rambling. We ended up walking a much wider range of the eastern ejido than I had expected, and much of the conversation that unfolded on those unhurried walks had little to no clear connection with my project. The community members were sharing memories and conversations about land, in the land itself, and with each other—in fact, most of those conversations remained in Yucatec Maya only, with only the occasional summary in Spanish offered for me. For some of the community members on the survey team, these were lands that they had not visited in years, or ever. I recognize now that these kinds of grounded conversations were opening possibilities for rooting in useless lands, for restoring histories in the edges of the ejido.

Indigenous practices of land-based education open additional possibilities for thinking about the potential alignment of archaeological practices, like the Tzacauil TEK-based survey, with anticolonial goals. Land-based pedagogies, as Leanne Simpson says, understand land as both the context and process for learning. They arise from the core premise that "if you want to learn about something, you need to take your body onto the land and do it."[37] She notes that "by far the largest attack on Indigenous Knowledge Systems right now is land dispossession, and the people that are actively protecting Nishnaabewin (all things Nishnaabe) are not those at academic conferences advocating for its use in research and course work but those that are currently putting their bodies on the land."[38] Echoing and expanding on this idea, Matthew Wildcat and colleagues say, "if colonization is fundamentally about dispossessing Indigenous peoples from land, decolonization must involve forms of education that reconnect Indigenous peoples to land and the social relations, knowledges and languages that arise from the land."[39] I can't say if the TEK-based survey in the eastern ejido had the effect of land-based pedagogy for the participants, but I do believe that the project created incentives to connect community members with land and with each other in the context of that land. Engaged archaeological practices designed to include opportunities for community members to connect with each other on land and with land, without any particular "use" for archaeologists or their research, create spaces for the restoration of history to lands cast as useless.

We didn't call what we were doing a "TEK-based survey" while we were doing it. After the first day, the Yaxunah community members recognized what we were doing under a different name: *xíimbal k'áax*, walking the woods.

ða   ða   ða

Our ambling conversations through the Yaxunah ejido were accompanied by many beings of the forest world. Earth and bedrock, wind and water, spiders and lichens: all have their encounters, and all have their histories. The area's really deep history might begin with the same asteroid that would later inspire the creation of a dinosaur theme park at Chicxulub. When that asteroid, itself a minor planet, plummeted into the planet sixty-six million years ago, its force rippled out from Chicxulub and punctured craters in the submerged limestone platform of the Yucatán Peninsula. When the peninsula began to surface above the sea during the Pleistocene (24–33 million years ago), the cratered wounds remained as cavities in the karst plain.[40] Many more millions of years later, the Maya would call these cavities *dzonot*. The Spaniards heard the word as *cenote*, and this is what most folks call them today. As the only permanent sources of water in the northern peninsula, these apertures in the bedrock give life to the Maya forest world.

This is a young land. On the continent to the north, the Appalachians were already more than four hundred million years old when Yucatán came out of the sea. The peninsula arose as a limestone platform from the water, and accreted more limestone, marl, and gypsum into its newborn landscape. In the north the peninsula is a flat, low plain, save for the squat rolling hills of the Puuc region in the west, and its soils are thin and pocketed in bedrock pits. Dry scrub forest and grasslands grow in the shallow, rocky earth, surrounded by the saltwaters of the Gulf of Mexico and the Caribbean.[41]

Bedrock is sometimes called in Spanish *la roca madre*, the mother rock. In Yucatán, bedrock forms the foundation of the forest world and is the foundation for Indigenous Maya ecological knowledge. The bedrock is often described as flat. But to walk the landscape is to witness with your feet just how many ways the mother rock defies generalization: bedrock bulges out into massive outcrops, crumbles into boulders, swings low into shallow depressions, drops off abruptly into crevasses. Where apertures in the bedrock open down to water, you have cenotes. Some cenotes are open with the water right at the surface like ponds. In others the water is at the bottom of deep columnar shafts, and in still others water is reachable only by plunging into caverns through porthole-like portals. And nearly everywhere, the bedrock holds caves, both dry and wet, honeycombed inside itself.

There are places where bedrock undulates and drops but does not break in upon the water table. These dips create soil traps, depressions that gather and pocket the earth. The largest of these depressions, known as *rejolladas*, can support much deeper root systems than soils on the surface (fig. 9). They shelter biodiverse microclimates by conserving moisture and enabling the growth of mature and multilayered forests. Trees find refuge in *rejolladas*, and for millennia Indigenous practitioners of arboriculture have tended fruit and cacao trees deep inside the depressions.[42] Smaller and shallow low places, called *bajos*, are important too for their capacity to shore up soil and moisture. The qualities of soil-rich depressions and their locations in

FIGURE 9. Deep depressions, known as *rejolladas*, conserve moisture and trap soil, allowing lush pockets of trees and plant life to flourish in the central Yucatán landscape. Photo by the author.

the forest world are curated carefully in the hyperlocalized TEK of the Yaxunah ejido.

Bedrock is exposed and abundantly visible on the surface of the central peninsula, and over the centuries the rock and Maya people have collaborated to shape the forest world. Outcrops—places where bedrock juts out of the ground—offer ready platforms for houses as well as the materials with which to build them. These natural rock florescences lend their mass to ancient monuments; the Tzacauil Acropolis, like many pyramids in the Yaxunah ejido, is essentially a husk of stone masonry stretched over a natural rock outcrop. Long stretches of flat bedrock stippled with cavities hold opportunities for temporary water storage during the rainy season (fig. 10). Those same cavities, when filled with soil, mimic *rejolladas* in miniature and are utilized for container gardening.[43] Larger pits pockmarked across the bedrock can be expanded or reinforced using clay and stone walls to increase their capacity as rain catchers. Openings into the subsurface world grant clandestine access to water, storage pits, and veins of *sascab*—a white marl

FIGURE 10. Natural cavities in bedrock create seasonal reservoirs and opportunities for container gardening. Photo by the author.

powder that can be used to make plaster and mortar. Caves are sacred in their role as portals into the earth's interior.[44]

The trees at home in this rocky terrain are shorter and scrubbier than the high-canopied rainforests of southern Yucatán and Central America. Forests in northern Yucatán hug the ground, shading the undergrowth of thorny brush below, except in places where soil traps gather stands of tall trees together. Maya forest TEK attends to the habitats and growth cycles of several kinds of hardwoods, especially *chaká* and cedar, as well as fruit-bearing trees. Trees are intrinsic to life in Yucatán—they give firewood, building materials (beams, posts, fronds), forage for animals, and foods both for festivities (tree bark for the alcoholic beverage *balché*) and for famine (*ramón* trees provide breadnut, a food eaten in times of desperation).[45]

The trees create homes for the animals. Yucatán has been called *la tierra del faisán y del venado*, the land of the pheasant and deer, and these creatures and many others have cohabited the forest world with humans for thousands of years. Not all species have survived the transformations of colonialism and industrialization: jaguars, ocelots, pumas, spider monkeys, and many other species once native to Yucatán have waned or vanished altogether from the region. The animals that have persisted hold important ground in Maya land relations. Life cycles of animals are reckoned along with the tempos of the milpa, as many creatures frequent the fields to eat weeds, blossoms, insects, or crops at specific points in the seasonal cycle.[46]

Humans are joined in the cocreation of the forest world by and with other mammals. Their names across different languages and nomenclatures create a chorus: there are deer/*kéej* (*Odocoileus virginianus yucatanensis*), peccary/*kitam* (*Pecari angulatus yucatanensis*), armadillo/*weech* (*Dasypus novemcinctus*), agouti/*tepezcuintle*/*jaaleb* (*Dasyprocta aguti*), rabbit/*t'u'ul* (*Sylvilagus floridanus yucatanensis*), coati/*chi'ik* (*Nasua narica yucatanica*), squirrel/*ku'uk* (*Sciurus yucatanensis*), raccoon/*k'ulu'* (*Procyon lotor L.*), and pocket gopher/*tuza*/*baj* (*Orthogeomys hispidus yucatanensis*).

Birds, too, cocreate the forest world, including wild turkey/*kuuts* (*Meleagris ocellata*), partridge/*nom* (*Crypturellus cinnamomeus*), quail/*beech'* (*Dactylortyx thoracicus sharpei*), grackle/*k'áaw* (*Quiscalus mexicanus*), woodpecker/*ch'uju'ut* (*Melanerpes pygmaeus*), vulture/*ch'oom* (*Coragyps atratus*), and *motmot*/*toj* (*Eumomota superciliosa*).

There are many others. Reptilian and amphibian cocreators of the forest world count among them the spinytail iguana/*t'ool* (*Ctenosaura acanthura*), box turtle/*áak* (*Terrapene yucatana*), many kinds of frogs and many kinds of snakes, several of which, like the *huol poch* (*Agkistrodon russeolus*), are dangerous to humans. Rich insect, arachnid, and microbial life abound and collaborate in the forest rhythms.[47]

ﻉﻭ   ﻉﻭ   ﻉﻭ

During our *xíimbal k'áax* TEK-based survey walks, my eyes and my feet began to adjust to the forest. I started to recognize patterns in the ground as the Yaxunah community members walking with me pointed out, again and again, the subtle shifts in the mosaic of bedrock and soil that makes up the

FIGURE 11. Burning reveals the mosaic-like terrain of the Yaxunah ejido: a patchwork of superficial bedrock, or *tzekeles*, interspersed with soil expanses, or *kancabales*. Photo by the author.

terrain. Bedrock, exposed on the surface with sometimes only a dusting of leaf litter, can easily make up half of the ground surface in a given area in the Yaxunah ejido (fig. 11). Where there are soils, it's pretty common for soil layers to measure only about twenty centimeters deep before they give way to bedrock, and often they're even shallower. Interlopers in this landscape have long derided the soils of Yucatán, from colonial friars to industrial agriculture corporations to archaeologists frustrated with poor preservation conditions.[48]

Yucatec Maya farmers remain unperturbed by these concerns and continue to curate a deep working knowledge of shallow soils, as they have for millennia. Only recently, scientific soil analysis has confirmed what practitioners of Maya soil traditional ecological knowledge have known for a long time: soils in northern Yucatán are incredibly diverse, shifting along variables of age, parent materials, rainfall, topography, atmospheric conditions, as well as the amount of organic materials and living organisms they harbor.[49] Coaxing crops out of this stony landscape for thousands of years, as Maya farmers have done, is a practice grounded in ecological intimacy with the land and a granular knowledge of its nuances.

Maya soil TEK is curated and communicated through the precision of specialized words. The Yucatec Maya language is a storehouse of soil types contained in a complex lexicon.[50] There are words to organize soils according to the qualities that shape their agricultural potential. Color, depth, granularity, and stoniness are accounted for lexically in ways that baffle the speakers of homogenizing colonial tongues. Two kinds of soil that are particularly important in the Yaxunah ejido's forest world are *box lu'um* and *kancab*.

Box lu'um (or *ek lu'um*; both mean "black earth") is a thin, rich, brown or black soil made dark from great amounts of organic matter. The darkness signals soil nutrients, and among many Yaxunah farmers today, box lu'um is the preferred soil for milpa agriculture. Box lu'um abounds in the Yaxuná archaeological site, the largest ancient settlement in the Yaxunah ejido and also the longest occupied, and so this zone is where many milperos look first when scouting the plot for their next planting. In doing so they participate in a multimillennial ecological conversation with farmers of the distant past.

Rather than inferring that the ancient city of Yaxuná was settled in this place *because* of these black soils, we should probably flip the causal link: the organic-rich soils covering the ruins were likely created through centuries of human life, enriched through generations of household refuse. At some Maya sites, as well as in the Amazon, such anthropogenic "dark earths" were at once by-products and sustainers of human settlements, as waste fertilized soils and enabled the practice of intensive agriculture.[51] Today's Yaxunah farmers who make milpa in the Yaxuná ruins are in a very direct way transforming generations of ancient, localized ecological intimacy into maize.

But out in the edge lands of the eastern Yaxunah ejido, we walked not on black earth but on the brilliant red soil called *kancab*. Kancab glosses to "yellow earth" but to my eyes its color is often closer to red. Around Tzacauil the kancab is a bright reddish orange, sometimes straight scarlet. Beneath the top layer of red clay, there is a yellow lower subsoil. You find kancab in low-lying depressions and in wide, level expanses called *kancabales*.

Most of the Yaxunah farmers I've talked to consider kancab a lower-quality soil for cultivation. That's partly why, people told me, no one really bothers to farm in the eastern ejido anymore, where red soil abounds. Yet researchers studying Indigenous soil TEK across the Yucatán Peninsula have documented that while kancab and other red soils may not be preferred by farmers practicing milpa agriculture, they are the primary soils used by farmers practicing *intensive* agriculture.[52] Intensification involves increasing inputs of time and energy—amending the plot with fertilizer, rotating crops to restore nitrogen back into the soil—to enable continuous cultivation of a single plot of land. That's a very different strategy from the shifting milpa, in which milperos plant on parcels (made nutrient-dense through the ash from controlled burns) for two years before they move on and allow forest succession to reclaim the old fields. Since most contemporary Maya farmers in the Yaxunah ejido practice milpa agriculture, it makes sense that kancab would be widely regarded as marginal compared to the black earth of box lu'um.

But we know that agricultural practices and ecological knowledge are not static; they change and transform through history. For past farmers, the kancabales of Tzacauil and the eastern ejido could have held a different meaning than they do in the twenty-first century—and in fact, this hypothesis would later be supported by excavations my team and I conducted at the first farming village that formed at Tzacauil about two thousand years ago. Casting these lands as useless holds echoes of Spanish colonial authorities' complaints about the poverty of Yucatecan soils: the useless land narrative depends on the uprooting of history.

࿐ ࿐ ࿐

The possibility that ancient Maya farmers were practicing agricultural intensification—farming in fixed plots over long periods of time, made possible through inputs like fertilizer, weeding, crop rotation, and so on—raises an important connection to current concerns about sustainability. Traditional Maya milpa agriculture requires that farmers have access to a lot of land in which they can shift from one forest patch to the next; for this reason, milpa and swidden farming more generally are considered extensive agriculture. Extensive agriculture inherently involves cycles of forest clearing, and so in some reductionist viewpoints, milperos are responsible for deforestation-related climate change along with industrial logging companies, plantation owners, and commercial cattle ranchers.

Climate change is already a reality for farmers in Yucatán: they feel it in shorter and erratic rainy seasons, more and more severe hurricanes, and unusual crop damage caused by insects and other creatures, whose own life cycles and habitats are impacted by unpredictable weather. These all make agriculture a more precarious venture than it used to be, especially for subsistence farmers who might lack resources to buffer against the risk. These stressors combine with the challenges of navigating the neoliberal and globalizing food landscape, and the result in Yaxunah is that many community members feel pressured to leave farming and migrate out to seek employment in hospitality or construction.[53]

Some sustainable development organizations have suggested that milpa agriculture is, at least in part, responsible for climate change. CIMMYT, the agricultural research nonprofit that partnered with the Fundación Haciendas del Mundo Maya to lay the groundwork for organic landrace tortillas in Yaxunah, sometimes lumps milperos together with the corporations and governments culpable for large-scale deforestation.[54] Because milpa farmers practice controlled burns that kill trees every year, they get painted with the broad brush of condemnation for the carbon emissions, soil erosion, and loss of biodiversity caused by deforestation writ large. It seems to matter little in this rendering that milperos are subsistence farmers practicing a form of Indigenous agriculture that is thousands of years old. I am troubled by this portrayal; I see in this narrative an erasure of history and a careless leveling of context. The controlled burns of traditional milpa farmers are not the same as the state-sanctioned logging, plantation agriculture, and industrial cattle ranching tearing through the forests of the Amazon, East Africa, Sumatra, Borneo, and many other wooded places around the world.

The alliance of CIMMYT and FHMM launched an initiative in a handful of Yucatecan farming towns to disrupt the Maya milpa in the interest of curbing deforestation: this is the same Sustainable Milpa Project I talked about in chapter 1.[55] Yaxunah was one of the towns where they piloted the project. The Sustainable Milpa Project set up a model farm to demonstrate the possibility of milpa with the "slash-and-burn" part excised altogether. Rather than a traditional extensive milpa, where the site of active cultivation shifts to a new location every couple of years, this experiment would be an intensive milpa, theoretically capable of continuous cultivation in a single, fixed plot. Instead of using ash (burnt vegetation), the soil of the model milpa would be enhanced by other kinds of fertilizers—certified organic, of course, so that the maize grown could be marketed as such in Noma Mexico and other high-end establishments. Organic agriculture has its benefits, and I think its practices would make sense to traditional Yaxunah farmers even if they were unfamiliar with the term itself.

But during our walking conversations of the *xíimbal k'áax* TEK-based survey, I began to wonder whether the Sustainable Milpa Project was more interested in organic certification and its appeal for outsiders (chefs, hipster foodies) than in sharing the root meaning and reasons for organic agricultural practices with Yaxunah farmers themselves. Don Tomás, one of the

Yaxunah elders on the TEK survey team, shows up often in the photographs used in CIMMYT's promotional materials. He is charismatic, holds within himself a deep archive of Indigenous ecological knowledge, and is a gifted storyteller and communicator.[56] Importantly for both CIMMYT and myself, he is also generous with what he knows and willing to share it with outsiders.

One day during the survey, don Tomás was telling me about the organic milpa practices he was learning from CIMMYT agricultural scientists on the Sustainable Milpa Project. He told me that organic—*orgánico*—just meant that you left the leaf litter on the ground before planting, rather than burning it. In Spanish, leaf litter is often called by Yaxunah community members "lo orgánico"—the organic, biodegradable stuff. So the explanation held a certain logic: the organic milpa promoted by CIMMYT was a no-burn milpa, which meant keeping the leaf litter intact on the ground. Don Tomás was satisfied with this explanation, and did not, when I asked, remember much about CIMMYT's communication of "organic" as a certification process that went beyond simply not burning (in fact, organic food can be produced through traditional milpa using burns). It's possible, of course, that CIMMYT technicians did explain the full meaning of organic to don Tomás and the other participating project farmers. But even if they did, it felt strange to me that the community elder so often invoked in the Sustainable Milpa Project's promotional materials had not been fully briefed on the meaning behind the pilot milpa and its push for organic certification.

࿐ ࿐ ࿐

Sustainable development initiatives like the Sustainable Milpa Project have a complicated relationship with ancient and traditional agriculture. Initiatives might co-opt ancient agricultural practices, like the milpa, to confer a sense of long-term sustainability and legitimacy to their programs, but they often seek to resurrect or improve those practices in ways that ignore the legacies of more recent history (like colonialism and neoliberal reform) and fail to take seriously the expressed needs and desires of farming communities themselves. In a 2019 report about the Sustainable Milpa Project pilot farm, I read that CIMMYT predicts the campaign for no-burn practices in communities like Yaxunah will continue long after the project formally ends.[57] Their optimism reminds me of another chapter in the story of sustainable development and ancient farmers, one that unfolded far from the Yaxunah forest world, high in the Andes mountains. I want to uproot us, for a moment, from the bedrock of the Yaxunah ejido and go to the ground around Lake Titicaca.

The plains around Lake Titicaca, a high-altitude body of water straddling the border between Bolivia and Peru, are ribbed and textured with acres and acres of oblong mounds and ridges.[58] These earthen constructions are the relic farms of ancient Andean peoples. Farmers built these raised fields by mounding up muck from the lake bottom, engineering artificial islands where planting could be possible. Canals interdigitated with the earthen platforms, providing channels for reed boats to pass through as well as a ready and replenishing source of water and nutrient-dense lake muck for the crops.

Raised fields like the ones around Lake Titicaca were innovated independently as a form of intensive agriculture by ancient farmers around the world. Raised fields let farmers regulate drainage and watering and they stabilize soil temperature, which in the Andes helps baby potato plants survive the frosts of early spring. Raised fields also enable farmers to coax crops out of swamps and marshes—places that otherwise might not allow for agriculture at all.[59]

But raised fields also take a lot of work. Intensive agriculture in the broadest sense is all about increasing energy inputs—weeding, mucking out canals, applying fertilizer, building fences, scaring away crows, planting cover crops, dredging up soil, hauling away rocks—to maximize what you can grow in each plot of land. Raised field farming requires a lot of labor to build and then maintain. Why would the ancient farmers of Lake Titicaca go to all that trouble? And, with relic raised field systems covering tens of thousands of hectares, why did they farm this way at such a huge scale?

The raised fields of Lake Titicaca had long been mysterious: even by the time the Inca Empire conquered the Titicaca Basin, the raised field systems were long abandoned and their history obscure. Later, sixteenth-century Spanish colonizers chronicled Indigenous Andean farming. They described irrigation and terracing but said nothing about raised fields. In the late twentieth century, archaeologists began researching them—right at the same time that sustainable development projects were first crystallizing.

An archaeology graduate student from the United States named Clark Erickson set out to investigate some of the raised fields on the Peru side of the border in 1981. Erickson quickly realized that just excavating the raised fields wasn't going to answer all his questions about the role they played in ancient Andean societies, so he decided he'd experiment with farming on raised fields himself. He used the ancient canals and ridges as a blueprint and enlisted local Quechua farmers to help build a modern raised field system with handheld farming tools. With the fields ready, the crew planted crops native to the highlands: potatoes, quinoa, and *cañihua*.[60] For five years Erickson and his team collected data on the experimental fields. They measured the soil-replenishing properties of "green manure"—lake muck dredged from the canal bottoms and spread on the fields—and charted the fields' capacity to regulate soil temperature and buffer against frost damage. They also measured crop yields, particularly for potatoes.[61]

The crop yield data got most of the attention because the raised fields produced bumper crop after bumper crop. Over five years from 1981 to 1986, Erickson's experiment grew an average of ten metric tons of potatoes per hectare. Neighboring potato farmers, not planting on raised fields, harvested on average only one to four metric tons per hectare. Erickson reported the results with buzzy excitement in 1988: "These larger yields are especially significant because we used local and improved potato varieties without fertilizers in the experiments, while most of the potato fields upon which the regional estimates for Puno are based were fertilized." He went on to say, "We have also demonstrated that high yields can be sustained for several years of continuous cropping."[62]

Erickson wasn't alone: another archaeologist from the States named Alan Kolata built and cultivated a separate set of experimental raised fields in the Lake Titicaca Basin in the eighties. Kolata's raised fields also produced surprisingly high yields. Using these results (and Erickson's), Kolata ventured that continuous potato cropping made possibly by raised fields had fed the vast Tiwanaku Empire (ca. AD 600–1000), one of the major Andean civilizations and a precursor to the Inca.[63]

The archaeologists believed that raised fields eliminated the need for land to rest between potato crops. They thought that adding lake muck to the planting beds replenished nutrients to the soil and took the place of fallowing. The promise of intensive, continuous, and high-yield farming in a region often dismissed as agriculturally unproductive was a big deal, and news of the experimental raised fields soon hurdled past the disciplinary boundaries of archaeology and into the sphere of sustainable development. A long-neglected ancient agricultural technology suddenly seemed capable of miracles; an end to global hunger, or at least to poverty and food shortages in South America, felt within reach.[64]

Erickson, who by this time had finished his PhD and gotten a job as a professor, soon partnered with agronomists, the Swiss government, and the

Peruvian Ministry of Agriculture with the mission to revive raised field farming among economically vulnerable Peruvian farmers. Erickson explained the reasoning for the raised field rehabilitation project in a 1988 article with the optimistic subtitle, "Putting Ancient Agriculture Back to Work," writing, "countries such as Peru and Bolivia often use models from more technologically advanced nations to develop their agriculture and industry." These models fail, explained Erickson, because they depend on synthetic fertilizers, expensive equipment, and cash cropping. But raised field farming would be an "appropriate technology" based on traditional and local modes of technology and labor organization. Raised field farming could rescue the poor of the Andes—if only smallholder farmers were willing to reclaim this ancient farming practice as "appropriate technology."[65]

Flush with support from the international aid community, the project partners sank a fortune into the raised field farming initiative. They spent millions of dollars rehabilitating ancient remnant fields, building new ones, and launching a campaign to convince (mostly indifferent) small-scale Andean farmers to get on board. Quechua-language promotional and educational materials invoked a (mostly fictionalized) narrative of cultural heritage by explicitly linking the splendor and symbols of ancient Tiwanaku civilization to the goals of the modern nation-state. The sustainable development folks ran an enthusiastic effort, but the people whose enthusiasm actually mattered—the farmers—remained at best lukewarm about the push for a "return" to a form of agriculture they had never practiced. The raised fields never gained traction with the farmers, and the initiative sputtered to an end.

Years later, the anthropologist Lynn Swartley reexamined the premature push of ancient raised field farming as "appropriate technology" for sustainable development. Swartley noted that for the sustainable development community, the branding of raised field farming as "indigenous" absolved it of the sins of Western industrialized agriculture, an echoing back to earlier reductive tropes of the "noble savage" and "ecological Indian." "The ancestral and indigenous pedigree of the raised fields led researchers to uncritically assume that the fields were ecologically compatible with the lake basin environment," she said. "The linking of sustainable development and theories that privilege indigenous knowledge is partially due to North American and European preconceptions of Native Americans as being natural environmentalists and conservationists."[66]

Assumptions that ancient raised fields were inherently sustainable based on their antiquity and precolonial status missed the importance of historical context. The excitement shared by the archaeologists and the sustainable development community was premature: true, the experimental fields overwhelmed expectations with their back-to-back potato harvests, but a five-year experiment doesn't justify the leap to advocate for continuous cropping, indefinitely. In practice, farmers who did agree to adopt raised field farming ran into crop failures after a handful of years of continuous potato cultivation. Later, agricultural scientists learned that fallow periods do more than just restore nutrients to the soil—they also work to curb the growth of pest populations, particularly certain nematodes capable of decimating potato plants.[67] Simply adding lake muck does not substitute for the ecological role of fallowing and crop rotation.

Archaeologists have continued studying the remnant raised fields of the Titicaca Basin. Through that work, an altogether different narrative has emerged than the one of well-fed farmers that first sparked the raised field rehabilitation campaign. Now archaeologists tend to think that the ancient farmers of the Titicaca Basin gained no direct benefits from raised field farming; the farms were a system designed to serve the political elites of the Tiwanaku Empire. Farmers may have been coerced or otherwise compelled to undertake the hard work of building, maintaining, and cultivating the raised field systems. This was not a way of life that empowered farmers, this was a system designed to extract tribute from the agricultural base of an expanding empire.[68]

In Swartley's postmortem on the raised field rehabilitation campaign, she calls the technique "invented indigenous knowledge." "Raised field agriculture was not an actual system of knowledge that was intact and in practice by contemporary inhabitants of the Lake Titicaca Basin," she points out. "The contemporary practice of raised field agriculture was an invented tradition, which maintained ethnic and class boundaries through the symbolic appropriation of the past."[69] In presuming inherent sustainability in the remnant raised fields and in pushing for a "return" to a form of agriculture that farmers had never in their lives practiced, the campaign accidentally crossed into the territory of neocolonialism.

The South American raised field rehabilitation projects proved untenable, but the optimistic link they fabricated between ancient agriculture and modern sustainable development lives on in initiatives like CIMMYT's Sustainable Milpa Project. Declaring intensive "no-burn" milpas sustainable by virtue of the trees not cut, the woodlands not murdered, misses the complex social and political nuances underlying the longevity—or collapse—of agricultural systems. Certainly, deforestation does release carbon into the atmosphere, trigger soil erosion, and cut down biodiversity—but when we fail to differentiate the impacts of traditional ecological practices, like subsistence milpa agriculture, from industrial-scale destruction, we move towards a definition of sustainability that is neither equitable nor environmentally just.

The narrative that intensive milpa would be more sustainable than traditional extensive milpa implies that Yucatec Maya communities would be better off abandoning the TEK of burning. This narrative insinuates that communities would themselves become sustainable if they cut off the traditional milpa's multigenerational conversation among forests and farmers in favor of small, fixed, continuously cultivated parcels dedicated, it seems, to growing certified organic produce for high-end restaurants and tourists. Followed through to its logical conclusion, the premise offered by the Sustainable Milpa Project and other sustainable agriculture initiatives is one in which communities like Yaxunah no longer have much use for their woodlands. Extractive land relations supplant mutual land relations. Unbound from engagement with the forest world, the edge lands of the ejido become cast as useless. Pressure builds to sell the lands to private developers who promise to make the land useful. Here is the useless land narrative, cropping up again.

෨ ෨ ෨

When I think about the useless land narrative in Yaxunah, my thoughts settle down next to the memory of a pile of rocks we encountered one morning on the *xíimbal k'áax* TEK survey.

The rocks weren't supposed to be there. The sun was already high overhead and scorching as we stood in silence contemplating the pile. Eighty miles to the east, the Noma Mexico team was halfway through their tenure in Tulum; they had just announced their plan to donate a portion of every bar menu ticket to the vaguely named Maya Mundo Foundation. But I wasn't thinking about any of that. All I could think about was the damn rock pile.

We were at Tzacauil, way out at the ejido's eastern edge, and it was one of those days at the cusp of the rainy season where the air feels crackly and alive and vibrating with both the possibility of giving rain and the possibility of withholding it for another day. I was locked in an existential standoff with the rock pile. It was early in the field season and I was still attached to the folklore that all would go according to plan, and this rock pile—clearly a collapsed structure—was not on the site map shining from the iPad I clutched white-knuckled in my hands. I stared from screen to stones and back. The still hot air vibrated in my ears as I searched the map's empty spaces for the stones in vain.

A yawn broke the silence and caught across the circle like a listless contagion. For the six Yaxunah community members with me, the rock pile posed no such existential crisis; it was one of thousands that lent its granular texture to the forest.

The map in my hands had been made a decade earlier by another archaeologist who had mapped Tzacauil and other sites in the ejido. Like most archaeological maps, this one's conventions—clean prismatic shapes standing in for amorphous rock piles like the one in front of us—had little to do with how Yaxunah community members themselves experienced their lands. I had spent hours gazing at this map and carefully superimposing it over grey-and-white lidar imagery of the area, and had planned out precisely how much time (and grant money) I needed to investigate each feature. Now, this pile of rocks, this collapsed structure that appeared nowhere on my map, threatened to throw off all that planning. Hence our standoff.

I pinched my fingertips on the screen, watching the familiar shapes of the Tzacauil Acropolis, its sacbe, and its house mounds grow and shrink as I zoomed in and out, willing the pile of rocks to appear on the map next to the dot that showed where we were standing. Finally, I cleared my throat.

"I don't see it on the map. Are you sure it's a structure?" I asked.

"Yes," don Tomás said, simply. He stood, one hand at the machete on his belt, confident, as he sized up the rock pile again for my benefit. He went on, "The ancient people stored their maize in it. We do the same today."

Turning to the others, Tomás switched from Spanish to Yucatec Maya, and the conversation immediately picked up, leaving me quiet and listening closely for words I recognized. Two of the other men, don José and don Mateo, joined don Tomás in talking all at once, gesturing expansively to illustrate their spontaneous debate about, I guessed, the proper construction of a good corncrib. Doña Noemí was mostly silent, though doña Laura periodically interjected a sentence or two into the conversation with a flourish of her hook-shaped *coa* blade. The seventh member of our group, don Crisanto, had taken a seat on a low boulder of bedrock and was fiddling silently with his sandal strap; he appeared utterly unmoved by the rock pile and the debate it had ignited. I listened hard and looked from face to face to rock pile and then back around again.

Suddenly Mateo seemed to have a revelation. His eyes widened and he clapped a hand on don Crisanto's shoulder, asking him a question and ending it with a lyrical phrase I recognized, "¿*ma si, no*?" Isn't that right? I watched as Crisanto blinked, then turned to look again, now with curiosity, at the rock pile. His eyes widened. He pushed his baseball cap back on his brow, his face suddenly opened, younger-looking with surprised recognition. He smiled, in pleased amazement, laughing as he answered Mateo's question. The six Yaxunah community members laughed, then turned and looked at me expectantly, forgetting, as they sometimes did, that I don't speak Yucatec Maya and was completely lost. "What happened? What is it?" I asked.

Mateo, still laughing and shaking his head, summed up for me in Spanish. "Yes, it's a building, but don't worry about this one," he said. "Don Crisanto built it for his milpa." He patted Crisanto on the back, and Crisanto, who didn't speak much Spanish, smiled at me sheepishly.

"I don't understand," I said.

"He built this to store his corn."

"So . . . it's not ancient?"

"No. It's, maybe, fifteen years old? He forgot he made it!"

I laughed too, then, my relief mingled with an uneasy wonder that a pile of rocks so young could play such tricks. Don Crisanto's ruined corncrib looked no different from the remains of ancient structures found all over the ejido. Without excavating, the rock pile was indistinguishable as a modern building, and even if we had excavated it, we might not have found any materials that could have been used to date it. Even the man who built it had forgotten about it.

The rock pile wasn't alone in being forgotten. This was my fifth season working in the Yaxunah ejido, and I'd long ago gotten the sense that for many community members, this patch of the forest world, out on the ejido's eastern edge, was a neglected sort of place. Now here we stood, talking over a relic from the last time a Yaxunah milpero had worked in this far hinterland of the ejido. The rock pile, ca. 2002 AD, wasn't primordial but old enough still to feel almost mysterious to me in its abandonment. Why, I asked the group, does no one farm out here anymore?

They gave me many reasons. This land is too far from the town. The soil is poor. There are too many coatimundis and they eat the maize. There are too many *aluxes* (spirit guardians, who often cause mischief and sometimes danger). The *aires* (air, wind, spirit) are too powerful. Lots of people don't really want to make milpa anymore, anywhere, because it is too risky and the chemicals are too expensive. It is better to carve wooden souvenirs for tourists than to farm. The reasons hung in the air, heavy like eulogies, as we stood again in silence around don Crisanto's corncrib.

Mateo broke the quiet by repeating, "You don't have to worry about this one."

The group stirred back to life. Don Tomás readied his machete and turned, eager to find something the actual *antiguos*, the ancients, had built. He started whacking through the thorny brush and waved for us to follow. "K'oox xíimbal k'áax," he called out. Let's walk the woods.

ﻋﯞ   ﻋﯞ   ﻋﯞ

The ejido edge lands hold, in their rocks and soils, their ruins and trees, a deeper archive of the long conversation still unfolding among farmers and the forest. In that archive, there are chapters of the conversation that took root long before colonialism, capitalism, and industrialization sowed a narrative that lands like these were useless. Archaeology is the way I learned to read that archive. If you know how to read them, stone and clay residues can transport you back to the beginning of agriculture in this land, to the deep histories of collaborative world making in these forests.

Yaxunah farmers now continue that ancient conversation with the forest. There are some new topics of discussion: no longer are the questions just about where and when to plant next, they are also questions about the offers from developers wanting to buy up the forests, and the possibilities of privatizing communal lands. *Xíimbal k'áax* was the name the six Yaxunah community members gave our TEK-based survey around the ejido edges. Later I learned that *xíimbal k'áax* is a specialized term used by milperos. It refers to the particular walk that milperos take in the forest when they are trying to decide where to burn and plant next.

The walking decision of the milpero, *aj kiimsaj káax*, murderer of the woodland, is a decision weighted with responsibility to the living forest world and a gratitude for its gifts; it is a decision rooted in mutual land relations. It is not a decision that can be made from home—it is a decision that is made on foot, in the forest, in communion with the beings of the forest world. *Xíimbal k'áax* embodies an ancient unfolding interview among farmers and forests, a series of questions still asked today but with a meaning that has changed: is it time to plant? Or is it time to move on?

THREE

Seeds of Permanence

THE GROUND WAS STEAMING, the sun was high. Damp earth exhaled into our faces as we gazed back into time. Two Yaxunah men and I were crouching beneath the trees in an open excavation. The men scraped their trowels carefully at the base of a stone wall that had been buried for the last eighteen centuries. By their side, I watched as jagged pieces of a smashed pottery bowl surfaced, blazing red against the ground. Even broken, the bowl held its shattered fragments close: we could see each piece in its place and imagine how hands had nestled the bowl, unbroken, here at the base of the wall.

Most things archaeologists unearth get buried incidentally, but some things are buried intentionally. Caches are one of them. The bowl at the base of the wall, and the food or drink it once held in its wholeness, was a cache—the material residue of an act of consecration.[1] What words may have been spoken, what songs may have been sung, what rituals may have accompanied the bowl into the ground had left no visible mark. But right after the bowl had been placed, both it and the base of the stone wall it consecrated were buried under a layer of rock and soil. I imagine the burial: the bowl surrendering first with a single splintering crack, then shattering, spilling its contents—pozole? *balche*? *caldo*?[2]—for the earth to drink in the darkness under the rubble. This was the rubble the two Yaxunah excavators had spent much of that morning, eighteen hundred years later, slowly digging out. With trowels these men midwifed the cached bowl into the twenty-first century, in land that had become the eastern edge of the Yaxunah ejido.

The bowl had been cached inside the stone foundation of the oldest house at Tzacauil. I call this house, really a large stone platform with stone foundations for three or four dwellings on top of it, the Jach Group; *jach* means big or great in Yucatec Maya, and not coincidentally, the oldest house was also the most grand. The Jach Group was the first permanent house in the early agricultural village that formed at Tzacauil in the time archaeologists call the Late Formative period (ca. 250 BC—AD 1) to Terminal Formative period (ca. AD 1–250).[3]

The people who lived here were among the earliest farmers to root in these forests. Yet the bowl itself was far older than the house it hallowed and the agricultural people who lived there. Months after the bowl resurfaced into the sunlight, a ceramicist examined its fragments and placed their origin in the Middle Formative period (ca. 900–250 BC)—a vast span of centuries when the ancestors of the first Maya farmers were living as foragers, and as transitional forager-farmers.[4]

The bowl and the house that swallowed it thread together distant moments. The bowl was formed by someone in a society that was learning to cultivate the forest while still following the seasonal shifts of wild plants and animals; the foraging people to whom this bowl first belonged were mobile and would have moved their homesites often. But the bowl was cached by someone in a society that had embraced farming, and along with farming the stone houses of permanent agricultural villages. When the founding farmers of the Jach Group planted the old bowl in their new house, they were seeding into their homesite a multigenerational connection made manifest in clay. The bowl was an heirloom.[5]

Heirloom bowls, stone houses, a pyramid and a road: some twenty centuries ago, the early farmers of Tzacauil planted rock and clay in the eastern edge forests of the Yaxunah ejido to express their deep commitments to land. The first agricultural land relations here emerged from these seeds of permanence.

The lineages of five homesites—Jach, P'aak, Chamal, Kaan, and Sáastun—together formed the first farming community at Tzacauil. Each homesite sits enfolded in a patch of open land. These open lands were not empty or unused ground: in the red soil around their homes, the early farmers of Tzacauil learned to practice intensive cultivation (fig. 12). Tzacauil farmers in this way participated in the wider genesis of Maya agricultural knowledge, including the urban agriculture that would later sustain many of the great Maya cities for generations.[6]

Centuries before the useless land narrative was sown in these woods, and centuries before celebrity chefs and dinosaur theme parks and wind farms landed in Yucatán, early farmers rooted down on the campsites of their foraging ancestors and began to cultivate the forests of Tzacauil. While the

FIGURE 12. The community of Tzacauil as it may have appeared during the time of the first farmers in Yaxunah ejido history: the Tzacauil Acropolis and initial stretch of the Tzacauil Sacbe are finished and active, and Tzacauil villagers practice intensive agriculture and arboriculture around their multigenerational homesites. This reconstruction shows Tzacauil at its peak population in the Terminal Formative, circa AD 1–250. Illustration by Kathryn Killackey.

permanence they seeded was ultimately temporary, the remains these first farmers left anchor a core chapter in the Yaxunah ejido's deep history of mutual land relations.

ॐ   ॐ   ॐ

Today, the ruins of the ancient farming village at Tzacauil are on the edge of the Yaxunah ejido. When the village was first formed by early farmers, it was also on an edge—out in the hinterlands of the ancient city of Yaxuná, the ruins of which are located just next to (and under) the modern town of Yaxunah.

Mobile foragers and early forager-farmers had been gathering in Yaxuná for generations before agriculture was widely practiced in the lands of the Yaxunah ejido. These mobile Middle Formative people came together to rearrange vast amounts of stone and earth into a plaza: a social and public space to meet and, archaeologists think, to participate in rituals linked to seasonal shifts and cycles.[7] Later, when Late Formative people took up farming, many chose to settle down close to the plaza. They built durable houses with stone foundations that would affirm connections with the plaza and its gatherings for generations. More farmers settled at Yaxuná, and together they shaped the landscape even more by building pyramids, road systems, and palaces. Yaxuná was urbanizing.[8]

Around the same time Yaxuná was really starting to grow, a small contingent of farmers decided to put down roots—not near the plaza, not in central Yaxuná, but in a patch of forest a little less than an hour's walk (about three kilometers) east of the young city. They settled to farm at Tzacauil. Their homesites formed a loose cluster around their own pyramid, the Tzacauil Acropolis, and their own little road system, the Tzacauil Sacbe. In this way they replicated the template for the neighborhoods of Yaxuná. The main difference was just that Tzacauil was not another neighborhood in the expanding city, but an offshoot apart on its own, out in the forest.

Why did these farmers choose to root in Tzacauil? I don't think they made the decision randomly; I think they rooted in these lands because they inherited a body of ecological knowledge that had been germinating and ripening long before settled agriculture took hold. There are traces of that earlier forager history in this land. It's stored in the archives of clay: in heirloom bowls like the one cached in the Jach Group, and in stray bits of broken forager pottery buried inside the houses of later farming families. These are residues of Maya people who knew the forests of the Tzacauil edge lands, long before anyone decided to stay there to farm.

Most of the Middle Formative ceramic fragments—forager pottery—that my team and I found buried inside the stone foundations of Late to Terminal Formative farmers' houses probably ended up there unintentionally. When farmers built stone platforms for their houses, they went looking for rubble to fill in the foundations. An old trash heap, or midden, made for ideal fill. Farmers gathered up middens near their homesites, inadvertently scooping up the scraps and sherds of earlier people in their baskets of cobbles and earth. When the baskets were emptied to fill the platforms, the relics of the older pots ended up together with the rubble. Even though these stray potsherds didn't get the same intentional burial as heirloom caches like the bowl at the Jach Group, their presence inside later dwellings still archives information about the early entanglements of foragers, forager-farmers, and forest worlds.

The makers of the oldest clay bowls and jars that were found, in fragments, at Tzacauil would have belonged to foraging communities. But the Middle Formative period to which those potsherds belong is vast (more than six centuries long!) and holds in its wide temporal container a couple dozen generations. Archaeologists working across the Maya region think that during some of these generations, foragers were experimenting with cultivation; they danced up to and across the porous threshold between gathering and farming and became, for at least a time, forager-farmers.[9] In Middle Formative Tzacauil and throughout the lands of the Yaxunah ejido, people easily could have been eating from half-tended gardens and groves of semiwild fruit trees. Yet these demi-domesticated places were likely only small pockets within a wider, wilder forest of untamed foods.[10]

Settled agriculture as a widespread practice was slower to root. Farmers far away in Central Mexico had domesticated maize thousands of years earlier, but the strange grass arrived unhurriedly in the Yucatán Peninsula.[11] Maya people and maize plants got to know each other for hundreds of years before they entered fully into the reciprocal relationship that continues, still sacred, today.

In this liminal time between mobile foraging and sedentary farming lived the foragers who stayed temporarily—I like to say camped—at Tzacauil. The foragers circulating through these forests were learning the granular details of local ecology and generating ecological knowledge adapted to specific places in the forest world. They were innovating the practices that would become, eventually, Maya agriculture.

All of this was happening on the move. Foragers lived light on the land compared to their farming descendants, setting up and breaking down camp across the forest as they followed seasonal wild foods.[12] I know of no house remains found in the Yaxunah ejido that can be dated securely to the Middle Formative, and this is because foragers seem to have made their homes almost entirely of ephemeral materials, wood and thatch right on the ground or directly on bedrock outcrops. These homesites lacked the enduring stone foundations that later farmers liked to use. The most durable stuff that these foragers did leave behind is broken pottery, the rubbish that accumulated at their favorite campsites. The buildup of Middle Formative forager pottery in certain places shows that groups of people, and then their descendants, returned to the same spots season after season, for generations and even for centuries. Read in this way, the buildup of forager pottery is a proxy for a deepening ecological intimacy between human lineages and land.

I compared the potsherd count and mass of Middle Formative ceramics found in excavations of each of the five homesites of the Tzacauil Late to Terminal Formative farming village.[13] The Jach Group, founded in the Late Formative as the oldest permanent homesite at Tzacauil, held in its rubbly fills the greatest amount of forager pottery by far, even with the heirloom bowl excluded from the count. Tzacauil's earliest farmers were drawn first to this place: the Jach Group incorporates a massive, naturally level bedrock outcrop—a perfect building site—surrounded by deep expanses of red soil on all sides, with a stretch of exposed bedrock just a short walk away to the north. The abundance of forager rubbish, inadvertently sequestered inside the Jach Group in its construction fill, tells us that this particular bedrock promontory had been a favorite place and perennial campsite for generations of earlier foragers. Their presence left residues as their relationship with this land deepened.

I imagine land relations developing in slow, incremental layers over the bedrock outcrop where these foragers came to camp, the outcrop itself becoming a stalagmite of their ecological intimacy with the land. I imagine a father and son pressing seeds into the red soil before breaking down camp, then returning late in the summer to harvest maize from spindly stalks. I imagine a grandmother slowly pouring a jar of water out for her tomato plants, each nested in a cavity in the bedrock outcrop that she filled with earth gathered nearby. I imagine children eating the bright orange flesh of papayas, picked from a tree planted near the promontory by their mother's mother, taking care to save the black seeds. The fragments of broken pottery these foragers left behind are not simply detritus, they are residues of break-fasts and dinners cooked and eaten around campfires, and relics of the oldest agricultural knowledge in the Yaxunah ejido. In these potsherds are the deepening roots of mutual land relations, growing slow and strong through the rhythms of everyday life.

❧   ❧   ❧

By about 300–250 BC in central Yucatán, the lives of people and the lives of maize had become so intimately entangled that land relations and society as a whole transformed: maize agriculture and permanent farming villages became foundational to life in the forest world.[14] Wild foods did not disappear from the diet. But from the traces left in the ground, archaeologists think that most folks in this part of the Maya region retired from the wideranging mobility of their foraging ancestors at the start of the Late Formative.[15] People were rooting into the land to farm, and they wanted homes that matched that rootedness, homes that would endure for generations. And so they started to build with stone.[16]

The beginnings of settled agriculture in the Maya lowlands correspond with a massive raising up of stone buildings of all sorts—house foundations, pyramids, roadways, plazas—that would be unmatched in the rest of Maya history.[17] This pattern was embraced by the earliest farmers living in the lands of the Yaxunah ejido. In the ancient city of Yaxuná, a template for agricultural settlement took root as stone buildings sprouted: people raised and repaved the earlier central plaza several times over, and they built up several huge complexes known by archaeologists as triadic group acropolises, basically C-shaped arrangements of buildings perched high above ground on massive stone and rubble platforms.[18] Builders connected these monumental stone complexes to each other via networks of raised limestone causeways, or sacbes. These monumental acropolis groups, along with palatial residences, encode in their stone signals that social hierarchies were rooting, too; many archaeologists accept the Late Formative as the origin for full-time farming and also as the origin for Maya royalty and stratified society. Pyramids and plazas became administrative centers and venues for political theater in the growing city.[19]

The farmers who settled in the city of Yaxuná stayed closer to the ground than the kings, but even they still raised up their homesites by rearranging the stony landscape into permanent homesites. The first settled farmers there chose to plant their homes on top of bedrock outcrops, which they elaborated by enclosing the outcrops with boulders and filling the resulting boulder boxes with rubble and soil to create rectangular platforms. On top of the platforms, farmers added simple stone foundations to support simple buildings, their dwellings and kitchens, made of wood and thatch. Several of these early Yaxuná farming homesites would be aggregated around a shared focal point, usually one of the acropolis groups or a soil-rich depression, creating loose clusters of homesites that replicated in scatters across the city. These clusters were the neighborhoods of urbanizing Yaxuná.[20]

If the ancient city of Yaxuná were like a tree, then each of these neighborhood clusters was like a branch. As the branches spread, the tree grew. And if you cut one of these branches from the tree trunk, took the cutting and transplanted it into a patch of forest three kilometers away, you'd have Tzacauil. Like the farmers living in Yaxuná, Tzacauil farmers planted their homesites around a shared focal point, the acropolis—a pyramid nearly identical to one built in Yaxuná around the same time—and the sacbe.[21] They built their homes the same way, boxing in bedrock outcrops with boulders, filling them in to make platforms, and placing their dwellings on top. The Late to Terminal Formative farming villagers that settled at Tzacauil faithfully replicated the same pattern of the neighborhood clusters at Yaxuná, with one main exception: they were way out on the edge of things, in the forest east of the city.

The early farming families living in the neighborhoods of Yaxuná and in the village of Tzacauil had something else in common: they preserved open lands between and around their homesites. While these open lands might appear, two thousand years later, as empty space on archaeological maps, they were far from neutral ground. These lands were being farmed. In Yaxuná, the people of later periods—the city-dwellers of the Classic (ca. AD 250–1100)—filled in these formerly open Late Formative farmlands with their houses. Later settlements make it difficult to recover archaeological evidence about how Late to Terminal Formative farmers lived in the lands around their homesites in Yaxuná. But in Tzacauil, the homesites of the earliest farming villagers remained relatively intact—so it is in these homesites at the edge of the ejido that this early history of rooting can still be read.

ह्र   ह्र   ह्र

Once a woman from Yaxunah told me the story of how she met her husband, who was from a different town. They fell in love and planned to marry. Her future husband had thought she would come live with him, but as he spent more and more time in Yaxunah visiting her, he eventually decided that he would move from his hometown to live with her. This happened a lot in Yaxunah, the woman told me. People come for a time and then decide to stay. She offered an explanation shared by many in Yaxunah: the *kancab*, the red soil of the ejido, sticks to people.

I think of this, of kancab's ability to make people stay, when I remember walking the forests of Tzacauil. Kancab predominates in the eastern ejido. In the Yaxuná ruins, closer to town, you find more black soil—the organic-rich *box lu'um*. But around the homesites of Tzacauil's first farmers, the terrain unfurls in a patchwork of yellow-red kancab interwoven with the gray and white of exposed bedrock. And like in the Yaxunah woman's story, the kancab does indeed stick, becoming a glue-like mud during the months of the rainy season. It gets difficult to walk on.

That's why the community members on *xíimbal k'áax*, the traditional ecological knowledge (TEK)-based walking survey that we conducted in the spring of 2017, were surprised to find that all five of Tzacauil's Formative farming households had chosen homesites that were surrounded by kancab. Each founding family built their house on top of a bedrock outcrop, but those outcrops float in small seas of reddish-yellow soil that would have been sloppy and sticky to walk on for several months every year. Later in Tzacauil's history, villagers favored homesites on terrain predominated by bedrock. This makes a lot of sense; bedrock offers rainy season advantages like stable walking surfaces, drainage, and access to natural cavities that can be used as reservoirs. But the first farmers of Tzacauil seem to have been determined to plant their homes directly in soil-rich—and for much of the year, mud-rich—patches of the forest.

The earliest two homesites settled in Tzacauil's Formative farming village were the Jach Group and the P'aak Group. Both are planted on bedrock promontories surrounded by expanses of deep soil just west of the Tzacauil Acropolis.[22] The soils around the Jach Group, the older of the pair, were among the deepest documented at Tzacauil. The founding families of the remaining three homesites in the Formative farming village came a little later. These three groups, Chamal, Sáastun, and Kaan, reflect the same preference for planting homesites in soil-rich places—even if they had to make compromises.[23] The founders of the Chamal and Kaan Groups staked out homesites close to the Tzacauil Sacbe. The Chamal farmers took up a bedrock promontory located in the same soil-rich expanse as the Jach Group, but settled for rockier lands to the south and thin-soiled ground to the west. The Kaan farmers chose a homesite on the opposite side of the sacbe, on a bedrock outcrop overlooking an expanse of deep soil to the west, with thinner soils and some bedrock on its other sides. The Sáastun founders sacrificed proximity to the acropolis and sacbe altogether in favor of a homesite surrounded by soil, choosing a bedrock outcrop enfolded by soil flats a few minutes' walk south of the acropolis. All five homesites in Tzacauil's early farming village are planted in soil-rich areas.[24]

Those early farmers found ways to deal with the muddiness.[25] Family members at both the Jach and P'aak Groups made the ground around their dwellings easier to walk on by arranging stones into makeshift pavements. Our excavation team found these rough stepping stones lodged into the soil while digging around the edges of the groups' boulder-lined platforms. Older Yaxunah community members pointed the stones out and explained that before cement became cheap in Yaxunah, their grandparents made informal walking paths out of stepping stones to get around outside during the rainy season. The look and placement of the stones around the Jach and P'aak Group platforms reminded these elders of the pavements they remembered from the ground outside their grandparents' homes.

On another day during the TEK-based survey of Tzacauil, two Yaxunah community members and I were walking the terrain around the Kaan Group. The Kaan Group's main platform, like the others at Tzacauil, had been built on a bedrock outcrop. But this particular outcrop came with natural walkways: an elongated stretch of bedrock connected the platform south to an expanse of flat bedrock riddled with cavities. The survey members pointed out that these natural corridors would have granted rainy season access to lands around the Kaan homesite. We walked down to the low soil flat just west of the Kaan Group—prime potential mud land. Then the two Yaxunah men noticed a line of boulders partly buried in the soil expanse, running parallel with the contours of a bedrock rise a few meters away. Outside the line of boulders, the kancab was loose and fine. Inside the line of boulders, on the side closer to the outcrop, the ground was packed and hard. Don Mateo, one of the community members on the survey team, walked back and forth stamping his feet on each side of the boulder line. I could hear the difference in the crunch of his sandal sole. The ground inside the boulder wall was too compact to be natural. We bent down and examined the surface: small pebbles had been mixed with the kancab and tamped down, with the line of boulders reinforcing the mixture like a terrace wall. Later excavations into this constructed surface revealed that it had been built towards the end of the Late Formative, around the same time the Kaan Group founders planted their homesite nearby.[26] The stretch of compacted, gravel-rich land provided a stable walking surface during the rainy season. Like the natural bedrock corridors, the gravel surface was part of a network of walkways created to enable Kaan farmers to access soil-rich land.

The Late to Terminal Formative farmers of Tzacauil put in work to be able to live surrounded by soil; centuries later, the farming families who founded the Classic period village at Tzacauil did not make these same commitments, choosing instead to live in bedrock-rich areas of the site. That early farmers went to such lengths to plant their homesites directly in soil hints at a set of land relations predicated on multigenerational connections among specific households and the precise ecologies of particular places. Something important was happening in these ostensibly empty soil-rich lands surrounding the early farming homesites of Tzacauil.

ə℈   ə℈   ə℈

For a long time, archaeologists imagined Maya sites as "vacant ceremonial centers," mostly empty places where hermitlike astronomer-priests meditated on the stars in solemn solitude, supported by an anonymous class of rogue farmers living in the forests.[27] The ancient Maya never developed true cities, reckoned early archaeologists, because Maya sites didn't look like anything the archaeologists would have recognized as cities. Cities were supposed to be dense and congested places. Ensconced in the grit and smog of London, New York, and Chicago, these archaeologists sat at their desks writing about empty Maya sites, unaware that their own definitions of urbanism were biased towards the chokeholds of medieval European fortresses—packed, enclosed, confined—whose legacies persisted in the industrial cities of the late nineteenth and early twentieth centuries.[28]

Years later, when archaeologists actually began to study those supposed empty spaces in Maya sites, they quickly found that the spaces weren't empty at all. Away from the pyramids and plazas, on-foot surveying teams documented sprawling settlements and complex infrastructure, networks of roads, canals and reservoirs, and engineered agricultural landscapes of raised fields and terraces.[29] Just in the past couple of decades, advances in lidar have further astonished the world by revealing that Maya settlements were far larger and more populated than we had guessed from the ground-level view alone.[30] Parallel discoveries in soil chemistry and paleobotanical analysis continue to clarify the emerging picture: the reason so many Maya sites appear empty is because their ancient residents interspersed settlement with intensively cultivated agricultural plots.[31] The open areas that give Maya settlements their dispersed appearance were not unused—they are relics of urban agriculture.

Tzacauil was out on the edge of a growing city and was always small. Permanent settlement in the village peaked in the Terminal Formative with a total of five homesites. The households probably would have included multiple generations and extended families, but even with generous estimates, the total inhabitants of Tzacauil likely numbered well under one hundred people and more likely ranged between forty and eighty villagers. Tzacauil was not one of the great urban agricultural cities of the ancient Maya world, like Caracol, Tikal, or Coba.

But Tzacauil does replicate the template of neighborhood clusters documented in nearby Yaxuná, an ancient city that by many measures did develop the characteristic "low-density" pattern of Maya urban-agricultural centers by the end of the Formative period.[32] Tzacauil's early farming homesites are surrounded by open lands, and unlike Yaxuná and most of the great urban agricultural Maya cities, Tzacauil's open lands remained relatively undisturbed during later periods of Maya history. Tzacauil, then, from its forgotten place out on the edge, might hold in its stones, soils, and clay the archives of land relations in the early lineage of Maya urban agriculture.

That lineage continues today in Maya *homegardens*. In contemporary Maya towns, almost every house is surrounded by a plot of land. This is the house lot. House lots in Yucatán are usually enclosed by *albarradas* (mortarless stone walls) and used regularly by resident household members for outdoor activities.[33] Homegardening is among the most important of these activities (fig. 13).[34] Maya homegardens are rich sites of Indigenous TEK, and the deep traditions of ecological interactions among current households and houselot landholdings are key to understanding the open lands in dispersed villages like Tzacauil and in the major urban agricultural cities of Classic Maya civilization.

Maya homegardens emulate the tropical forest in miniature. They intricately layer biodiverse companion species from the tree canopy down to the ground.[35] In a given homegarden in Yaxunah, you might find stands of papaya, sour orange, guaya, and avocado trees lending their leafy shade to the land, while below, hollow logs filled with black earth run raucous with green

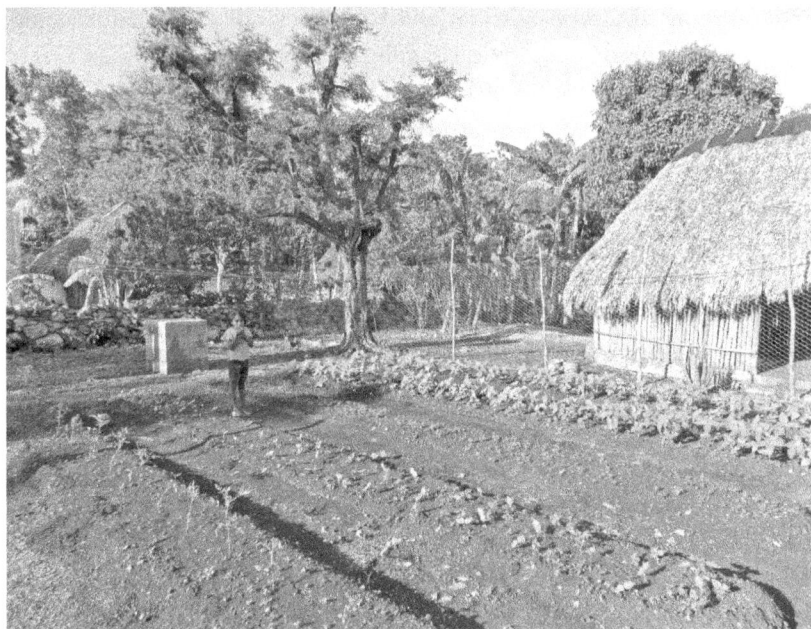

FIGURE 13. A modern homegarden in Yaxunah. Contemporary Maya homegardens inherit the ecological knowledge of ancient Maya intensive agricultural practices, including urban farming. Photo by the author.

chaya, onions, and bright red chiles. You might see buckets nesting on sunny patches of bedrock, some holding ripening tomatoes and others spilling over with flowers. Cilantro, epazote, mint, oregano, *hoja santa*, and other herbs for cooking and medicine you'd see sprouting in trays (known as *k'aanche*), filled with soil and lofted on slender, stiltlike branches to keep the plants out of pecking range of the turkeys and chickens strutting underneath. You might hear honeybee hives buzzing, tucked in a distant corner of the house lot. The ecological knowledge embroidered into the Maya homegarden is rooted in deep histories of multispecies entanglements and localized in the land of the homesite. Because the homegarden is situated around the dwelling, the connections between people and land that the homegarden seeds are intimate, personal, and continuous.

Homegardening, though, has not been a static constant in Maya history. Anthropologists working in Yucatán during the first decades of the twentieth century noted the presence of Maya homegardens, but in their quest to tabulate the caloric breakdown of Maya diet, they usually dismissed homegardening as only a negligible source of food.[36] Homegardens were good for garnishes and seasoning, anthropologists reckoned, but not really adequate for supplying the staples needed to sustain a family. Probably part of this dismissal of homegardens as inconsequential had to do with the fact that, traditionally, homegardens are the domain of Maya women. The picture became more nuanced when later ethnographic and historical research on homegardens across Mesoamerica showed that in some communities, homegardens could be critical contributors to household subsistence and even used for growing maize, long thought to have been a crop only grown away from the home.[37]

The supplemental, rather than central, role of modern homegardening traces to colonial land reforms. Colonial authorities in Yucatán worked actively to undermine Indigenous homegarden practices. There are records of an order that forced Maya communities to live in tightly gridded towns, which meant smaller house lots and smaller homegardens. This order also meant the breakup of multigenerational and extended family households, and with this the breakdown of intergenerational transmission of homegardening knowledge. Clearly, though, the Spanish had a difficult time getting communities to comply; that same order was issued repeatedly, hinting that many Maya people quietly resisted the dismantling of their spacious house lots and sprawling homegardens for generations.[38]

Cultivated plots, localized directly around homesites and interwoven with settlement, contributed a bigger role in Maya subsistence practices before colonialism. There are vestiges of ancient walled house lots, nearly identical to those seen in modern Yucatecan towns, in precolonial Maya cities like Coba, Mayapan, and Chunchucmil.[39] Archaeological studies of soil chemistry and artifact patterning have been able to link particular places inside these ancient walled house lots with intensive agriculture and gardening; these studies show that the walled homegardens of contemporary Maya towns trace back into deep lineages of ecological knowledge.[40]

However, this tradition of walled houselot gardens—a tradition that has survived into the present—is only one of many expressions of homesite-localized agricultural practices that existed in the precolonial Maya world. Many of these ancient traditions do not have clear analogues in the present. The more archaeologists investigate the apparently "empty" and "unused" lands in Maya settlements, the more heterogeneous and dynamic the picture of Maya agricultural landscapes becomes. To understand how Tzacauil and the edge lands of the Yaxunah ejido fit into this picture, I'll take you through some comparative cases of homesite-localized agriculture elsewhere in the Maya world.

The management of these ancient agricultural landscapes was as much—or more—a political question as it was an ecological one. In some Maya cities, systems of state-level governance steered homesite-localized agriculture with a heavy hand. At the urban agricultural city of Caracol, in Belize, early farmers buffered against environmental stress by intensifying their agriculture: they started building and farming on terraces.[41] Terraces enhanced soil health and empowered Caracol farmers to stave off the risks of year-to-year climate unpredictability. But before long, terraces evolved from a grassroots-level buffer against seasonal crop damage to a top-down strategy for accruing crop surplus, political stability, and prosperity.

Caracol's political leaders began to depend on the terraces as the basis of their power. They took on the burden of expanding and maintaining the vast infrastructure that terrace farming in a growing city demanded. Lidar has revealed that the sprawling settlement of Caracol is almost completely engineered, blanketed with the ghostly ridges of ancient terraces.[42] At the same time, perhaps keen to the precarity of their situation, Caracol's political leaders promoted a strong sense of shared social identity across all households in the city, even as social inequalities entrenched and deepened. All households ate the same way, lived in similar dwellings, and used the same kinds of pots and stone tools. These shared practices, enforced from the top down, insisted on a veil of egalitarianism to mute the concrete hierarchies of the centralized Caracol state.[43]

Caracol's terrace agriculture may have started as ecologically sustainable, but it became politically rigid. What had begun as a flexible adaptation became a dependency: the more Caracol's leaders benefited from the terraces, the more they became reliant on them and the specific demands of infrastructure they required. Caracol leaders had to sink increasingly more resources into expanding and maintaining the terrace system, all while promoting their image of social cohesion. When extra burdens of climate and political stress arose at the end of the Classic period, the demands of urban agriculture proved to be too much for Caracol's leaders to handle. The terraces, and the city they had fed, were abandoned.[44]

But not all homesite-localized agriculture worked like that—in some places, political power was decentralized and authorities did little to intercede in the daily lives of farmers. In the urban agriculture of the Río Bec region of Campeche, each household was embedded in its own autonomous agrarian domain.[45] From about AD 600–900, each Río Bec household managed the landholding directly around its homesite. Households marked their domains off using natural and artificial boundaries, sometimes even competing over land with neighboring households. Each adopted various practices of intensive agriculture, like terraces, in the lands around its homesite. Unlike Caracol, Río Bec homesite-localized agriculture was decentralized; like Caracol, climate and political stresses associated with the end of the Classic period pushed this urban agricultural landscape to abandonment.

Meanwhile, rural farmers in the village of Chan, an ancient Maya site in Belize, lived among a complex system of homesite-localized terrace agriculture for two thousand years (ca. 800 BC—AD 1200).[46] Chan was small, a hamlet in the hinterlands of the ancient city of Xunantunich, but despite its size (or perhaps because of it), Chan managed to persist through the political and ecological stress that led to the abandonment of many of its larger contemporaries. Community cooperation and flexibility formed the core of Chan's social and ecological sustainability.

Farming families at Chan lived surrounded by the terraces they cultivated.[47] Unlike in Río Bec, there are no signs of property division among the terraces, and many terraces even reach across the house lots of multiple homesites; Chan terraces were managed collectively by the community instead of by separate households. To keep the terraces watered, Chan farmers engineered small-scale water management infrastructure, including a springhouse, irrigation canals, and reservoirs, and even learned to manipulate underground streams. Farmers in Chan amended the soil of their terraces with ash and organic food waste, cycling the refuse of daily life back into the land as fertilizer. The adoption of these intensive practices did not come from an outside, top-down order—the Chan farmers themselves innovated intensification through organic and incremental growth over dozens of generations.[48]

Social institutions lent structure and continuity to Chan's agricultural practices. Ritual in the village evolved from an early emphasis on individualized ancestor veneration to later ceremonial practices that emphasized the community as a whole and affirmed intergenerational connections with land. Social stratification was unpronounced or absent altogether: everyone lived in perishable houses, goods appear to have been distributed equitably, and bioarchaeological analysis of skeletal remains found that health was consistent across the village. This was not like Caracol's homogenized community identity, enforced from the top; Chan's community identity seems to have developed organically from the grass roots.

At Chan, a strong sense of community identity and equality created the social foundation for land relations, enabling the long-term management of soil, water, and forest. Farmers maintained access to favored hardwoods, namely *chico zapote* trees, throughout the village's long history. The continuous presence of chico zapote remains, recovered from Chan hearths by archaeobotanists, points to the ongoing persistence of mature forests around the village. This was not the norm: that same tree species, chico zapote, disappears abruptly from the archaeological record of the powerful Maya capital of Tikal, to be replaced instead with less preferred woods. Chan's forest management practices, and the community institutions that supported them, empowered the village to mitigate the massive upheavals faced by larger Maya cities.[49]

ॐ   ॐ   ॐ

Out at Tzacauil, the seemingly "unused" grounds between and around the village's five Late to Terminal Formative homesites hold residues of agricultural intensification, readable in the physical traces farming families left behind. These residues are quiet in the ground; to interpret them, and to connect them to the social dynamics that originally created them, is the challenge of archaeology. One place to begin seeking answers is to look among smallholder farming societies alive in the present.

The anthropologist Robert McCormick Netting spent years living in twentieth-century smallholder societies, meaning communities that practiced intensive, permanent, and diversified farming on plots of land localized within their settlements, or what I'm calling homesite-localized agriculture. Netting studied smallholders around the world, from high-altitude herders of the Swiss Alps to Kofyar terrace farmers of Nigeria, and observed the diverse ways that smallholder households use ecological knowledge to grow food in fixed locations over many generations.

Netting found that smallholder farmers intensified their agricultural production by tinkering around with inputs—practices like weeding by hand, mucking out irrigation ditches, mending fences to keep hungry animals out of the garden, applying dung to restore soil nutrients—so that they could cultivate a plot of land over a sustained period of time. Unlike shifting agricultural practices (such as the Maya milpa), when you're practicing intensive farming, you're localizing and concentrating your labor, time, and energy in one particular place. In the case of homesite-localized intensive agriculture, that place is the land right around where you live.

Farming households that practice this kind of intensive homesite-localized agriculture deepen their relationships with particular plots of land.

Netting found that this deepening of relationship took two forms: in material improvements to the land and in the more ephemeral but vitally important accumulation of ecological knowledge.

Material improvements involved investment in physical stuff. Netting noticed smallholder farmers building fences, digging canals and drainage ditches, spreading manure, pruning fruit trees, and shoveling up soil into raised beds. Intensification is a lot of work. When you think about all that work, it becomes clear that a main reason why smallholders cultivate the land close to their homes is that it's simply easier to keep up with all those tasks when you live right there on the land. Because of this enmeshment, the tempos and materials of daily life become entangled with agriculture. Food scraps and waste fertilize the earth. Kids playing outside scare away crop-hungry creatures. The rhythms of weeding, checking crops, and picking vegetables, herbs, and fruit are woven into the cycles of cooking meals. Over time, this all becomes more than a matter of convenience. Netting found that siting the dwelling directly in the cultivated plot of land acted as a powerful expression of land tenure in smallholder societies. The house itself becomes the lineage materialized, rooted and rooting into a particular patch of land.

The members of the household become the repository of ecological knowledge, intimately localized in that particular patch of land. Netting observed that smallholder families learn through generations of trial and error how to combine multiple, complementary agricultural practices within a single plot of land, choreographing complex nested schedules of planting and harvesting for diverse species. Family members learn which places in the homesite landholding get the best sunlight and which get the shade, they learn the granularity of subtle soil differences and the vagaries of rainfall and wind peculiar to their plot. This ecological intimacy matters: a smallholder household's ability to grow enough food is contingent not just on the physical improvements its members make to their land, but on their localized and cumulative familiarity with the nuances of their land.

Together, physical improvements and localized ecological knowledge explain why multigenerational households are so common in smallholder societies, and why landholdings are almost always transmitted as inheritances, rather than sold. As a plot of land accumulates physical improvements and localized ecological knowledge, the land pulls in and roots down multiple generations of the household living there. Elder family members curate ecological knowledge and are cared for in their old age; younger family members provide their labor and benefit from the ecological knowledge and physical improvements their elders first seeded.

The ecological knowledge is ephemeral, but its corollary and counterpart, the physical improvements to land, leave traces in the ground. Sometimes these traces can be recognized through archaeology. The residues of the Late to Terminal Formative farming village at Tzacauil, out at the ejido's edge, match the patterns for a smallholder community: planting the homesite in soil-rich land mattered, and living in houses that affirmed connections with that soil-rich land mattered. In Tzacauil I read the echoes of deepening, multigenerational ecological knowledge written in the stone houses of the first farmers and in the lands around their homesites—not "unused" or "empty" spaces, but archives of rootedness.

ご   ご   ご

To trace out the rootedness of the first farmers in the Yaxunah ejido edge lands, I'll follow one homesite, a cluster of dwellings and the open land around them, that formed part of the first farming community at Tzacauil. This homesite is the Chamal Group, and it was the first area our team of Yaxunah community members and archaeologists excavated at Tzacauil, back in the summer of 2015. Later, in 2017, we revisited the Chamal Group during the *xíimbal k'áax* walking survey of the eastern ejido, and again during a series of trench excavations in the open lands around homesites to look for signs of houselot activities like cultivation (fig. 14). The traces and residues we documented at the Chamal Group exemplify the multigenerational commitments to intensive, homesite-localized agriculture that shaped land relations at the edge of the Yaxunah ejido nearly twenty centuries ago.

The farming family that chose to live at Chamal planted their homesite during the transition from the Late Formative to Terminal Formative. When they began building their home, the Tzacauil Acropolis had already risen above the trees and the Jach and P'aak homesites had been founded and farmed for a long while. The Chamal founders began to build their home just like their neighbors out at Tzacauil, and also like their more-distant neighbors back west in the growing city of Yaxuná. They chose a bedrock outcrop west of the Jach homesite and planted their home in part of the same deep red soil expanse that had drawn Tzacauil's very first farmers, the Jach founders, to root down permanently.

FIGURE 14. A trench excavation investigating the *kancabales* (soil expanses) surrounding one of Tzacauil's Late to Terminal Formative homesites. Photo by the author.

The Chamal founders burned limestone to make mortar. They mixed the mortar with red soil and packed the mixture down on top of their bedrock outcrop, encrusting and leveling the rugged contours into a compact surface. On top of this, they arranged a layer of large stones like a three-dimensional jigsaw puzzle, setting the bases of the stones into the burnt lime mortar and reinforcing the lot with boulder walls. The builders added no soil or rubble to stabilize these large stones, relying instead entirely on the points of contact among the rocks to steady the layer. Many of these stones were not the amorphous rocks used in most construction fills at Tzacauil, but rather semi-carved into rough blocks. These blocks caught our attention, as did thin sheets of limestone we found near the top of this fill layer. Once the Chamal founders had finished placing the layer of large stones, they sealed off some of the gaps left between rocks by laying down thin, tabletlike slabs of limestone. These slabs then supported a ballast of fist-sized cobbles. The builders spread earth across these cobbles and tamped it down to make a floor. The thin slabs of limestone were there to stop this floor from slumping down into the crevices of the large rock layer below.

Both the thin limestone slabs and the semi-formed blocks we found in the Chamal Group's earliest construction stood out to a few Yaxunah community members who were working on the excavations and who were also experienced stonemasons. These masons pointed out that the slabs and blockish stones looked like the by-products of stonecutting. Throughout excavations at the Chamal Group, our team continued to find more residues of quarrying, cutting stone, and burning lime. These are traces of deep ecological knowledge of limestone, and by extension, of land. They suggest a fluency in karst that enabled Chamal family members to rearrange their localized landscape into new expressions of rooted permanence.

With their bedrock outcrop expanded and elaborated by the construction of this stone platform, the Chamal founders arranged the stone foundations for a rectangular dwelling overlooking the patch of surrounding land. The dwelling itself would have been made of wood and thatch—much like most houses in Yaxunah today—and would have faced a substantial stretch of exposed bedrock that connected the Chamal homesite to the Tzacauil Sacbe.

The next episode visible in the history of the Chamal homesite came when its people undertook a massive renovation in the Terminal Formative period. The Chamal householders gathered an enormous amount of stone and rubble to expand their platform, nearly doubling its area and covering most of the underlying bedrock outcrop. This gave them enough room to put up more foundations, made of neatly cut stone, to support an additional one or two more dwellings on top of the platform (fig. 15). The householders also dressed up the platform's entry point by adding a few wide, terracelike stairs along the southern edge, so that people walking by on the Tzacauil Sacbe would see a stately entrance. Away from the eyes of passersby, the north end of the platform remained privately rough with craggy bedrock.

Around the same time they embarked on these renovations, the Chamal householders built a little kitchen—which may have also served as an extra sleeping room or storage building—on a patch of exposed bedrock off the back corner of their platform. Centuries later, when our team excavated the remnants of this kitchen—by then just an oval ring of stones—we found that it had been built on top of a deep pit cut into bedrock and filled in with rubble. This kind of pit would have been used as a kiln to dig out and burn limestone. The negative spaces of this pit and the many others like it that remain hidden are mirrored in the above-ground aggregations of stone that formed the houses, pyramid, and road of Tzacauil's early farming village.

The Chamal householders expanded their homesite from one dwelling to potentially four. This is important because the growth of the physical house is a proxy for the growth of the household, an observation Netting made among

FIGURE 15. Yaxunah community members excavating the Late to Terminal Formative house foundations of the Chamal homesite at Tzacauil. To the bottom and right of the image are the remains of the homesite's original dwelling. Above and to the left are remains of the Chamal homesite's renovation: the stone foundations of an additional dwelling and the platform's expansion towards the Tzacauil Sacbe. Photo by the author.

smallholder societies and made also by anthropologists in early twentieth-century Yucatecan towns. A 1934 ethnographic study of the Yucatec Maya village of Chan Kom, for instance, recorded that the most respected and prosperous old men in town headed the largest households. The house compounds themselves materialized the cycle of household growth. In one Chan Kom house compound, the founding couple settled down in 1906 to live in a single wooden dwelling, which they used both as a kitchen and as a sleeping room. In a few years they added a second wooden dwelling and a separate little building, mostly used for cooking during the day but also by some of their kids for sleeping at night. By 1928 the founding couple had nine children, and two of their eldest were already married and starting their own families, while still living at home. As the family expanded into new generations, so too did the house compound grow: the household added a new kitchen and an extra dwelling made of stone. Everyone continued to shuffle around the dwellings, since the founding couple didn't like how hot the stone house could get, and many family members ended up preferring to sleep in the new kitchen or the second wooden dwelling. They had decided to let the first kitchen slide into abandonment, had just added an addition to the new kitchen, and were in the process of building another stone room when the anthropologists showed up. All those changes had happened in just a few decades.

When you project these kinds of temporal rhythms and family sagas onto a Late to Terminal Formative homesite that might have been inhabited for centuries, like the Chamal Group, you can start to see how the humble foundations of old dwellings hold in their stones the dynamic cycles of household history. The physical growth of the Chamal homesite suggests that multiple generations of household members were committed to rooting in place in this particular patch of soil and bedrock.

There's something else about the Chamal homesite renovations: their timing coincides with major renovations at the Tzacauil Acropolis. From a test pit dug into the acropolis platform, our excavation team could see that a burst of construction had raised and expanded the acropolis with a thick layer of rock and rubble. Like the Chamal renovations, as well as renovations in other Tzacauil homesites, the building activity at the acropolis happened in the Terminal Formative.

One way to interpret this growth is through the negative space that all that stony architecture left behind in the land; these constructions essentially lock up stone the way a glacier locks up water. Contemporary Maya farmers gather up loose stones from the ground when preparing a parcel for cultivation, because the stones can break or wear away the wooden tips of agricultural tools. The farmer's practice of gathering fieldstone piles together even has a particular name, *mul tuntah'*. Yet the small stone piles created by modern Maya farmers are likely only an echo of the massive stone moving that likely accompanied the first several generations of permanent agriculture. In this burst of renovations materialized in the Tzacauil Acropolis and in the Chamal homesite, I read a history of early farmers in rocky ground, who sponged up the fieldstone from the land and reorganized it into physical expressions of rootedness. Shored up in the stony monuments of house platforms, vestiges of the original farming TEK of the Yaxunah ejido reside and remain.[50]

The open lands of the Chamal homesite hold still other vestiges of that knowledge. In the soil flat north of the main Chamal house platform, Yaxunah community members excavated a trench. In some places the soil was deep for Tzacauil—up to half a meter—but elsewhere bedrock was right below the surface. The bedrock our team uncovered in this trench was

FIGURE 16. A skilled Yaxunah mason demonstrates how ancient residents of the Chamal homesite would have cut stone. Photo by the author.

unusual, smooth and worn off into curving points and edges. As soon as this bedrock began to surface, a few community members on the excavation team pointed out that it was the preferred kind of bedrock for cutting stone. Not far away, the excavators found large pieces of rock that bore the hallmarks of human workmanship. The rocks had chisel-like edges, similar to small scraping tools our team found sometimes in Tzacauil excavations, but these were much bigger—about the size of an arm. One man on the excavation that week happened to be one of the most skilled stonemasons in Yaxunah. He at once identified these large chisel-shaped rocks as stone-cutting tools, and he started to show us how they would have been used to break off chunks of limestone from the bedrock (fig. 16). As excavations in this area continued, the team continued to find broken fragments of bedrock. Like the semi-formed blocks and thin slabs documented in the Chamal house itself, these were remnants of stone cutting.

During the *xíimbal k'áax* walking survey of Tzacauil, Yaxunah community members identified bedrock features around the Chamal homesite that match the kinds of physical improvements Netting observed in smallholdings. Between the main platform of the Chamal Group and the Tzacauil Sacbe to the south, there is a stretch of exposed bedrock. Although bedrock is easier to walk on than soil and can be used to collect water, the first two homesites settled in Tzacauil (Jach and P'aak) were planted in places with little surface bedrock. The founders of the Chamal homesite came a bit later and worked within the mosaic of soil and bedrock patches to choose a place with good access to soil, yet with some bedrock, too. The bedrock between their house and the Tzacauil Sacbe would have made it easier to come and go, even during the rainy season.

In that stretch of bedrock, Yaxunah community members on the survey team pointed out that the karst was flat and riddled with cavities. These, they explained, were ideal for seasonal water storage: they would fill with water during the rainy season. The community members found, too, that a larger depression in the bedrock had been modified to hold more water than it would have naturally contained. Around the depression's rounded edge, a few community members brushed away leaves to reveal a few simple lines of stones placed along the rim, and others contended that the depression had been dug out to increase its volume. These modifications point to this pit's perennial role as a reservoir for those dwelling in the Chamal homesite. Here, they could rely on a semi-irregular and ready supply of rainwater for crops, cooking, or washing.[51]

Red kancab soil surrounds the Chamal homesite on every other side, though the depth of these soil flats before you'd hit bedrock could range from just a scant few centimeters to more than half a meter. The soils tend to get thinner the further you move away from the Chamal house lot; the deepest soils immediately surrounded the house itself. While many household activities would have been happening in these open lands—stone quarrying and carving, for starters—the preference for planting the homesite in soil-rich lands shown by the Chamal homesite, and by all the homesites of Tzacauil's early farming village, tell us that homesite-localized cultivation was important in this community. The traces of agriculture are ephemeral, but these red soils were not "empty" or "unused" lands. Red kancab is the preferred soil for agricultural intensification—the permanent, homesite-localized cultivation of Netting's smallholders—among contemporary Maya farmers. When considered alongside the more durable residues of smallholder life, like the growing number of dwellings, the use of long-lasting stone architecture, and physical improvements to the landholding, these red soils were what rooted Tzacauil farmers in place for generations.[52]

To read the Chamal homesite is to trace a history of multigenerational relationship with a specific patch of land. The durable residues left behind by that history—rock, clay, soil—hint at the dynamic and entangled practices of dwelling and farming, of rooting deeply in land. Chamal's people expressed their rootedness physically in their homesite, in their houses and in the open lands around them. These expressions materialize the ecological intimacy that was accumulating in the family that lived there. While the orchards, gardens, and intensive plots that the Chamal farmers grew with that ecological intimacy appear to leave only empty space, their residues remain in markers of permanence and in the open lands themselves.

ॐ   ॐ   ॐ

Five groups of people sunk deep roots into the five homesites that formed the early farming village of Tzacauil, and together they formed a community. There are signs of shared tradition and shared identity. There are also signs of growing social inequality.

All five house groups share a common template: each is perched on a bedrock outcrop, each in a soil-rich patch of land. All are oriented to face the village's heart, the acropolis, and its central artery, the sacbe. All five are built in a similar style, and all five preserve open land between and around their dwellings.

Left behind in each of the five homesites were similar remnants of stuff, a common bundle of culinary practices and daily rhythms legible in the discard of domestic life. Excavations in the five homesites recovered fragments of metates (portable stone basins) and manos (handheld grinding stones) to go with them. All were made of local limestone and would have been used to grind maize and prepare other ingredients for cooking. All the grinding equipment across the homesites shows signs of habitual use; many of the grinding stones bear faint indentations of a thumbprint and finger grooves, stone ghosts of their owners' right- or left-handedness.

Pottery fragments found in all five homesites hold the same sense of shared culinary traditions. Across our excavations, we found a pretty consistent ratio of about two bowl fragments for every one jar fragment for this early farming time period.[53] To figure out how different pottery vessel shapes were used in ancient Maya cooking, archaeologists working at the site of Sihó in northwestern Yucatán conducted a chemical residue analysis on ceramics collected during excavations. Their team found chemical markers of maize, beans, and proteins on jar fragments, which, along with the globular bodies and restricted necks of jar-shaped vessels, suggest that jars were typically used to cook stews, with or without meat. Bowl fragments, meanwhile, bore traces of maize, sometimes with markers for chile pepper and starchy tubers, which point to their use as serving vessels for seasoned maize beverages, like the pozoles and *atoles* consumed in Mexico today. If these findings from Sihó can be extended to Tzacauil, then we can imagine the five Tzacauil homesites sharing a cuisine of stews and corn-based beverages, seasoned with garden herbs and chiles and supplemented with occasional game meat.

Shared customs muted emerging differences. The founders of the Jach and P'aak homesites were first and second, respectively, to plant permanent houses at Tzacauil. They claimed patches of ground with deep soils, minimal bedrock, and close access to the Tzacauil Acropolis and Sacbe, the most visible signs of the village's political connections with the new royalty presiding at Yaxuná. When the founders of the Chamal, Kaan, and Sáastun homesites later looked to plant their own permanent houses, they faced some competition for soil-rich lands. They had to make compromises. For the Sáastun founders, finding an open patch of soil-rich ground meant sacrificing proximity to the acropolis.

Markers of multigenerational permanence in the land were likewise not distributed equally across the five early farming homesites of Tzacauil. While all five homesites likely housed multigenerational families, only three households—those based at the Jach, Chamal, and P'aak homesites—marshaled the kind of major renovations associated with a major growth in members. Heirloom caches, relics from Middle Formative foraging ancestors, were found only in the two oldest house groups, Jach and P'aak.[54] The Jach Group had not only the greatest amount of Middle Formative potsherds sown throughout its construction fills, but the greatest density of potsherds from across the Late to Terminal Formative, too.[55] When viewed in context, this buildup of broken ceramics isn't because the Jach family had more pottery vessels than their neighbors at any given time—rather, the buildup is so great because they had been rooted in Tzacauil the longest.

The open lands of the five homesites also register social differences. With the help of a soil scientist friend, I ran some basic soil chemistry tests on samples taken from the kancabales surrounding the five homesites.[56] Soil chemistry in Yucatán's thin earths poses challenges, but we found that the lands around the Jach Group registered some of the highest phosphate and pH levels of all the sampled areas. Higher phosphates can be caused by the repeated discard of household refuse, from food scraps to human waste, and are both a by-product of daily life and a documented form of soil-enhancing fertilizer, as compost.[57] Elevated pH indicates more alkaline soils, which can result from household activities like the habitual deposition of wood ash, again both a by-product of daily cooking fires and a known fertilizer, or from the regular spilling of limewater used in maize processing.[58] Both chemical signatures materialize a long-term entanglement of waste management and homesite-localized intensive agriculture. I don't think the people of the Jach homesite were living with the land differently from their neighbors—but I do think they were living with that particular patch of land for more time.

There are differences, too, in the physical improvements distributed around Tzacauil's early farming homesites. The Jach and P'aak householders arranged stones into makeshift pavements to help their members get around their homesites when it was raining. The Kaan householders shored up gravel and soil behind a boulder wall and tamped it all down to create a compact walkway. The Chamal householders modified a natural bedrock depression into a seasonal reservoir. And the founders of all five homesites, by building with stone, sponged up the loose rock from the land and in this way made the earth easier to farm with wooden-tipped tools. For the people living at the three homesites that underwent major renovations—Jach, P'aak, and Chamal—expanding platforms and adding more dwellings removed still more stone from the ground.

All of this to me suggests that social inequalities were calcifying around how long each household lineage had been living and farming in Tzacauil. The longer a lineage lived in a particular homesite, the more its people rooted in the land through material improvements and localized ecological knowledge, and the more its status grew.

In this early village, then, are echoes of the same vulnerabilities that would later disrupt Maya urban agricultural cities. Tzacauil's household autonomy and competition for soil-rich homesites resonate with the urban agriculture practiced in the Río Bec region. And as in the urban agricultural neighborhoods of Caracol, Tzacauil households muted their emerging differences through a shared community identity, which may have been developed alongside political centralization. The Tzacauil Acropolis grew to its final massive size during the same period that the forest around it was filling in with the Chamal, Kaan, and P'aak homesites. So little, still, is known about the acropolis and the road that materialized a physical relationship between the urbanizing center of Yaxuná and the small hamlet seeded at Tzacauil, but the presence of these grand civic-ceremonial buildings hints at intervention and attempts at political centralization. The early farmers of Tzacauil may have been out on the edge, but as their village grew, they were actively integrated into the political web reaching out from the city of Yaxuná.

ಶಿ   ಶಿ   ಶಿ

The first farmers to root down in the edge lands of the Yaxunah ejido committed to permanence. Their stone houses and intensive agricultural plots became entangled expressions of multigenerational and localized land relations. From the ground-level view of the early farmers, these entanglements were permanent; from the vantage of the twenty-first century, they were temporary.

By the very end of the Formative period, Tzacauil was abandoned. The community dissolved or relocated or both, and the stone houses and carefully tended agricultural plots were left behind. Tzacauil was not alone: archaeologists have documented many instances of abandonment all occurring around this same time, and climate unpredictability and environmental stress, mainly from droughts, helped to catalyze this wave of desertion.[59]

Farmers would never again root into the edge lands of Tzacauil with such localized, permanent, and multigenerational interactions as they had in the Late to Terminal Formative. When people did return to live and farm the hinterlands of Yaxuná centuries later, they were no longer practicing the homesite-localized intensive cultivation characteristic of smallholders. Why was that? Small villages could and did manage intensive agriculture through the turmoil of widespread societal collapse and environmental strain. In the village of Chan, rural terrace farmers weathered turbulence through grassroots-grown community identity and collaborative ecological management.

Like Chan households, the households of Tzacauil also developed deep intimacy with their homesite lands, but political leaders in Yaxuná might have undermined bottom-up community cooperation in the hinterlands with their efforts to centralize power. The rise in markers of social inequality at Tzacauil coincides with the burst of labor and energy invested in elaborating their acropolis and sacbe, the clearest physical expressions of the village's links with Yaxuná. Deepening hierarchies among the households could have seeded barriers to community collaboration, especially given that household status appears so entangled with autonomous intensive agricultural plots, localized in homesites. These factors made intensive cultivation out in the edge lands of Tzacauil a rigidity trap, not because intensive cultivation was ecologically unbalanced but because it became politically and socially inflexible. When the strain of climate vulnerability and drought entered the equation, Tzacauil's villagers uprooted. They walked away.

⁍ ⁍ ⁍

Farmer hands seeded an heirloom bowl, formed and fired by forager hands, deep inside the stone foundations of the first permanent house in Tzacauil's early agricultural village. Centuries later, farmer hands unearthed the bowl, and it emerged into a forest still shaped by the relations of an edge land. I photographed the bowl and recorded its location on the excavation drawing. Then I uprooted it piece by piece into a plastic bag, tagged with the details of its provenance. The bowl, sheathed in plastic, waited for the field season to end.

The bowl traveled with me to Mérida. It reemerged into the light for lab analysis, then rested again, back in a plastic bag, along with other "special finds," each in its own plastic bag, in a five-gallon gray plastic bucket. For a few months this bucket and a dozen others holding bagged artifacts from Tzacauil lived with me in a house I was renting in the city. Then it was time for me to leave, and for the bowl to go back to Yaxunah for temporary storage in the archaeological camp, right at the overlap between Yaxunah the modern town and Yaxuná the ancient city. I left the bowl, buried in its robe of plastic, somewhere inside one of the lidded buckets that I stacked neatly in the bathroom of the small house where I had lived during the last months of my research at Tzacauil; the bathroom, unlike the rest of the thatched house, had a solid roof that wouldn't leak. I blanketed the buckets with a clean tarp and left.

Time passed. The director and permit holder for our regional archaeological project emailed to say he was in Mexico wrapping up loose ends for the investigations in the Yaxunah ejido covered by his permit, of which my work at Tzacauil had been one part. He asked if I had any pressing need to work with any of the Tzacauil artifacts again in the immediate future. I didn't, and told him so. Were they ready for long-term storage then? Yes, I guess, I answered, imagining the heirloom bowl and its companions journeying across the country in their buckets, to be packed into a warehouse somewhere in Mexico City.

That's not what happened. Artifact storage is an ongoing challenge for a country as rich in archaeological heritage in Mexico, and perhaps especially so when you're dealing with the broken pots and humble grinding stones from a tiny site like Tzacauil—not exactly museum-caliber stuff. The solution the state archaeology offices have found is to return the artifacts to the places they come from. The buckets and all they contained would be buried in the lands of the Yaxunah ejido. The project would pay Yaxunah farmers to deposit the Tzacauil buckets, along with the buckets resulting from ten years of other investigations in the ejido, inside a *sascabera*—a large depression in the ground where limestone marl had once been mined—and inter them with cement and earth. Theoretically, if anyone ever wants to run new tests on the reburied artifacts, they can be dug back up. I feel a peculiar certainty this won't be happening in my lifetime.

When I was nearly done writing this book, I returned to Yaxunah for the first time in years to start a new program of research with the community. There were plans now to turn the archaeology camp back into an ecolodge and restaurant, and the director of our old project was paying community members to fix up the place after a few years of pandemic-related neglect. One day after work, an archaeologist friend and I entered camp to see the *sascabera* where all the artifact buckets were buried. She had helped me for two seasons at Tzacauil and, like me, had known the camp as a vibrant little village of archaeologists; to walk through it now, deserted and in semi-decay, felt strange and haunting and full of the residues of memory.[60] We approached the *sascabera* and looked in. I saw only a cement plug marking the portal into the subterranean storage, already nearly hidden under dead leaves and new vegetation. The buckets were quiet underground, reburied once more by the hands of farmers.

The heirloom bowl and all those other clay and stone creations of the earliest farmers in the edge forests have been replanted back into ejido land, enrobed in plastic, a souvenir from their brief surfacing into the twenty-first century. This was its own kind of caching, a seeding through materials once again a story of continuity among past and future generations of people and land. What will the world be like when the bowl emerges again?

Someone someday will find the heirloom bowl buried among the other stuff, planted in soil, sticky now with the emotional residues of not just the foragers who made it and the early farmers who planted it but those of the Yaxunah community members and archaeologists who dug into the red soil to retrieve it for a short while, only to bury it again. Someone else will unearth it. The ground will be steaming, the sun will be high. Damp earth will exhale into their faces as they gaze back into time.

FOUR

———

Taproot to Fibrous Root

IN THE FIRST WEEKS after its germination, a *Brosimum alicastrum* seed sends a taproot down into the earth. The seedling is a tree in infancy, one known by many names: in English, breadnut; in Spanish, *ramón*; in Yucatec Maya, *óox*. Creating the taproot is óox's first main task of survival. The taproot starts as a small filament, questing downward, a subterranean explorer in search of water. In Yucatán, this quest is crucial. Water is scarce during the long dry season from November through April. The taproot of the óox seedling plunges down to pull moisture up into the young tree, drinking from deep subsurface soils where water is held even during the months of drought. By the time some Yucatecan óox trees reach maturity, their taproots can reach depths of fifteen meters.[1]

But some óox saplings are different: some begin by rooting down but then transition to rooting outward, spreading their roots horizontally through the top layers of soil. In one study of *Brosimum alicastrum* in Yucatán, biologists used oxygen isotope analysis to track the water sources taken up by óox root systems during times of drought stress.[2] The researchers wanted to see how the tree's root systems were able to find water in the kinds of shallow soils and exposed bedrock patches that are so common in Yucatecan forests. They predicted that early investment in deep taproots, plunging down to the level of waterlogged subsoil or groundwater, would be the deciding factor for drought-time tree survival in shallow soil. The research team tested this hypothesis by measuring the water intake of two groups of the trees, one cohort of five-year-olds and another of nine-year-olds, during peak dry season in a patch of thin Yucatecan soils near Mérida.

To run the experiment, the researchers first had to get to the water table. They excavated a pit into the bedrock near the óox trees, digging down through the hard limestone crust known as *laja* and into the soft, weathered limestone marl known as *sascab*. They finally hit groundwater at nine meters below the surface. Having reached the water table, the researchers could then sample that particular groundwater to measure its oxygen isotopes. They would compare that measurement to the oxygen isotopes of the water they found stored inside the *Brosimum alicastrum* saplings. If the isotopic fingerprints of the sapling water and the local groundwater matched, it would mean that the tree roots had indeed tapped all the way down to the water table.

The bedrock pit dug by the researchers also allowed them to get a look at tree root growth, just by examining the walls of the excavation pit. They were surprised when they could see the óox roots concentrated in the upper layers of soil and bedrock: the thin topsoil was dense with roots, and root mats filled pockets and fissures in the rock. When they looked a little farther down, the researchers could see that the top layers of soft limestone marl had likewise been threaded with fine roots, but below that, they could see no signs of root growth. All of the roots were a fibrous mat contained in the top two meters of the ground, with no roots visible in the seven-meter stretch of bedrock between these surface root mats and the subterranean water table. This presaged what the researchers would later confirm with their isotope analysis: these óox trees were not drinking groundwater.

The isotopic fingerprint of the water contained inside the trees themselves showed that none of the trees, regardless of their age, had tapped down to drink from the water table. Instead, their roots were sipping in the moisture held in just the top few meters of bedrock.

This was unexpected, and so the researchers came up with a way to measure tree stress to figure out what was going on. They measured the water content inside the sapling shoots right at the peak of the dry season. The amount of water each sapling had stored up could be used to quantify how much stress it was experiencing during the drought. The team discovered that the younger *Brosimum alicastrum* trees were much more water stressed than their older counterparts. The younger trees were having a harder time pulling in moisture.

The researchers realized that the older trees were experiencing less water stress because their root systems had more time, not to root down but to root out. The four-year head start of the older trees went not towards plunging taproots down to the water table but to exploring the top layers of soil and bedrock and spreading out in search of pockets of moisture. As the younger cohort of trees matured, they too would learn to adjust their root growth to spread out horizontally like this, in fibrous root systems. This capacity for flexibility turns out to be key to the resilience of *Brosimum alicastrum* in Yucatán.

Óox is not alone: many trees begin their lives with taproots but later transition to fibrous root systems. For the *Brosimum alicastrum* trees growing in Yucatán's thin soils and harsh dry seasons, the shift from sending taproots down to sending shallow fibrous roots out can mean the difference between death and survival in times of extreme drought.

Óox is not alone: in the edge lands of the Yaxunah ejido, the forest holds an analogue, a story of farmers learning to spread out after first sinking down. After walking away from the intensively cultivated plots and multigenerational boulder-lined stone houses of Tzacauil's first farming village, the people who remained in the hinterlands of the ancient city of Yaxuná—today's Yaxunah ejido edge lands—adapted. They gave up the taproots of permanence, concentrated in particular plots of land, and embraced instead a less rigid and more mobile way of life. The people shifted to milpa agriculture, and with that shift they enabled their survival through turbulent times of political and climate upheaval. Archived in the ground of Tzacauil is this: the rootedness at the core of mutual land relations is flexible, adaptable, nimble.

This shift in what it meant to be rooted is legible in the remains left by sporadic waves of farmers who lived in Tzacauil during the periods archaeologists call the Late Classic (AD 550–700) and Terminal Classic (AD 700–1100).[3] These more transient farmers had moved away from the intensively cultivated plots and multigenerational homesites of their Late Formative antecedents; they embraced instead the agricultural practice and accompanying mobility of the milpa. Like óox roots in thin soil, the farmers of the Yaxunah edge lands began with the taproot strategies of smallholders before adjusting to the fibrous root strategies of milperos. The practices changed, but the rootedness of mutual land relations remained.

ॐ ॐ ॐ

Centuries passed and the Late Formative village founded by the first farmers of Tzacauil transformed in the absence of permanent human settlement. The wood and thatch buildings collapsed, then decayed. Trees rooted into the interstices of stone foundations, making them slump, spilling out their rubble cores. Mosses and dead leaves were laid like mantles over the mounds. All the while, people kept living in the area, and many were still living in the city of Yaxuná. When people would have walked out to the forests of Tzacauil—as surely they did, to gather firewood, to hunt, to pull up water from the underground spring beyond the ruins to the east—they don't seem to have stayed for long, certainly not long enough to leave a trace that archaeologists could decipher more than a millennium later.

The edge lands of Tzacauil became even more of an edge. Earlier, the Tzacauil Sacbe had marked the Late Formative farming village as a destination: the causeway ran like an artery straight into the village's monumental heart and gave structure to the community that formed around it. Though the sacbe was never finished on its western side, follow its trajectory out through the forest and even today you'll see that the course was set for Yaxuná's central plaza.[4] The sacbe materialized the link between the two settlements, one urbanizing and the other a far-flung branch, marking in stone the movement of people, goods, and ideas that flowed across the forest between them. The link was lost with the abandonment of the village at the end of the Terminal Formative, and the Tzacauil Sacbe was left to the woods.

As the forest quietly reclaimed Tzacauil, a new road came slashing white through the lands east of the city of Yaxuná during the Late Classic. This road, a limestone causeway called Sacbe 1 by archaeologists, would later be recognized as the longest ever built in the ancient Maya world.[5] It spanned just over one hundred kilometers and connected Yaxuná with the city of Coba, a powerful capital that rose amid lush forests and lakes in the modern state of Quintana Roo.

Hieroglyphic inscriptions found at Coba suggest that this exceptional road was commissioned under the reign of a Coba queen, Lady K'awiil Ajaw.[6] During her reign, Lady K'awiil Ajaw led several successful military campaigns and expanded Coba's territory. Some archaeologists think that she ordered the construction of Sacbe 1 to consolidate control of the central northern lowlands region. With Yaxuná subordinated and incorporated as the western outpost for Coba's expanding territory, this new sacbe would have allowed military forces to reach the interior peninsula quickly and efficiently on a straight-line trajectory.

Though a military function might have catalyzed the causeway's construction, once it was built, the road would have held many roles for many kinds of walkers. Pedestrians of all sorts probably walked Sacbe 1, not just to get between Coba and Yaxuná but also to get to the many settlements stationed along the causeway's length.[7] Journeys that began or ended in Yaxuná would have taken travelers right past the abandoned village of Tzacauil; Sacbe 1 clips just south of the Tzacauil ruins, running nearly parallel with the centuries-older Tzacauil Sacbe for a stretch before shooting on to the east.

The Late Formative farmers of the first agricultural village at Tzacauil planted their homesites around a causeway that marked their community as an origin and a destination. Centuries later, the Late to Terminal Classic farmers of Tzacauil lived on the wayside of a road that, by all clear measures, ignored them completely. In these years, farmers of the edge lands were transforming their relationship with the forest in ways that appear, at first, of no clear interest to the powerful players in the region's larger political campaigns.

છ ઢ ઢ

A small group of farming families decided to make their homes at Tzacauil in the Late Classic (fig. 17). They came to the expanses of bedrock in the southwestern part of the old village, leveled the bedrock, and laid the stone foundations for a cluster of dwellings made of wood and thatch.

A millennium or so later, I looked at lines representing those stone foundations on a map and broke the cluster into three separate group designations, named Pool, Kaan, and Mukul. The people who dwelled here likely wouldn't have recognized my groupings as meaningful divisions; I'm inclined to believe that this cluster of dwellings and kitchens was the shared homesite for a single extended family. Our team of Yaxunah community members and archaeologists investigated two of these groups, Pool and Kaan, through survey and excavations.[8]

The Pool Group perches on the highest bedrock outcrop in Tzacauil. For walkers approaching from the west via the abandoned, but still serviceable, Tzacauil Sacbe, the three Pool dwellings would have been the first they encountered in the Late to Terminal Classic homesite cluster.[9] When our team started excavating at the Pool dwellings in 2016, we figured it would be pretty simple to work out their construction history because we could see bedrock right at the surface on all sides. The remains of the three dwellings were straightforward, single-course stone foundations, and I predicted we'd need only to dig about twenty centimeters before we would hit bedrock and be done.

But once digging began, the excavators and I learned quickly that the Pool dwellings were more complex than the visible patches of bedrock had seemed to promise. Soon we were far back in time, finding traces of earlier activities

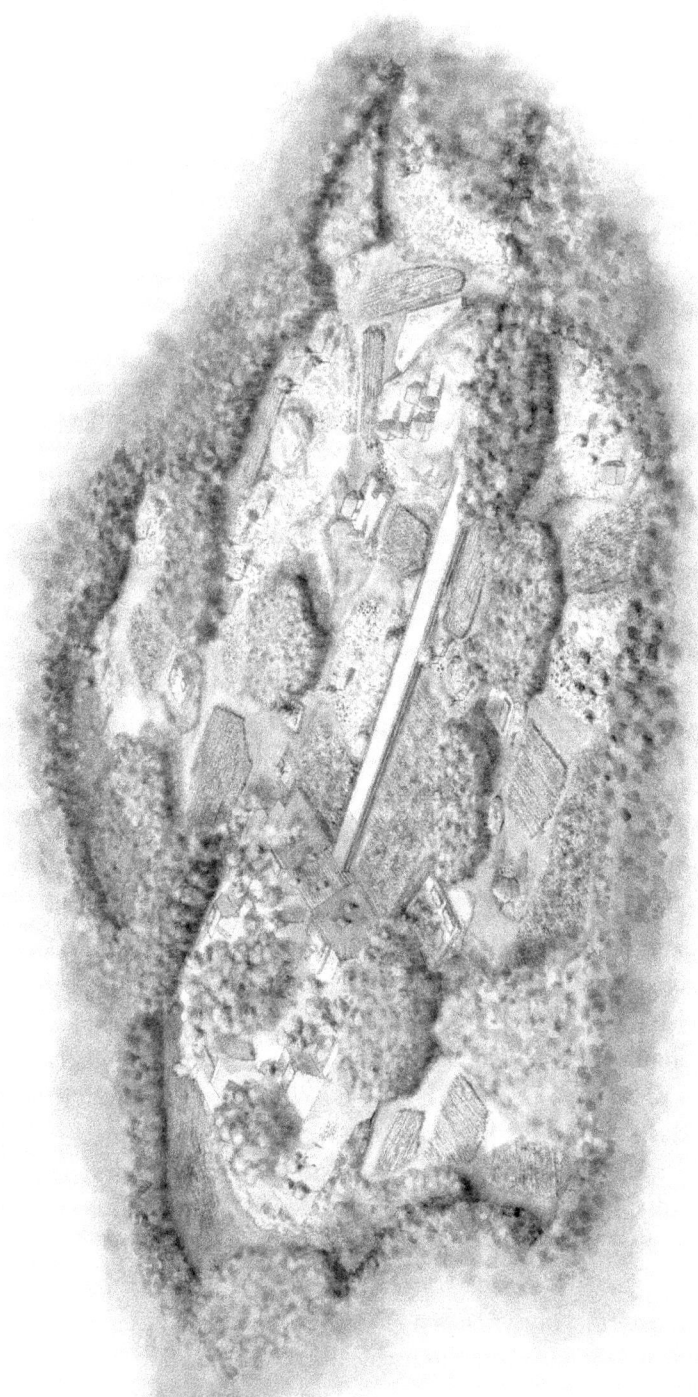

FIGURE 17. The community of Tzacauil as it may have looked during the time of mobile milpa farmers in the Late Classic (AD 550–700) and Terminal Classic (AD 700–1100). Earlier buildings, like the Tzacauil Acropolis and most house platforms, have been abandoned to the forest. A small group of farming families cluster their homesites on a high bedrock rise and reoccupy (and renovate) the nearby Kaan Group. Through the practices of their shifting milpa cultivation, the land becomes patchy with fields and forests in various stages of succession. Small field huts, temporary camps for milpa farmers, can be seen below the Tzacauil Sacbe. Illustration by Kathryn Killackey.

that had taken place on the bedrock outcrop in the era of Tzacauil's first farming village. Beneath one of the Pool dwellings, we found a filled-in hole cut into the bedrock. It was a pit kiln, like the one we had found under the Chamal Group's kitchen on the other side of the Tzacauil Sacbe. Based on the broken ceramics we found in the pit rubble, the kiln was dug during the Late Formative period, the era of the first farming village at Tzacauil. This pit kiln might have been used to make mortar or plaster to be used in the sacbe construction.[10] After the pit was filled in, Late Formative villagers—perhaps the family living at the nearby Kaan Group—continued to use the elevated vantage point of this bedrock outcrop for some time, though how exactly they did this was hard to determine. Everything had been moved around and reshaped by the farmers who resettled the outcrop in the Late Classic.[11]

The Late Classic family who chose this bedrock outcrop for their dwellings began, then, with a rocky surface that had already been modified somewhat by the Late Formative villagers centuries earlier. These later people set about completely remodeling the bedrock outcrop, raising and expanding the elevated surface to support new dwellings. To level everything up to the highest point of the outcrop, they added large stones and pushed some of the rubble fill from earlier buildings into the gaps. They finished this fill with a packed layer of fist-sized cobbles and tamped earth to make a floor, but in many places they left flat patches of bedrock uncovered, a natural and ready-made living surface.

They planted stones on this newly raised surface, the simple foundations for three small houses made of wood and thatch (fig. 18). To the southwest sat a rectangular dwelling of wood and thatch on low stone foundations, its door turned in to face the other two buildings of the group.[12] To the north, a second wooden dwelling perched on a low mound of fist-sized cobbles.[13] The cobble mound the Pool builders created for this dwelling's foundation was an oval, though somewhat amorphous as it lacked any clear stone walls; many houses in the city of Yaxuná from this time followed a similar design. To the northeast, the Pool builders laid simple stone lines to support a rectangular hut—one of the only buildings our team would document at Tzacauil that didn't have a cobble floor inside its walls. Cobble floors mean that a building probably once had a plaster floor; the plaster erodes and disintegrates over centuries in the open air, but the cobbles laid as a ballast underneath remain. Yaxunah community members on the excavation team pointed out that in traditional Yucatecan kitchens, earthen floors are pre-

FIGURE 18. Yaxunah community members excavating one of the dwellings of the Late to Terminal Classic homesite known as Pool. Photo by the author.

ferred. A spill on a plaster floor, they said, sits there until it's mopped up, but a spill on a dirt floor simply seeps into the ground. This simple building may indeed have served as a kitchen for this homesite: during excavations inside its walls, our team recovered nine handheld grinding stones used for processing maize and preparing ingredients for cooking.[14]

The people of the Pool Group lived high on the tallest bedrock rise at Tzacauil. Just below their outcrop lay the low soil flats where, generations earlier, Late Formative farmers had shored up earth and gravel behind a terrace wall to create a stable walkway to reach their intensive agricultural plots. When our team excavated a trench through that walkway and into the soil-rich expanse beyond it, we found traces only of Late Formative villagers. Up above, excavations at the Pool Group recovered the highest density of potsherds documented for any Tzacauil homesite; people living at the Pool homesite in the Late to Terminal Classic clearly owned—and broke—a lot of clay pots and jars.[15] But still we found no ceramics from that period down below in the soil flat. These later farmers were not interacting with the soil-rich patches of Tzacauil in the same ways that their antecedents, the Late Formative smallholders, had before them. The residues of their land relations concentrate on bedrock alone.

Bedrock offers many gifts, and throughout the history of land relations in the Yaxunah ejido, people have collaborated with karst in creative ways.[16] Flat rises of bedrock present stable surfaces that drain well during rains. Even as Late Formative farmers were drawn to earthy *kancabales*, they still chose to plant their houses on the bedrock outcrops that stud the soil flats. As a rule, those earlier farmers preferred to root their homesites at a distance from the flat expanses of bedrock that lend their rugged texture to much of Tzacauil's landscape, even while those stone lands offer opportunities for seasonal water storage and container gardening. Farmers made these choices to ensure that the future generations in their smallholder lineages would retain access to soil-rich ground. But by the Late Classic resettlement of Tzacauil, farming in the Yaxuná hinterlands had changed. That change is written high on the rocky outcrop where the Pool people made their home: farmers no longer felt the same obligation to plant their houses directly in the soils they planned to cultivate. The constraint to root the home in soil had been relaxed. And so farmers chose to live among the gifts of bedrock.

෨ ෨ ෨

At the Yaxuná archaeological site, I can't name a single Late Formative home-site that wasn't renovated and reoccupied by new generations of Late to Terminal Classic city dwellers; if those homesites are there, archaeologists haven't found them.[17] Yet at Tzacauil, only one Late Formative homesite was revived in this way.

The Kaan homesite had been planted by smallholders during the heyday of Tzacauil's first farming village, right around the same time that the Sáastun and Chamal homesites were founded. The Late Formative Kaan founders chose a patch of land just south of the Tzacauil Sacbe. They were near soil, but also linked to great stretches of exposed bedrock. The bedrock near the homesite formed natural corridors, ready walkways into a network of rock and low soil, which the Kaan homesteaders expanded by making an additional walkway of tamped gravel and earth. No other Late Formative homesite at Tzacauil incorporated natural and built walkways in this way. This, I think, was precisely what attracted later people to reclaim this home-site but more or less ignore the muddy soil-rich places so valued by the first farmers of the ejido's edge.

These newcomers revived a small community at Tzacauil during the Late Classic. When they got there, the residues of the earlier farming village—the houses, the acropolis, the sacbe—would have already been ruins, cut out of the forest and then returned to it hundreds of years in the past.

I read a story of quiet forgetting written in the rubble of the Kaan home-site. The Late Formative founders of this house had chosen this place partly because it put them right on the Tzacauil Sacbe: they were steps away from the central artery that connected their village west towards the city. Processions and parades would have passed on this avenue. Beloved visitors would have stepped down from the road to greet the Kaan family, bringing with their footsteps the current of news and gossip that flowed east and west.

These ephemeral moments didn't leave detectible traces in the landscape, but material traces of the sacbe's importance to the early Kaan residents remain in stone. When our team excavated the north side of the group's main platform, we found that the Late Formative residents had dressed up the front of their homesite with low stone steps running the length of the plat-form. None of the other three sides of the platform had steps like this. Only the north side, just a few steps away from the sacbe, invited formal access—and attention. The dwellings on top of the platform were positioned to face the road. The people who first lived here took great care to emphasize their connection with the Tzacauil Sacbe.

But by the time Late Classic folks came to live at the Kaan homesite, the sacbe was no longer charged with the same potency it had commanded dur-ing Late Formative times.[18] They would have known that the road had never even been finished, after all; the new arrivals would have seen that the old sacbe fizzled out with a few rocky gasps of stray and semi-finished segments, about halfway between the acropolis and Yaxuná.

Besides, new settlements were springing up all over the place in the lands east of Yaxuná, and plenty of folks were robbing stone from the old Tzacauil Sacbe to use for their new dwellings.[19] The crumbling stone causeway could still be traversed, and rainy season travelers probably gave thanks for its raised passage above the muddy soil flats. But it was no longer the artery it once was. And so the Late Classic newcomers to the Kaan homesite set about remod-eling their living space to communicate not with the defunct road to the north, but with the small new community being seeded to the west at the Pool and Mukul homesites.

The Kaan homesite had new people now, and they took the old boulder-lined platform as raw material and began to mold it. Huge stones from the old platform's western wall came crashing down, pushed mightily from above or tugged down with ropes from below. The renovators re-formed the boulders into a container, stretching the old perimeter of the platform out to the west. They wasted no time worrying about a well-dressed wall: they poured baskets of soil and armfuls of rubble on top of the slumped-out Late Formative fill, leaving a sloping mound that shored up the widened surface on the platform above. Set into the slope's middle, the renovators crafted a rough stairway, or maybe a ramp—it was hard to tell—to make it easier to climb up and down from the platform. They cobbled this entry together from rough stones and finished it off with a thick layer of crudely made plaster that was crumbling and chunky and not at all like the hard burnished surfaces found in the finer architecture of Yaxuná. And while the Late Formative entry to the platform had been wide and spanned the entire north wall, this later entry was narrow, more private.

For Kaan residents who walked down this little stairway, they would have noticed that on their right, the platform edge was farther back and recessed, while on their left, the platform jutted out like a swollen lip of stone and rubble. Centuries later, our team excavated this bulge in the platform's western wall south of the small staircase (fig. 19). As the Yaxunah community members on the excavation cleared rocks and earth to get a sense of the platform's construction, a neat row of loaf-shaped stones surfaced at the base of the rubble.

Don Sebastián, an older Yaxunah man on the excavation team who was usually always laughing and joking on site, now brushed the loaf-shaped stones in silence. He whisked away soil and flecks of dead leaves with uncharacteristic solemnity as he prepared the excavation unit for a photograph. I stood nearby with my camera and considered the stones. Don Nazario, passing by with an empty bucket on his way back from sifting soil at the screens, paused next to me and likewise considered the stones. We exchanged a glance. "*Sí, es,*" was all he said. Don Sebastián gathered up his tools to move them out of frame and came to stand next to us. Brushing his hands together to get the dust off, he said quietly, "*Sí, es.*" Yes, it is—the answer to the unspoken question we were all thinking: was this row of loaf-shaped stones covering a grave?

Everyone working at Tzacauil knew what a Late to Terminal Classic grave looked like because a few kilometers west, the city of Yaxuná holds hundreds of burials honeycombed within the stone foundations of its many dwellings.[20] Yaxuná's population reached the highest levels in its history towards the end of the Classic period. The city filled in with stone foundations for wood and thatch houses, often planted on earlier homesites, on bedrock rises,

FIGURE 19. Excavations of the Kaan homesite's main platform at Tzacauil. The platform was built in the Late to Terminal Formative and then renovated to add a narrow accessway during the Late to Terminal Classic. Beneath the fill of those renovations, the excavation team uncovered a row of stones characteristic of Late to Terminal Classic graves—a household member may have been buried here. Photo by the author.

or right on the ground. And within these stone foundations, the city dwellers buried their dead in shallow crypts, roofed with loaf-shaped capstones and sealed beneath floors.

When the first major archaeological project ran at Yaxuná in the 1980s and 1990s, its excavations unearthed dozens of Classic period burials within houses.[21] For many of the older Yaxunah community members working with me at Tzacauil, like don Nazario and don Sebastián, memories of excavating these household burials were highlights from a different era of archaeology in the ejido—to say nothing of the royal tombs found in the Yaxuná North Acropolis. Even in my own era of research in the ejido, my fellow archaeologists were leading investigations that regularly found and excavated burials inside Yaxuná homesites. The majority of Yaxuná houses remain unexcavated; that so many burials had been found with such limited sampling makes it strikingly clear that the archaeological site of Yaxuná is a cemetery of staggering size. You walk differently through the ruins, knowing this.

The burials investigated in the ancient city of Yaxuná have generated valuable insights into past Maya life, health, and ritual practice during the Classic period.[22] The individuals buried in homesite graves were accompanied with precious belongings: painted ceramic vessels, jaguar teeth, greenstone tools, and bone perforators used in bloodletting. The patterns in these mortuary goods let us glimpse Classic period practices of identity, of gender, and of status.[23] Bioarchaeologists—specialists in the study of human remains—have learned from bones and teeth, for instance, that the Classic-era city dwellers of Yaxuná were mostly vegetarian, eating a regular diet of maize, squash, and beans, supplemented only once in a while with meat. And bioarchaeological analysis of royal individuals buried in the North Acropolis has revealed that a faction of Classic-era Yaxuná nobility came from far away, perhaps from the lush rainforests of the southern Maya lowlands. Many of these royals died violent deaths, the histories of political upheaval written in the traumas of their bones.[24]

Even the fact that the burials are under house floors says a lot. Ancient people throughout the Maya region interred their dead beneath the floors of their homes. Like the practice of caching heirlooms, burying the dead inside the home might have activated a sense of deep continuity among lineage and land.[25] Living in close communion with the remains of great-grandparents, grandparents, and parents seems to have reaffirmed for the living generation a connection with ancestry and with place.

This practice goes back to the Formative period in some places in the Maya region, but in the Yaxunah ejido, no documented burial has been decisively dated earlier than the Classic: none at Yaxuná, and none even at Tzacauil with its relatively preserved Late Formative homesites. The first farmers of the Yaxunah ejido forests, it seems, enacted their connections with ancestry and with place through the stone of their homes and, sometimes, through the caching of heirlooms. No one knows how the people of this land honored their dead during the first several generations of settled agriculture. But by the final centuries of the Classic, Yaxuná city dwellers had adopted the custom of living with their ancestors nearby. They lived on top of bones, buried under rows of loaf-shaped rocks, the stone rafters shielding the sacred space of crypts.

The stones uncovered beneath the Kaan platform fill, neatly brushed up by the experienced hand of don Sebastián, were identical to the familiar capstones found in homesite burials at Yaxuná. We never lifted them. I photographed the stones, drew them, and then the Yaxunah community members reburied them that same day. While I value the insights bioarchaeology provides about the past, for me the decision not to excavate the Kaan Group burial was simple: I did not want to disturb the single grave found at Tzacauil. Logically I knew that a sample size of one meant that whatever could be taken from that grave would not be statistically robust enough to say much of anything meaningful about life there.

There were other reasons not to open the grave. In the United States, legislation passed in the nineties created legal protections for Native American grave sites.[26] The laws are different in Mexico, and many Mexican people hold attitudes towards death and human remains that are very different from mainstream attitudes in the States; take, for instance, the tradition of Day of the Dead celebrations in many parts of Mexico and the local version, *Hanal Pixan*, celebrated in Yucatán. My decision to rebury the loaf-shaped stones at the Kaan homesite came less from concerns about sample size and more from tangled ethical questions about disturbing the dead.

While I won't ever know for sure if that row of stones sheltered a burial, I feel convinced enough to say with some confidence that I think the remains of one or more of the Kaan homesite's Late to Terminal Classic residents are resting there. If I'm right, this single possible burial, contemporary with many, many more like it in nearby Yaxuná, suggests that the mortuary practice of burying the dead inside houses had reached the Classic community living at Tzacauil. But then why, when the Classic houses at Yaxuná often include multiple burials each, did we only find one possible burial in all of the Classic dwellings of Tzacauil combined?

ॐ   ॐ   ॐ

There were other differences between life in Yaxuná and life in Tzacauil, differences pronounced enough to leave traces in the ground. When our team excavated Tzacauil's Late to Terminal Classic period houses, we found very few artifacts that came from far away. Obsidian, a black volcanic glass used to create blades, comes from just a few places but made its way throughout ancient Mesoamerica as a valued trade good. The Yaxuná archaeological site is sown with glittering black flakes and fragments of obsidian that came into the city during the Classic period from far away. You can find obsidian at nearly every Classic homesite in Yaxuná, suggesting that almost all households in the city could access the material.[27] You'd probably find more obsidian in a single two-by-two-meter test pit dug into almost any homesite in Yaxuná than what our team recovered from hundreds of square meters excavated at Tzacauil: a single obsidian flake at the Kaan homesite, and a couple of stray fragments found on the ground, out of any clear context.

Up on the Pool homesite, we found a few isolated examples of other kinds of nonlocal goods. A polished greenstone celt, a broken perforating tool made of fine quality chert, and a small scrap of marine shell all materialize links between the people of the Pool household and the flow of goods coming into Yaxuná from afar.[28] Yet the relative scarcity of nonlocal goods found in Classic Tzacauil homesites, compared to what's been found in contemporary homesites at Classic Yaxuná, hints at social differences. The hinterland folks living at Tzacuail may have been only marginal or occasional participants in regional trade networks. Another possible explanation could be that the Classic people living at Tzacauil didn't stay in place long enough to accumulate the amount of waste that their urban contemporaries did. Perhaps if their access to nonlocal goods was uncertain, then Tzacauil farmers might have taken better care of the objects they did manage to obtain, taking even worn-out tools with them when they moved.

I said before that nearly every Late Formative homesite in Yaxuná was reoccupied, and usually remodeled, when the city reached its population peak near the end of the Classic. Walk around Yaxuná and without even needing to dig you'll see these layers of life collapsed on top of one another: the humble stone foundations of Late to Terminal Classic period houses perch everywhere on top of the massive boulder-lined platforms of Late Formative houses.

You would start to see, too, that in some of the boulders lining those old platforms, smooth-sided clefts had been ground into the stones, making them into basins. When the basins are shallow, archaeologists identify them as metates, the stones used for grinding plants with the help of a handheld stone tool called a mano. Use a metate for a long time and eventually the groove will deepen to the point where grinding gets difficult. Those deeper-grooved basins are called *pilas*, and they become used as small cisterns for holding water.

These metates and pilas ground into the boulders of Late Formative platforms tell a story like the one written in the Kaan homesite's turn away from the Tzacauil Sacbe: the recycling of an earlier tradition into new uses, in this case, the transformation of Late Formative boulder walls into Late to Terminal Classic maize grinding and water catching equipment. The deepening grooves of the metates and pilas found throughout Yaxuná hold in their clefts the residues of new histories of Classic people and land, rooting down in the urban landscape.

But we found no metates or pilas ground into the old boulder walls of Tzacauil, not even at the Kaan Group, where there was clear evidence of a Late Classic family taking over a Late Formative homesite. People living in Tzacauil's cluster of Late Classic homesites were certainly grinding maize; we found a dozen manos at the Kaan Group, and three dozen more at the Pool Group.[29] If these tools were being used to grind maize in boulder basins or depressions in the bedrock, the practice was too short-lived to wear down the rock into the characteristic troughs of metates and pilas. The excavation team found a fragment of a portable metate at the Pool homesite, which could mean that the people living there usually used equipment that could be carried around—not immoveable boulders. In either scenario, there's a sense that the farmers living in this small community out in the Tzacauil edge lands were more mobile than the folks living in the urban heart of Yaxuná.

The differences in burials reinforce this idea still further. The Late to Terminal Classic homesites of Yaxuná hold in their stony cores so many more ancestors than the homesites of the Tzacauil hinterlands. The small community of farming families that planted their homesites at the Kaan, Pool, and Mukul cluster lived there for a relatively short time, perhaps a decade, perhaps a generation. Not enough time for many ancestors to be seeded into their houses, not enough time for many hands to grind deep clefts into old boulders.

In the last chapter I compared the city of Yaxuná in the Late Formative to a tree. The tree grew, branch by branch, neighborhood by neighborhood, each replicating a pattern that extended out across the urban landscape. Tzacauil in the Late Formative was like a cutting from that tree, replanted to replicate the same pattern in the edge lands. Yaxuná boasted more public venues and more inhabitants, but the qualities and textures of daily life might not have been so different in the two places during the first few generations of small-holder farming.

Yet differences that might have been muted in earlier years became pronounced in later years. Yaxuná became something categorically different from the small hamlets, like Tzacauil, that sprang up in its hinterlands. A dichotomy of urban and rural deepened in the ejido landscape through a series of bundled changes.[30]

One of these changes had to do with permanence and transience. In urban Yaxuná, the many dead buried inside houses and the gradual grinding down of old boulder walls into metates and pilas are residues of both lineage and permanence. Late to Terminal Classic folks rooted in Yaxuná's urban core, solidifying generational relationships with land in the proclamations of bone and rock.

For those living outside the city, life and death went on. Maize grinding went on. But the material traces of these rhythms read quieter in the edge lands because people weren't staying in the same place for several generations anymore. Late to Terminal Classic farmers of the edge lands weren't as mobile as their foraging ancestors were, but neither were they as tethered to single parcels of land as their early agricultural ancestors had been. They planted homesites. They made milpa, engaging the forest patch by patch in the ongoing reciprocal relationships of ritual and offering that survive in the ceremonies of milpa farmers today. They lived in a particular place for a time—how long exactly, I don't know, maybe a few seasons, a few years, a few decades—and then moved on to continue the rhythms in another part of the forest.

ঌ   ঌ   ঌ

The transformation from farming lineages who tethered themselves to particular places to farming lineages who moved through the forest is written in the edge lands of the Yaxunah ejido. North of the Tzacauil Sacbe, the ruins of two small buildings archive within their rock foundations an important piece of this story. They are the Jaltun and T'uup Groups, and their stones were among the last laid by precolonial people in Tzacauil.

You'd find Jaltun by walking west from the remnants of the Chamal homesite, over a shallow soil-rich *kancabal* and onto an expansive stretch of bedrock riddled with frying-pan-sized cavities.[31] The Jaltun Group isn't a group exactly—it's a single heap of stones mounded on top of this flat bedrock expanse. The shallow apertures in the rock all around the mound host large trees inside their pockets of soil and moisture. Elsewhere on the bed-rock, our excavation team found deeper crevices plunging through the sur-face stone. We found that the builders of the Jaltun Group had dealt with these by capping the crevices with flat slabs of rock to prevent fill from slump-ing down. During excavations, some Yaxunah community members used the same method to refrigerate big bottles of Coke underground. The bottles were sealed into bedrock shafts first thing in the morning and retrieved, still chilled and beaded with condensation, hours later.

Every time I referred to the Jaltun Group's lone mound as a house during excavations, Yaxunah community members working on the project would gently chide me, saying there was simply no way this tiny building had been a house.

"It's barely big enough for a single person to lay down inside of it," some-one would say.

"And look at those stones," someone else would add, pitching a pebble at the chaotic rubble in the building's crowded interior with a flourish. "How could somebody walk around on all that?"

After carefully digging the mound and studying the jumble of stones jut-ting out from the surface, the Yaxunah excavators concluded that the dra-matic unevenness of the interior could be blamed mostly on the building's collapse. The walls of the Jaltun building were not simply single courses of stone. They had gone higher, built by positioning progressively smaller stones on top of a base of large rocks, just like the dry-laid stone walls known as *albarradas* that weave through Yaxunah and most Yucatecan towns today. Trees and time had churned up the Jaltun walls and spilled them out into a mess. But even with this insight about the walls, the inside of the Jaltun building was still puzzling: it lacked the stable, flat floors we had gotten used to finding in Tzacauil dwellings, whether early or late. I came around to the obvious conclusion that the Yaxunah community members had been patiently pointing out all along: this was almost certainly not a house.

Over to the east, the T'uup Group likewise seemed too small to sleep in, which is probably the bare minimum you'd ask for in a dwelling. This was the last group our team excavated at Tzacauil.[32] It turned out to be the simplest. T'uup's single small mound had been planted near the stately remains of the Late Formative Jach homesite, on a patch of bedrock adrift in the same soil-rich expanse that had been favored by Tzacauil's earliest farmers. The T'uup builders had arranged an oval ring of large stones on the bedrock, and inside the walls they packed down a thin layer of soil mixed with stones. They raised up the walls by fitting smaller and smaller rocks on top of the base stones, reaching somewhere around waist or chest height.[33] The walls had long ago collapsed into a jumble, but some Yaxunah community members—themselves experienced *albarrada* builders—could see how the stones had once fit together.

These two tiny buildings, Jaltun and T'uup, had the fewest artifacts of any of the groups our team excavated at Tzacauil.[34] I was accustomed to not finding much at the site, since ceramics and stone tools were already pretty scarce in the Late Formative homesites. But these two buildings dated to the Classic period, when I would have expected relatively more abundant access to pottery, and by extension, greater amounts of broken potsherds lying around or buried with construction fills. Whoever was involved with Jaltun and T'uup left behind only a scant few potsherds to mark their presence, even as the contemporary Pool and Kaan homesites were practically overflowing with pottery.

Among the few potsherds our team did find at Jaltun and T'uup were enough identifiable pieces to confirm that these two buildings indeed overlapped with the cluster of Classic homesites up on the high bedrock rise. It's worth getting a little more granular with ceramic dating here. The pottery found in excavations at Jaltun points to an initial construction in the first window of the Late Classic, around AD 550–700. But there are also potsherds from the final centuries of the Classic, a period sometimes called the Terminal Classic. Jaltun had pottery from the first part of the Terminal Classic, around AD 700–850, as well as from the second part, around AD 850–1100. Likewise, T'uup's minimal ceramic assemblage included pieces from both the Late Classic and from the first part of the Terminal Classic, a range up to three centuries long. Both T'uup and Jaltun yielded, on average, fewer than a single potsherd per square meter excavated. For comparison, the Pool homesite yielded on average about nine potsherds per square meter.

There simply didn't seem to be enough refuse at these two little huts for them to have been full-fledged homesites. The scant stuff we did find points to a gaping window of time, but if the Jaltun and T'uup Groups had been sites for the robust diversity of domestic tasks—food processing and preparation, cooking, gardening, tool manufacture, household repairs and renovations—for continuous centuries, there would be a lot more garbage. What we found in the ground backed up the initial impressions of the Yaxunah excavators: these probably weren't houses.

So what are these humble buildings? I think there's an answer in accounts of colonial-era Maya milpa farmers. In her book *Maya Society under Colonial*

Rule, historian Nancy Farriss writes about Yucatec Maya milpa agriculture as a kind of centrifugal force in the colonial landscape.[35] Colonial authorities desperately wanted to keep Indigenous Maya populations concentrated in tightly gridded towns. If the Maya stayed in place, then the Spaniards could more easily tax them and monitor them for signs of resistance or uprisings. But in those years, the milpa was the primary means of Maya subsistence. Milpa, as a shifting and extensive agricultural practice, required that farmers go out into the forest, sometimes great distances from those tightly gridded towns, to find land that was ready to be burned and planted. This unnerved the Spanish authorities, so they worked harder to bind Maya milperos and their families to the towns through mechanisms like compulsory attendance at Sunday mass.

There are times in the milpa cycle when the work intensifies and requires all-day labor for several days in a row. Making the walk back and forth between homesite and field every day becomes impractical past a certain threshold of distance. So colonial-era milpa farmers living far from their fields would sometimes set up temporary field huts and camp closer to their crops, returning home only on Sundays to go to the mandatory mass. Some farmers might have put up with this back and forth indefinitely. But often, farmers apparently grew tired of living on their own in the field huts, and tired, too, of having to regularly subject themselves to increasing demands whenever they did go back home. And so many farming families would eventually decide to relocate entire households—men, women, children, other relatives, animals, and possessions—out to the field hut. "For some the move was permanent," Farriss writes, "and the new house site became the nucleus of a new satellite settlement."[36]

While Farriss shows that this cycle of homesite relocation coded resistance to colonial rule, it also coded enduring Indigenous ecological knowledge. The cycle she describes—founding a homesite, then the gradual lengthening of the walk to milpa plots over the years, then the raising of temporary field huts, then relocating completely to the field hut and founding a new homesite there, and repeating again—is inextricably entangled with the ecological tempos of the milpa itself.

The origins of these cycles are materialized in the edge lands of the Yaxunah ejido. Rhythms of homesite founding, growth, and abandonment are encoded in the stone and clay left by farmers who lived at Tzacauil in the last centuries of the Classic. Jaltun and T'uup were field huts. They were temporary camps, set up by milperos near active fields and used as needed for shelter or storage of tools and harvested maize. The clustered dwellings of the Pool, Mukul, and Kaan Groups were full-fledged homesites: farming families lived there, slept there, renovated and repaired dwellings, cooked meals. They left behind the cumulative refuse of their lives, lived on the bedrock outcrop. They buried a family member. The archaeological record makes it look like all these things were happening at once, frozen in place and glimpsed dimly through the imprecise timing of ceramic chronologies. But they were not. Look past this static picture and you'll see the dynamic cycles of multigenerational milpa farming as it may have first developed in the Yaxunah ejido.

The cluster of dwellings high on the bedrock outcrop would have started as a temporary field camp. It might have gone like this: a Late Classic milpa farmer goes walking to find a patch of forest ready for cultivation. He and his family live somewhere else, in another hamlet in the forest maybe, or perhaps in the city of Yaxuná. The last few years he's been having to walk longer to find woodlands that are ready to be burned again; the city keeps growing. He reaches Tzacauil. The trees are thick. It's clear no one has lived or farmed much in these woods since the days of the ancestral farmers and their big stone houses and pyramids. The farmer sets up a temporary field hut on top of the old Kaan homesite—the foundation stones of an old dwelling work well and save him some work—and he camps there for a few days at a time as he raises a crop. The harvest is good.

He convinces his family to move out to Tzacauil the following year, not just his wife and children, but a few of his siblings and their families, too. They pack up their houses, move their belongings out to the forest, and set up a new cluster of dwellings—the Pool, Kaan, and Mukul Groups—on the site of the farmer's field camp. The families renovate and build new homes. They stay for years living on the high bedrock outcrop, burning and planting parcel by parcel, year by year leaving old fields to reintegrate back into the forest. They stay a while. Long enough, perhaps, for one family member to become an ancestor, buried in the sloping fill of the Kaan platform, but not long enough for others to join them. Not long enough for the daily grinding of maize to wear deep basins into the boulder or bedrock, and not nearly as long as the first farming families had remained in this land, anchored by taproots sunk deep into the red soil for generations.

Eventually the farmer and his relatives find themselves again walking farther and farther into the woods in search of ready land. Field huts spring up out in the forest. They are the seeds of new homesites. One day these field huts will pull the families out to them, and they will leave Tzacauil to repeat the cycle. In their wake, the forests of the eastern edge lands will be restored. The stone foundations of the dwellings the families left behind will be used for the temporary field huts of farmers who come later. Their cluster of old dwellings is visited off and on through generations as the forest grows and burns, grows and burns.

Jaltun and T'uup were temporary field huts that never amassed the gravity to pull in the rest of their farmers' families. These huts didn't become full-fledged homesites but continued instead to provide periodic shelter to farmers who lived elsewhere in the forest. Where the farmers lived is probably impossible to know. But for farmers to build field huts at Tzacauil hints that the forest here had returned to maturity; Jaltun and T'uup, I suspect, were built long after the families of the Pool, Mukul, and Kaan dwellings had moved on.

Farming families moved through Tzacauil, and throughout the forests of the ejido edge lands, for centuries. Seeded through the remnants of their homesites and field camps are potsherds, whose origins span the final four or five centuries of the Classic period. Colonial-era Maya milpa farmers were known to sometimes reoccupy abandoned houses if their fields were too far from their homes.[37] The broken pottery of later periods hints that these temporary stays continued in Tzacauil for a long time. Stone foundations laid in AD 800 might have been revived with fresh-cut wooden poles and green palm frond roofs in AD 1000. Farmers raised crops from the forest, light on the land, moving often, and always in communication with the old shelters and old fields of the farmers who came before them. Embodied in the stillness of the rock and pottery they left behind are the rhythmic land relations of milperos and forests, working collaboratively over hundreds of years.

ॐ ॐ ॐ

Like the changing root systems of *Brosimum alicastrum*, the changing land relations of farmers allowed survival in times of great stress. The drought that ended the first farming village at Tzacauil ended, too, the taproot practices of smallholder intensification in the edge lands—and catalyzed the shift to the fibrous root practices of the milpa. Milpa farming and its accompanying mobility empowered hinterland farmers with flexibility. Because of that flexibility, hinterland farmers were able to carry on their lives during an era of extreme upheaval and societal breakdown: the turbulent events sometimes known as the Maya Collapse.

The city of Yaxuná was not spared the turbulence of collapse.[38] Even through the droughts that made Tzacauil villagers abandon their homesites at the end of the Late Formative, Yaxuná maintained its primacy as the most populated center in the region. But its grip as the political center was loosening. Most of the great monuments of the early city fell into neglect. In the first part of the Classic (AD 250–400), there are signs that a foreign usurper seized control of the city and went on to legitimize the political takeover by appropriating the hallmarks of earlier Yaxuná kings.[39] From AD 400 to 550, the pottery vessels in circulation at Yaxuná abruptly shift from a tradition with strong stylistic links to the southern Maya lowlands to a tradition based in Oxkintok, a rising city in the Puuc hills region of western Yucatán. At the same time, a military outpost was founded at Xkanhá, a site located just two kilometers north of Yaxuná's urban core.[40] These signs of political upheaval are echoed in bone: a mass grave found in Yaxuná's North Acropolis from this period contained a dozen people, probably overturned nobles, whose remains bore signs of violent wounds inflicted at or near death.[41]

By the time a group of milpa farming families came to live high on a bedrock promontory at Tzacauil, another political upheaval was rocking Yaxuná a short walk to the west. Lady K'awiil Ajaw, conqueror queen of Coba, incorporated Yaxuná into her kingdom and consolidated control with the construction of Sacbe 1. Now Coba military forces could make a quick march across the forest and arrive in Yaxuná in only a couple of days. Unlike the previous few power shifts, no clear signs of violence accompany the Coba takeover, and population in urban Yaxuná actually began to grow.

Yaxuná reached its peak in the last centuries of the Classic. Houses sprang up on nearly every surface to accommodate city dwellers. New renovations began on the North Acropolis, and an influx of new ceramic traditions materialized strong ties, once more, with the Puuc region.[42] Yaxuná had been eclipsed by a rising center, or confederation of centers, to the west; some archaeologists even think that the rise in Yaxuná's population at this time could be a product of interregional migration.[43]

Yaxuná changed hands again for a final time in precolonial history sometime during AD 850–1100. Armies from the north invaded to take control of the city and claim it as territory for a growing empire based in Chichen Itza. Yaxuná's political leaders marshaled fortifications to be built around the North Acropolis, but their hasty defenses could not hold the invaders back. The army razed the acropolis and desecrated the tomb of a royal Yaxuná woman. With this takeover, the ancient city of Yaxuná was finally abandoned after a run of well over a thousand years.[44] The displaced residents may have been relocated to live closer to Chichen Itza, or they may have scattered out into the forest.

ə♥   ə♥   ə♥

These kinds of upheavals were endemic to the Maya lowlands during the critical years at the end of the Classic. Environmental degradation and climate shifts intensified preexisting political tensions, leading to the widespread abandonment of cities throughout the Maya area. When people refer to the Maya Collapse, this abandonment is what they mean. But rather than a singular event, the collapse is more accurately understood as a series of transformations and feedback loops, multiple waves of entangled change that swept through the region at different times and with different tempos. Many of these transformations were seeded by agricultural practices and political management of labor and land.[45]

In popular media accounts of the Maya Collapse, unsustainable agricultural practices are often blamed for causing civilizational demise. But the more archaeologists study subsistence practices from this transformative time, the more complicated the picture becomes. The same agricultural practice that persisted for centuries in one city could be completely disastrous in another. Deforestation accelerated past the point of no return in some places, triggering catastrophic damage to soil health and forest biodiversity; elsewhere, communities enjoyed long-term access to mature forest through selective clearing and careful land management.[46] Some Maya settlements let their soils degrade, while others combated soil erosion by farming on terraces.[47] Farmers in areas prone to natural disasters, like the coastal plain of Belize, became more adaptive to climate and environmental shifts than their inland neighbors because centuries of water table fluctuations had taught them to diversify their subsistence practices.[48] Rural farming villages were often more resilient in their agricultural and water management strategies, even as urban political institutions crumbled around them.[49] Farming practices at the end of the Classic were not inherently unsustainable, but political and environmental dynamics could render them rigid and vulnerable.

While Classic Maya rulers were trying desperately to salvage their authority, hinterland farmers were embracing a new kind of land relations. Greater attention to the archaeology of rural hamlets and villages is revealing that even while once-powerful urban centers were being depopulated, hinterland farming communities were carrying on. What their persistence looked like on the ground could vary—but what they have in common is flexibility.

Archaeologists studying societal collapse in past cultures around the world have found that flexibility is key to making it through times of great ecological and political stress. The breakdown of many civilizations can be traced to rigidity traps: vulnerable situations that occur when societies respond to stress by going all in on a narrow range of practices when they really should be diversifying. The disintegration of Norse colonies in Greenland can be traced back to an overreliance on climate-sensitive seal hunting.[50] The abandonment of Angkor Wat in Cambodia goes back to an inflexible, costly, and increasingly vulnerable dependence on a centralized hydraulic network.[51] The warfare and suffering that depopulated some Ancestral Puebloan communities in the American Southwest can be linked to the decision to double down on irrigation-dependent farming in the desert.[52] Likewise, early intensive agriculture in the Yaxunah ejido edge lands became rigid and eventually led to collapse, yet the flexibility of mobile milpa farming soon followed. Land relations changed: taproots gave way to fibrous roots.

Milpa enabled farmers of the edge lands to be flexible and thus to survive the turbulent centuries of the Maya Collapse. This isn't just true of Tzacauil. In the hinterlands north of Yaxuná, between the city and its rival Chichen Itza, a small hamlet known as Popolá likewise weathered the upheavals at the end of the Classic. Archaeological investigations at Popolá found that before Chichen Itza conquered Yaxuná, there was a contingent of elite families living at Popolá. These families maintained strong ties to the elite families of Yaxuná. With the rise of Chichen Itza, all evidence for this elite faction disappears from Popolá; they were likely forced out of power, or worse, along with the rulers of Yaxuná. But for the rest of the people living at Popolá—the farmers, the commoners—life continued much the same way after Chichen Itza invaded Yaxuná as it had before.[53] Like Tzacauil, the political turmoil that plagued the city and its rulers is muted in the farming hamlets of the edge lands.

My sense is that the string of political leaders moving through power at Yaxuná had learned to leave hinterland farmers to their mobility. They wouldn't try to lock farmers down, as colonial authorities later would. Perhaps they recognized that not only would this be a fight they wouldn't win, but that food would be more plentiful if farmers were empowered to move as they wished. The many power shifts of the Late to Terminal Classic brought with them no sign of direct intervention in the lives of the farming communities who moved through the forest. No great acropolis loomed overhead, as it had at Tzacauil before. To me it seems that rulers tolerated—even embraced—the mobility of the farmers living in the edge lands.[54]

Farmers still participated in the greater political landscape. The nonlocal goods, though few, found in the Pool and Kaan Groups hint that Late to Terminal Classic farmers of Tzacauil were involved in Yaxuná's regional economy. There's also some evidence that hinterland milpa farmers were still expected to pay tribute to political leaders even as they moved around.[55] But the farmers of the edge lands were themselves political agents. Rulers had little choice but to work with farmers, because they knew that at any point, the farmers could disappear into the forest (as many vexed colonial authorities would discover in a few more centuries). The direct governance that had been possible in the permanent villages of the Late to Terminal Formative would not work for the ephemeral hamlets of the Late to Terminal Classic. Amid Yaxuná's volatile political history and the environmental stress associated with the collapse, edge land farmers just kept moving, just kept making milpa, with little evidence that their lives were much affected by the entity at the receiving end of their tribute.

Just as óox, the *Brosimum alicastrum* tree of Yucatán's thin soils, responds to drought by adjusting its growth from downward taproots to outward fibrous roots, so too did the edge land farmers adjust their practices from intensive smallholding to the mobile milpa. Óox is a tree for hard times: Yaxunah and other Yucatec Maya communities still rely on its nuts as a fallback food in times of famine.[56] In lean times, the adaptability of the óox tree enables it—and the people it feeds—to survive. In the Late to Terminal Classic farmers of the Yaxunah edge lands, whose communities adapted their land relations and embraced flexibility during a time of climate strife and institutional breakdown, I sense a clear kinship with the nimble roots of óox trees.

The underlying reason that the mobile milpa could sustain edge land communities, even through hard times, was that those communities had secure access to great expanses of forested land. Even as power changed hands, hinterland farmers maintained relations not just with their active fields each year, but with all the "unused" lands of the forest where future fields might someday be cleared. Land sovereignty empowered farmers to innovate flexible and adaptive forms of mutual land relations.

But new institutions of power, carrying the germ for an entirely different set of land relations, were moving west across the sea. The edge lands were at the threshold of colonial encounter.

FIVE

———

Lines in the Forest

FEW YUCATEC MAYA HISTORIES got written down by colonial chroniclers. Here's one that did.[1]

Nachi Cocom intended to feed the guests first. The guests were members
of the Xiu lineage, who had arrived weary and weakened from weeks of eating
little else but tree bark. Now the Xiu sought the cenote at Chichen Itza—the
well of the ancient city, a sacred place within the boundary of Cocom lands.

The cenote promised blessings: rain, maize, and respite from the bearded
intruders and their hoofed beasts. For eight years those intruders had
appeared from the sea, disappeared back into the sea, and appeared again,
crashing down like a wave each time they landed. They had just left again. In
the wake of the intruders, the Xiu—Nachi Cocom's guests—had left their
own drought-stricken and war-ravaged lands in Maní. The Xiu came as pilgrims, delivering themselves into Cocom lands, seeking consolation from the
mouth of the well.

The Xiu contingent petitioned Nachi Cocom for permission to pass
through Cocom lands so they could reach the cenote. They knew their request
had to be made delicately: almost one hundred years earlier, the Xiu and
Cocom families had been rulers of a vast realm together when, in a moment
of political upheaval, the Xiu had slain nearly the entire Cocom lineage, save
for one man who escaped the slaughter because he was away on a trading expedition. The Xiu destroyed the Cocom house and burned the Cocom fields.

The one man who survived the betrayal was Nachi Cocom's grandfather.
He returned home from the expedition to find his world destroyed. He gathered the remnants of his line and fled to the province of Sotuta, in lands that
held the ruins of the once-great city of Chichen Itza and its sacred cenote.
They called their new town Tibolon. It is said to mean: "We have been

tricked, there is still time to retaliate." The Xiu left, too, and made a new home in Maní. It is said to mean: "Now it is over."

Ninety-six years had passed and Nachi Cocom was prepared to receive his guests. With the Cocom guards he met the Xiu pilgrims in the edge lands of Cocom territory, out in the forest. Nachi Cocom said: You are our guests. Eat with us. On the threshold, just inside the border, the Cocom gathered the wary Xiu into a house. There a banquet waited. The Xiu pilgrims wondered, was this a trick? The tree bark turned in their stomachs and their mouths filled with water at the sight of food. They let down their guard and began to eat.

For three days Nachi Cocom fed the Xiu. The Cocom entertained their guests and got them drunk. On the fourth day, Nachi Cocom sealed the house with the feast-stupefied Xiu inside and set it on fire. Every single Xiu inside was killed. "Now it is over."

Four years later, the bearded intruders and their hoofed beasts drifted ashore once more from the sea. They were the same intruders who had driven the desperate Xiu pilgrims into Cocom hands and a vengeful death. This time was different: the surviving Xiu sought their own revenge. The Xiu offered the bearded intruders their friendship.

Together, the Xiu and the Spaniards united to carry out the conquest of the Yucatán Peninsula. "Now it is over."

    ❧　　❧　　❧

Distill down the colonial project in Yucatán to its essences and one essence will be this: a long campaign to draw lines around land. Lines have power. Lines institutionalize edges. Lines distinguish "used" and "useful" land from "unused" and "useless" land, and the desire for this distinction has driven five centuries of colonial decrees and neoliberal agrarian reforms in Yucatán and across the Americas.[2] With an imaginary gash on a map, a line can deracinate history from land and cast the land as waste. Lines enact extractive land relations, make them real on the ground.

The story of Nachi Cocom was told by Xiu descendants to Spanish chroniclers; that the story survives into the present is, perhaps more than anything, a testament to colonial enthusiasm for any Indigenous narrative that referenced provincial boundaries—lines around land. Maya interlocutors selectively communicated histories that clarified certain elements while concealing others, and the Spanish chroniclers selectively preserved accounts that confirmed and aided the colonial interest in establishing borders.

There is another layer to this story. The foreign invaders befriended the Xiu in a move to use preexisting rivalries to their advantage (a strategy that served the Spaniards throughout the Americas),[3] but under colonialism and its systems of racialized extraction, the Xiu were pushed into subjugation along with the rest of the peninsula's Indigenous population.[4] Knowing this context of betrayal, the story of Nachi Cocom holds a tacit kernel of subversion. I hear the Xiu storyteller sending a message to the Spaniards in this tale of patience and revenge: "We have been tricked, there is still time to retaliate."

The past five centuries in Yucatán have been shaped by a saga of cyclical efforts to draw lines around land. The lines cut through the forest and are marshaled like weapons to parcel up woodlands and strip down Maya land tenure. To understand the ongoing campaign to uproot mutual land relations and install extractive land relations instead in the ejidos of Yucatán, you have to reckon with lines.

Lines cut through land and divide time. Not long ago, some scientists drew a line in time and called our side of it the Anthropocene.[5] The term was originally offered to describe a new geological epoch, an era in which humans have become primary drivers of planetary change. Different camps disagree about when to place the starting point of the Anthropocene line. Some say the Anthropocene began with the Industrial Revolution. Others scratch the line way back at the beginning of agriculture, ten or twelve thousand years ago. Still others draw it in 1945, at the first tests of the atomic bomb.

As Anthropocene entered the public parlance of a society rife with climate anxieties, the term morphed to mean an age of environmental destruction caused by the human species; the *anthropos* root of Anthropocene seems to suggest that all humankind collectively shoulders the blame for our age's storms, its melting ice, its fires, its warming and rising seas. But, as other voices soon pointed out, not all humans share equal responsibility for the crisis, nor are all humans equally impacted by the unfolding destruction of that crisis. The Anthropocene concept, with its blanket blame on the human species, fails to account for the complex and entangled roles of racism, colonialism, and capitalism in the human-driven damages wrought on the environment.[6]

To mobilize attention towards these inequalities, some scholars are drawing the line five hundred years ago at a particular watershed event in human history: the emergence of plantation agriculture. These voices call our current age by a different name—the Plantationocene, a term first proposed by a group of scholars led by Donna Haraway and Anna Tsing in 2015.[7] Since then, other scholars have enhanced and expanded the Plantationocene concept by centering the roles of race and resistance and by correcting tendencies to flatten particular histories into universals.[8] Key to this evolution has been a more deliberate incorporation of the deep tradition of plantation criticism developed by Black feminist, Afro-futurist, and Indigenous scholars, among them Sylvia Wynter, Katherine McKittrick, and Édouard Glissant.[9] The Plantationocene concept catalyzes a framework for restoring historical context to modern environmental justice conflicts.

When we center the plantation in our reckoning of human-driven environmental change, the ongoing roles and legacies of structural violence start to crystallize. Plantations arose five hundred years ago in colonial quests to implant extractive land relations and produce wealth. In a plantation system, plants, animals, and people alike are rendered interchangeable and, often, alienated from their original homelands. Industrial monocrops deplete the land and destroy biodiversity—the goal is fast profit, not long-term ecological balance—and labor is extracted through violent systems of racialized oppression. The Plantationocene is still unfolding; the extractive logics and land relations first refined on colonial-era tobacco, tea, cotton, and sugarcane plantations live on in twenty-first-century oil palm plantations, monocropped cornfields, factory farms, land grabs, and essentially all modern environmental justice conflicts.

The plantation flattens and universalizes; the antidote is granular particularity. We talk about ecological restoration, but what about the restoration of histories deracinated by extractive land relations? Specific histories counter Plantationocene narratives of used up, unused, and useless lands. For the lands of the Yaxunah ejido, some of the history of the last five centuries can be recovered in documents. Some of it must be found in the ground. These lands make only a few appearances in colonial-era records, but the land itself retains traces of lines drawn through its woods, residues of a five-hundred-year campaign to extract wealth from the forest and to separate Maya people from their land. The land holds residues, too, of Maya resistance and resurgence against and through those lines.

When I follow, in my mind, the lines through the Yaxunah forest, I keep ending up in the ghost of a pop-up restaurant, watching women hand-form tortillas by the sea. The lines drawn in the forest become the paths that led celebrity chefs to Yaxunah.

ॐ　　ॐ　　ॐ

I last took you to the lands of the Yaxunah ejido during a difficult time.[10] The armies of Chichen Itza had invaded the ancient city of Yaxuná, forcing city dwellers to migrate out and abandon Yaxuná after more than a millennium of continuous inhabitation. Urban Yaxuná was abandoned, but small hamlets of mobile milpa farming families living in the edge lands—like at Tzacauil—carried on. People returned to the great ruins of Yaxuná occasionally to practice rituals and leave offerings, but they don't appear to have remained for long.[11]

As early as 1511, Spanish explorers—the bearded intruders described in the Nachi Cocom story—first landed in Yucatán. They would stay temporarily, leave, then return again. This went on a handful of times before the Spaniards undertook a more earnest campaign of conquest. Decades later, Spanish chroniclers began recording accounts from Yucatec Maya interlocutors to learn more about Maya history and politics before colonial contact. Since the Spaniards also burned most of the Maya books, these accounts preserve information available nowhere else.

Maya interlocutors told their Spanish interviewers that before the ships started to arrive, the entire Yucatán Peninsula had been unified, first ruled from a capital at Chichen Itza and later ruled from a capital at Mayapan. When Chichen Itza subdued Yaxuná, the hinterland communities of the Yaxunah ejido lands would have been brought under pan-peninsular government for the first time. Later, power shifted to Mayapan. Authorities based at Mayapan governed the unified peninsula through a system of joint rule, known in Yucatec Maya as *mul tepal*. Delegates, representing lineages hailing from each of the sixteen provinces across the peninsula, lived and ruled together at Mayapan. The Cocom and the Xiu were two of the most powerful lineages in the *mul tepal* system, and there was tension between them. Competition among the lineages came to a boil when the Xiu revolted against the Cocom— as captured in the Nachi Cocom story—causing the abandonment of Mayapan and the dissolution of the unified peninsula in 1441. The peninsula split into sixteen provinces, each with its own autonomous government.[12]

This meant that when the Spaniards showed up in the early 1500s, the Yucatán Peninsula they encountered was politically fragmented. Fighting, raiding, and rivalries were frequent among the sixteen provinces. The conquistadores would have compared this situation to reports coming from Spanish encounters with the rich and powerful Aztec and Inca Empires. Considered alongside the Aztec and Inca, the Maya region was not only decentralized and chaotic but devoid of the mineral resources—gold, silver—

that motivated most conquistadores. The "conquest" of the Maya, then, was not a clear event. It started and ended uncertainly.[13] Over decades, a dynasty of conquerors named Montejo, first deployed from Spain in 1527, slowly pitted the Maya provinces against each other to erode Indigenous leadership.

There was no surrender, no clear moment of victory to satisfy the Spaniards. The year 1547 is sometimes cited as the end of the conquest, but even a cursory reading of colonial accounts reveals that the forest and the ways Maya people moved in it frustrated Spanish attempts to consolidate power well through the end of the sixteenth century. Maya families could virtually disappear from Spanish oversight by slipping away into the woods. By the time of European contact, Maya farmers of the edge lands had been practicing milpa agriculture for centuries. They knew how to disperse out into the forest, coming together and breaking apart again as they followed the seasonal and multigenerational life cycles of the woodland.

Historian Matthew Restall has studied the notarial record (documents like wills and petitions) of colonial Yucatán to gather insights into the lives of Maya communities from 1550 through 1850. Restall contends that allowances for farmer mobility were embroidered into the *cah*, a Yucatec Maya concept related to geographical, political, and personal identity.[14] When Maya people used the cah to talk about a geographical place, they referred to settlement: both a well-defined core (which Restall calls the residential cah) and a patchy, extensive collection of lands that could be located many kilometers distant from the core (Restall calls this the territorial cah). Farmers usually planted their fields within a day's walk of the residential cah, but in places where rich soils were scarce, as many as half the farmers belonging to a given cah could scatter into the forests to live closer to their fields. Even though these dispersed farmers lived and cultivated far outside the core settlement of their cah, they still maintained personal relationships, identities, and political affiliations linking them to their cah. The patchiness and malleability of the cah's political boundaries defied colonial conceptions of land tenure. How do you draw a line around a territory when its extent is based on the changing positions of mobile farmers?

This was the first fundamental tension between mutual land relations and colonial-era extractive land relations in Yucatán. To deploy their full ecological knowledge, milpa farmers had to be supported—and mostly left alone—to move frequently through vast tracts of forest. Spanish colonial authorities did not recognize the relationship between Maya mobility and agricultural sustainability.

That basic misunderstanding is preserved in documentary evidence like tax lists.[15] Tax lists specified and scheduled the amounts of tribute (goods like maize, beans, cloth, poultry birds, fish, and salt, as well as the labor of servants) that every town in Yucatán was expected to pay the colonial government each year. The first colonial tax list was put together by a team of Franciscan friars. The Spanish Crown dispatched the friars to survey the villages of Yucatán and, in each village, to interview Maya people about their tribute customs before the conquest. The friars reported that prior to European contact, Maya provincial leaders had collected maize tribute based on plantings: each farmer was required to plant a certain amount of seed every year and to give the harvest from that planted seed as tribute. The amount of seed varied depending on local conditions. The friars recommended that the Crown continue this tradition, and so in 1549 the first colonial tax list in Yucatán called for maize taxes by plantings, not by harvested crops, and adjusted the amount of maize to be planted based on local conditions. The 1549 tax list gave Maya farmers some flexibility to rely on their localized traditional ecological knowledge (TEK) to plant the prescribed amount of maize seeds. It didn't hold farmers living in marginal agricultural lands to the same standards as those living in fertile areas.

But in every tax list after that first one, colonial authorities set fixed amounts of maize tribute for all Maya farmers, regardless of the agricultural conditions where they lived, and demanded maize tribute based not on seed planted, but on crops harvested. Tribute orders now flattened the complex realities of irregular weather patterns, crop damage from pests, and uncontrollable variations in soil quality. Farmers faced extreme pressure to deliver the harvest tax or suffer the consequences. To cope with this stress and to reduce competition over farmable land, the natural solution would have been for farming households to spread out from the residential cah into the territorial cah. Yet at this same time, colonial authorities were cracking down on Maya mobility. New laws coerced Maya communities to live in condensed, gridded towns where they could be more readily controlled by priests, soldiers, and tax collectors.[16] The earliest colonial misunderstandings of Maya TEK are preserved, then, in the old papers of tax schedules and ledgers.

If there was a community living in the lands of the Yaxunah ejido when the 1549 tax schedule was compiled, it hasn't yet been identified among the dozens of village names listed. The lands of the Yaxunah ejido are mostly absent from the documentary record of colonialism's first two centuries in Yucatán. No census documents can be linked to Yaxunah lands until 1784, when both a town named Yaxunah and a cattle ranching estate named Hacienda Cetelac (located nearby) are listed.[17] As early as 1600, a set of Maya prophecies mention a settlement called Cetel-ak; this old Cetel-ak might be the same place as the later Hacienda Cetelac, and thus located in the lands of the modern Yaxunah ejido. After the fall of Mayapan in 1441, the breakdown of the unified peninsula into autonomous territories had left the Yaxunah ejido lands right on the border between two provinces, Cupul and Sotuta. This Cetel-ak may have sat on contested ground. The Maya prophecies recorded as the *Chilam Balam de Chumayel* say that Cetel-ak was a place where tribute was gathered.[18] Little else is recorded about Cetel-ak or any other place known to be in Yaxunah ejido lands throughout the early documentary record.

The inland scrub forests of the Yaxunah ejido and central Yucatán bear few clear traces of the early colonial presence. Yet the impact was no less insidious: diseases brought by the Europeans decimated many Maya communities living in the forests before 1700, without even requiring direct contact. For the survivors, transience—the practiced ability to scatter into the forest—became a critical strategy for survival in the first generations following European contact.[19] Read in this way, the scarcity of obvious traces of Maya presence in the Yaxunah forests from this time is perhaps best interpreted as a testament to Indigenous resistance.

ॐ ॐ ॐ

By the late eighteenth century, the population of Yucatán was rising fast. The original divisions between Indigenous Maya people and Europeans had been blurred by generations of intermarriage, and there was a strong presence of Afro-Latino populations in Yucatán and the surrounding Caribbean as well.[20] Even so, sharp lines of status continued to divide wealthy elites of predominantly white European descent from everyone else; this powerful class became known as the Yucatecos.

With the rapid increase in population, demand for food escalated.[21] Centuries earlier the conquistadores had complained with disgust and despair about Yucatán's rocky soils. Now their descendants, the Yucatecos, had to reckon with the problem of feeding growing cities like Mérida and Campeche, as well as the noble families and Indigenous populations attached to rural estates, from those same derided soils.

The ruling class of Yucatecos began to restructure the peninsula's agricultural systems—and with their reforms, they further eroded Indigenous land tenure.[22] To the Yucatecos, the tempos and practices of Maya agriculture looked lazy and inefficient. Rather than trusting milpa farmers to manage the land according to centuries of Indigenous TEK, they intervened. Yucateco nobles seized Maya-owned landholdings as private property and established for themselves a flurry of estates, the progenitors of later haciendas, to ramp up agricultural production.[23] The Maya farmers who had previously claimed those lands as their own were now ordered to work them for the benefit of Yucateco landholders, without pay, one day out of every week. The laborers were called *luneros*, after the Spanish word for Monday (*lunes*), as that was often their day of forced labor.

Still, Yucatán remained something of a backwater in the Spanish colonial world. There were no fabulous minerals to enrich the Crown's coffers, no soils that could take a plow, and even the clergy had struggled to convert souls among the scattered Indigenous population. Seizing Maya lands for private estates and enforcing agricultural labor would keep food on the table, but it wouldn't make the Yucatecos rich.

That changed with the Spanish crown's enactment of the Bourbon Reforms in the eighteenth century.[24] The Bourbon Reforms liberalized the Spanish colonial economy by relaxing trade regulations and modernizing industry. For the first time, the Yucatecos realized they would be able to acquire real wealth through the export market. Finally, they could see a pathway out of their backwater status—and that pathway started with haciendas.

Haciendas worked like plantations and factories: they concentrated production and labor in the same place.[25] The laborers at most haciendas were Indigenous Maya families, though in some cases immigrants were conscripted from China, Korea, and northern Mexico. Laborers lived in villages attached to the hacienda complex itself, which also typically included industrial infrastructure and elegant quarters for the Yucateco landowners. With the liberalization and industrialization sparked by the Bourbon Reforms, haciendas sprang up across the Yucatán countryside and began mass-producing meat, tallow, leather, lumber, and henequen (an agavelike plant used to make fiber). These goods provisioned growing urban markets right in Yucatán, while also generating surplus to export to buyers elsewhere in Mexico, Cuba and the Caribbean, and the United States. More and more lands were taken from communities and privatized as more and more haciendas were established.[26]

Desperation forced many Maya families into the haciendas. At the same time Indigenous communities were left without their forests and fields, they were also getting slapped with increasing taxes and mandated church fees.

How were Maya families supposed to pay these charges? Wealthy Yucatecos stepped in to offer a solution: they would loan Maya families the money, and the families could pay off their debts by working at the haciendas. Most families had little choice but to accept these loans. Once in debt, there was virtually no way for families to leave the haciendas. When hacienda laborers were paid, they were often paid in scrip, not cash. Scrip could only be redeemed for food and other goods at the hacienda—and hacienda owners controlled the prices to ensure that debts increased. This system, known as debt peonage, was slavery in everything but name.[27]

Even as haciendas started to spring up, much of the peninsula at first remained undisturbed by economic development. Forests continued to be sites of refuge and sovereignty for Indigenous Maya farming families and practitioners of the multigenerational milpa. But by 1825, Yucatán's political authorities had decided this was wasteful. The state government passed laws to authorize the seizure and sale of what they called empty lands, or *terrenos baldíos*. Privatizing what they believed to be inactive and unproductive forest lands, the thinking went, would promote cattle ranching and generate income.[28] These laws addressed for the first time the large swaths of land that had been of little concern to the colonial project prior to liberalization. But they were of great importance to Indigenous ecological knowledge. For milpa farmers, the forests were not empty or unused: they were part of a carefully coordinated, collectively managed, multigenerational, and ecologically balanced system of Indigenous agriculture. To the Yucatecos, the forests were simply unproductive land, wasteland, useless land.

The *terrenos baldíos* actually had to be defined before they could be sold. When colonial authorities assessed the lands surrounding a Maya town, they had to decide where "productive" farmland used by the community ended and where "empty" lands began. But how did they know where to draw that line? Historian Inés Ortiz Yam says that the Yucateco government's systematic attempts to resolve this question laid the groundwork for land privatization to escalate later.[29] Yucatecos tried out a wide range of methods for drawing lines in the forest. Most methods failed, frustrated by the incompatibility of Indigenous land relations, which were mutualistic and mobile, and colonial land relations, which were extractive and fixed.

The deceptively simple task of drawing a line to separate communal farmland from empty land turned out to be nearly impossible. According to Ortiz Yam, Maya communities had long-established rules about land tenure.[30] In a given town, each Maya family's agricultural practices were contained within specific plots of land defined by the *rumbo familiar*, or family route. These familial claims were respected and recognized within the larger community and landholding. Yet familial boundaries changed all the time with the seasonal, yearly, and decadal rhythms of the milpa cycle. While these fluxes were carefully coordinated and known within communities, it was a different matter entirely to try to explain all this to a Yucateco cartographer waiting impatiently, pen poised, to draw a line on a map. To Yucateco surveyors, the Maya farmer's fluid and relational concept of land tenure looked itinerant and just plain wasteful.

Yucateco political authorities grasped desperately for a solution to the empty lands–communal farmlands boundary issue. Until the empty lands were defined, they could not be sold, and until they could be sold, Yucateco landowners could not start making money. The governor of Yucatán, José Tiburcio López Constante, proposed legislation to standardize the amount of communal farmland endowed to each Maya community at a rate of five hundred mecates (twenty hectares) per family; this proposal was soon scrapped. Another proposal avowed that the clear solution was to fix a standard radius for communal lands: go beyond two leagues from the town center in any direction and you leave farmland and enter sellable empty land. Other Yucatecos argued that the simple answer was to force the Maya to build fences around their communal farmlands—make them sort it out.[31] That failed, too. With each doomed proposal, the disparity between Yucateco and Indigenous land relations calcified.

After several tries, the Yucatecos finally managed to push through enough legal wedges to begin the work of taking Maya lands in earnest. A law passed in 1841 affirmed a fixed equation for calculating the boundary between communal farmland and *terrenos baldíos*: a square league in each cardinal direction, radiating out from each town's central church, would define the edge of a town's landholding, its ejido.[32] Everything beyond that would be declared empty, ready to be parceled up and awarded to soldiers or sold to private buyers. The law dramatically restricted the communal farmlands previously held by Maya villages.[33]

But as had happened before, when brought to the ground, colonial law was ill-equipped to do battle with Maya ecological knowledge. The laws stalled again when confronted with the practicality of a simple question: drawing a line between farmland and empty land on a map was easy, but how, exactly, was that line supposed to be made real in the forest? The Yucateco government tried to solve this riddle in 1844 by levying taxes on milpa land

and ordering Maya villages to hire official surveying teams to map out boundary lines.[34] The prospect of paying outsiders to draw a line around any given year's milpas as a fixed and finite entity must have seemed ridiculous to Maya farmers. For them, looking only at fields under active cultivation missed the point of milpa agriculture entirely; the active plots were inextricably embroidered into a shifting patchwork of old fields, young woodlands, and mature forests.

There is a story of Indigenous resistance in the quiet fact that no record of any Maya village complying with the order to pay for an official survey has ever been found.[35] Through 1846, the Maya effectively blocked privatization of their lands through noncompliance. Under the pretext that they had not yet gotten around to measuring out their ejidos, Maya communities resisted the formal sale of their lands.[36]

The transformations and tenuous uncertainties of the Bourbon Reforms unfolded, too, in the lands of the as-yet-undefined Yaxunah ejido.[37] A land sale dating to 1773 deeds the lands of Cetelac, not far from the colonial town of Yaxunah, to a Yucateco named Dámaso Santana.[38] Santana established a cattle-ranching hacienda at Cetelac and began transforming the forest into beef. About a decade later, Catholic clergy based at the nearby county seat of Yaxcabá started making official pastoral visits to hinterland villages in the parish, which included Hacienda Cetelac and Yaxunah. The priests collected census counts during these trips, and from these records we know that in 1784 the town of Yaxunah registered a population of 205, the Hacienda Cetelac a population of eight.

A few Maya families lived as laborers attached to the hacienda, their dwellings embedded within the ranching compound and its landscape of corrals, troughs, canals, and water tanks. As they raised cattle and crops for the Yucateco landowner, the Maya families living at Cetelac would have maintained relations with the land, but how those relations adapted to the economic structures of the hacienda remains unknown. Some things can be gathered just from walking through the hacienda ruins. Maya families living at Cetelac used the stones from ancient houses to build their dwellings; the hacienda sits on the southern edge of the old city of Yaxuná. The hacienda is centered around a large *rejollada*, a natural depression that traps soil and moisture and makes ideal conditions for arboriculture, and includes several stone rings that would have been used as tree planters. Maya homesites at Cetelac include livestock pens and open lands for gardens. These are all testaments to continuing and changing Indigenous land relations.

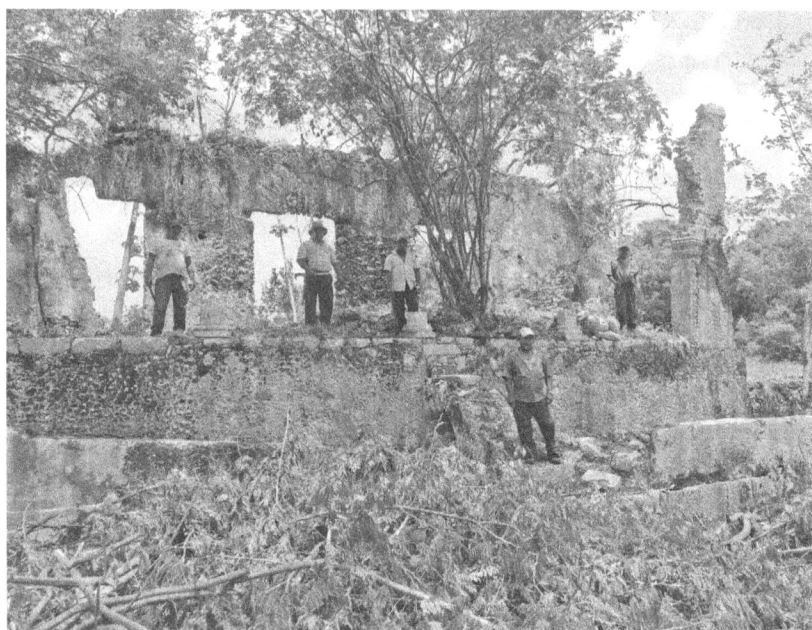

FIGURE 20. Yaxunah community members standing in the just-cleared remains of the manor house at Hacienda Cetelac. Troughs for watering cattle run alongside the house in the foreground. Photo by the author.

The Yucateco landowner's stately two-story manor house presided over all at Cetelac, sitting directly alongside the hacienda's true source of power, the *noria* (mechanized waterwheel), which pulled water from underground and sent it down to the cows and the laborers (fig. 20). Over the decades, the population living at the hacienda increased: priests registered twenty-five people living there in 1804 and fifty-one in 1828, the last year census counts were recorded at Cetelac. The increase in labor force likely signals an increase in production.

A short walk away, the town of Yaxunah was growing, too. Though the first pastoral visit to Yaxunah didn't happen until 1784, it's likely that the colonial town had been founded much earlier, perhaps as early as the six-teenth to seventeenth centuries during waves of forced Indigenous resettle-ment.[39] Yaxunah peaked at 1,121 inhabitants in 1821, a population even larger than the town would have two centuries later. Population at Yaxunah dipped to 896 in 1828, then to 500 in 1841, before rising again to 620 in 1846. Colonial-era Yaxunah boasted a small Catholic church, dedicated in 1817 and still mostly standing today, walled house lots arranged along the neat right angles of a European-style street grid, and a central plaza located just next to a large cenote. The cenote provided a permanent source of freshwater, and some houses had wells too.

With population rising in both the town of Yaxunah and at Hacienda Cetelac, Maya farmers living in these lands would have organized among themselves to manage the forest carefully and collectively. Sometimes that organization conflicted with the economic priorities of the hacienda landowner. A rare mention in the notarial record states that at one point in 1818, the landowner authorized two individuals to settle a land dispute between himself and the Maya living in Yaxunah.[40] Glimpsed in this note are the tensions of Bourbon-era privatization playing out on the ground: the cows of the Yucateco landowner vying with Maya milperos for sovereignty over field and forest.

The edge lands were part of this tension. No clear signature from the Bourbon era and its aftermath remains legible in the forests of Tzacauil, where the ruins of precolonial farmers were quietly decomposing far away from the hacienda and town, but these edge lands were precisely the ground at stake during the boundary disputes of the *terrenos baldíos*. If the 1844 order to delimit communal lands by measuring out a square league in the four cardinal directions from a town's church had been carried out at Yaxunah, it would have drawn a line just short of Tzacauil. Sitting just a few hundred meters into the "empty lands" zone, Tzacauil and the forests of the edge lands were immediately vulnerable in the Yucateco mission to privatize.

The Yucatecos wanted to turn empty lands into wealth, and they wanted to be taken seriously by the rest of the world while they did it. Yucatán and the Yucatecos had gotten used to a certain level of autonomy when they abruptly found themselves subsumed by the Mexican Empire in 1821.[41] Almost immediately after becoming Mexican, a faction of Yucateco elites started stoking dissent and crafting experimental forays into what their own independence could involve. Yucatán was geographically removed from Mexico City's influence, and many Yucatecos felt deeper roots in the cultural soils and seascapes of Central America and the Caribbean than in the emerging Mexican nation. The Mexican Empire was centralizing fast, and some Yucateco factions embraced integration, while others resented the prospect of forever remaining a peripheral frontier zone. The Yucatecos were not alone in feeling this sting: another peripheral zone in the Mexican Empire called Texas revolted in protest and declared itself an independent republic in 1836.

The Yucatecos launched their own rebellion. Most Yucatecos were concentrated in the peninsula's two largest cities, Mérida and Campeche, both on the west side of the peninsula. Farther east, Yucatecos were scattered sparsely in haciendas and small towns, but most of the surrounding population remained Indigenous Maya. Estimates place the ratio at as many as five Maya people for every Yucateco in these eastern hinterlands.[42]

As the Yucatecos dabbled in forming rebel governments, they accidentally fertilized an already-building Indigenous uprising in the frontier lands of the eastern peninsula.[43] In 1839, an upstart Yucateco landowner named Santiago Imán declared rebellion against Mexican sovereignty from his base in the lush eastern forests. Imán felt that his fight for autonomy required an army. He reached out to Indigenous communities in the eastern peninsula, promising Maya men tax exemptions and land grants in exchange for military service. Such offers were hard to ignore in the constant crush of tribute demands and privatization. Many Maya men agreed to fight, and they suddenly found themselves armed for the first time since their ancestors picked up weapons during the Spanish conquest. Imán, protected by the Maya army, marched on Mérida and declared Yucatán an independent republic.

The Mexican government, of course, heartily disagreed with Imán's declaration and soon dispatched forces to subdue the uprising. As the Mexican army struggled to retake Campeche and Mérida, the debate over independence versus reintegration captivated the full attention of the Yucatecos. Divisions deepened. A faction based in Campeche favored breaking away from Mexico for good, while a faction in Mérida pushed for joining back up. Both sides vied for the peninsula's political fate, and both sides stumbled forward with the recruitment efforts launched by Imán, swelling their ranks with Maya men—well-armed Maya men. The Yucatecos were so distracted by external threats that they failed to snuff an insurrection that was growing from within.[44]

る❧   る❧   る❧

Maya communities had reached a breaking point—and now, they were armed. Through the mechanisms of extractive land relations, the colonial project had disenfranchised Indigenous Maya people of their lands, trapped them in debt, and enslaved them as plantation laborers for more than three centuries when, in 1847, the Maya of eastern Yucatán launched the most successful Indigenous uprising in the history of the Americas.[45] The Maya Social War, also called the Caste War, began in the summer of that year when three Indigenous leaders—Jacinto Pat, Cecilio Chi, and Manuel Antonio Ay—

mobilized and armed a battalion of Maya soldiers outside Valladolid, the largest Yucateco city in the east. Panicking, Yucateco political leaders in the western cities suddenly realized the vulnerability of their situation and flailed to squash down any hint of revolt. The Yucateco forces publicly executed Ay. Then they ignited a campaign of terror to punish Maya villages, seemingly at random, across the eastern peninsula. Yucatecos burned Maya fields, sacked Maya towns, and killed Maya people with indiscriminate violence.

Late in July of that terrible summer, Chi and Pat decided to match the Yucatecos with force of their own. They issued an order that all non-Maya be killed. The uprisings that followed were swift and coordinated. An army of Maya men sacked and burned the haciendas of the eastern and central peninsula. They killed or drove out the Yucateco landowners, and they then turned west to march on Mérida.

By 1848, it looked like the Maya army would win the war. The army had arrived outside Mérida and launched preparations to lay siege to the city when—for reasons still not fully known or revealed—the soldiers split up and started to retreat back east. In the years to follow, stories arose to explain this decision. Some said the Maya soldiers left the fight and scattered because it was time to plant their crops; the rhythms of the milpa overpowered whatever tactical advantage the army had achieved. Whatever the reason the siege was abandoned, the Maya rebels would never again regain the advantage they had held in that moment.[46] The Yucatecos reasserted control, begrudgingly rejoining the Mexican Empire in exchange for reinforcements in August of 1848. Mexico revived the Yucateco military campaign and together their armies pushed the Maya out of the cities and back into the forests.

Even contained, the Maya rebellion stayed strong in the eastern peninsula for far longer than the Yucateco and Mexican governments would have liked. Maya leaders founded and governed sovereign states in the lands today known as the Mexican state of Quintana Roo and the nation of Belize. The largest of these states, anchored at the town of Chan Santa Cruz, maintained its autonomy well into the late nineteenth century.[47] The Yucatecos realized their powerlessness to intervene in the affairs of the eastern resistance, and they doubled down instead on their investments in the western peninsula.

The divide between east and west left a large buffer region splitting the halves of the peninsula, a swath of mostly unpopulated forest separating the Indigenous Maya and settler Yucateco states. The Yucateco government declared (optimistically and preemptively) the end of the Maya Social War in 1855, but this buffer zone continued to see regular skirmishes well into the first decade of the twentieth century. The forests of the Yaxunah ejido formed part of this buffer between east and west.

Yaxunah and Hacienda Cetelac sat deserted for decades after the volatile summer of 1847.[48] The year before there had been 620 people living in Yaxunah and likely dozens more at Cetelac (no census data is available for the hacienda after the 1820s)—and certainly, Maya people greatly outnumbered the Yucatecos. Met with the terrorism of the Yucateco forces, Chi and Pat had ordered the killing of all non-Maya. No records exist to say how word of this order reached the Maya of Yaxunah and Cetelac, nor to report how the events of their localized revolt played out in town and forest. The uprising appears to have started and ended suddenly, and the Maya of the town and hacienda wasted little time in leaving. No records say where they went. Some, perhaps, walked to join the rebel leaders and build up the independent nation of Chan Santa Cruz, while others may have scattered into eastern forests to farm again, away from the demands and debt slavery of peonage labor. Remaining would have been deadly, given the tactics of Yucateco soldiers.

In this depopulated and contested ground, the forests of the Yaxunah ejido waited for the drawn-out conflict to sputter towards its end. Census data show eleven people living in the town of Yaxunah in 1862, but there is no sign that anyone lived there again until about 1920, when the ancestors of today's families chose to settle there. The manor house at Hacienda Cetelac still stands in crumbling ruins, bearing the scars of the burning and sacking that accompanied its desertion in 1847. With few farmers around in the decades that followed, the multigenerational dance of the milpa paused and the forest grew back wild. The limestone of ancient structures weathered in the rain and wind, sighing out slumps of rubble as tree roots grasped down into the soil gathering between stones.

ॐ   ॐ   ॐ

All those years that the forests of the Yaxunah ejido were left as a wartime no-man's-land, politicians and peasant farmers across Mexico's vast entirety were churning through a new era of agrarian reforms. Porfirio Díaz took seven turns as president of Mexico during 1876 to 1880 and 1884 to 1911. Díaz used his decades in office to transform agriculture and earn along the way, some say, a reputation as a dictator. The civil unrest sown in the Porfiriato, the tenure of Díaz's presidency, led directly to the uprisings of the Mexican Revolution.[49]

Díaz leveraged agrarian reform as a tactic to stabilize Yucatán after the Maya Social War had (mostly) calmed. His prescription: more privatization would mean more peace and more progress. Communal milpa agriculture again came under fire, condemned as wasteful and backward. Instead of collectively managed milpas, the government wanted to seed the landscape with, as one historian puts it, "industrious, individualistic farmers working in a free enterprise system."[50] Authorities began parceling up Maya landholdings into fragments. By the early twentieth century, 134,000 hectares of communal land had been atomized into twelve thousand private plots. One percent of the population owned 97 percent of the land; and 96 percent of the population owned no land at all.[51]

Land tenure dissolved out from under the feet of Maya farmers as the rush to buy up splinters of the peninsula pressed on. The *terrenos baldíos* surrounding villages were deeded to private companies faster than Maya farmers could file their own claims. When Maya people did attempt to pursue formal title to these lands, they were often rejected outright by the courts.[52] Most of the land grab concentrated in the arid, rocky terrain of the northwestern peninsula, a region under firm Yucateco control that had been derided as marginal since the conquest. The sudden entrepreneurial interest in terrain once regarded as wasteland came down to a single plant: henequen.

Henequen is a kind of agave. Unlike Spanish conquistadores, henequen quite likes the scant and stony soils of northwestern Yucatán. Indigenous Maya people had long utilized henequen to make fiber, and Yucatecos learned to process henequen fiber into rope. By the Porfiriato, machinery had been invented that could transform henequen into mass-produced twine—which turned out to be an unassuming but absolutely essential ingredient in the emerging technology of industrial agriculture. The rise of mechanized agricultural equipment manufacturers, like the Chicago-based International Harvester Corporation, transformed farming in the late nineteenth and early twentieth centuries. The demand for farming equipment catalyzed demand for twine. Many of International Harvester's machines, especially its mechanized reaper, required cheap, biodegradable twine to bind bundles of harvested crops. The sudden need for vast amounts of binder twine spawned haciendas and plantations to grow henequen and similar fibers in Cuba, the Philippines, and Yucatán.[53]

The henequen boom transformed Yucatán.[54] Planters bought or confiscated communal farmlands and founded haciendas across the northwestern peninsula. Now landless, Maya farmers had few choices but to gravitate to those same henequen haciendas to make a living. Many Maya families became, once again, essentially enslaved as hacienda laborers through the insidious trap of debt peonage. Monocropped fields replicated like viruses across the rocky terrain of the henequen zone. To the south and east, agricultural and livestock-based haciendas absorbed the desperate labor of landless Maya people and pumped food back into the urbanizing northwest. Railroads ensnared the forest. Locomotives gobbled up trees and belched black smoke into the air. For a few gilded years, Mérida may have been home to the most millionaires per capita of any city in the world.[55]

The bust came quickly. After about forty years (1880–1920), the market for henequen rotted out: the monocropped haciendas struggled to adapt to even slight fluctuations in demand and could not compete at all once the industry discovered synthetic fibers. In a relatively short time, the transformations wrought by the henequen boom had amplified the long-felt tensions between landed elites and landless peasants. The suffering caused by these deep divides reverberated in similar sagas of disenfranchisement unfolding across Mexico. As the reign of Díaz at long last barreled to its finale, the anger of Mexico's landless peasants frothed up into a full boil.

ॐ   ॐ   ॐ

When Díaz's presidency ended, calamity ensued over questions of succession. With the nation's politicians and wealthy elites distracted by this tinderbox of political uncertainty, the agrarian uprisings known collectively as the Mexican Revolution ignited. The Revolution, which lasted for about ten years (1910–20), was a direct response to the deep inequalities among the landed wealthy and landless poor that had become rampant in Mexico. Those same inequalities were suffered in Yucatán, but the region's participation in the uprisings was minimal; the traumas of the Maya Social War were still fresh and impacted Maya communities' ability to organize. As a result, many of the policy victories won by the revolutionaries initially bypassed Yucatán.[56]

The modern ejido system emerged as one of the most significant outcomes and legacies of the Mexican Revolution.[57] Outlined in Article 27 of the post-revolutionary Mexican Constitution, the ejido system reshaped systems of land tenure in answer to the grievances of millions of landless peasants. Ejidos were legally defined as tracts of land granted to peasant communities by the federal government. Community members, known as *ejidatarios*, would own and work the lands collectively. Ejidatarios could not buy, sell, or rent ejido lands (a clear rejection of privatization) and had to be the ones to work the land themselves—they could not pay others to work it for them. All ejidatarios had a say in decisions about ejido lands. They formed official committees to govern their ejidos, and every ejidatario had the right to elect committee members and vote on the committee's internal rules. When they died, ejidatarios transferred their rights to ejido membership through wills, thereby ensuring generational continuity in communal land ownership. The ejido system remained basically faithful to the vision outlined by the postrevolutionary reformers into the late twentieth century.

Yucatec Maya farmers faced a long lag between the declaration of postrevolutionary agrarian reforms and their actual implementation on the ground. The ejido system took decades to make inroads into the peninsula. After the Revolution, the Mexican government installed a string of hand-picked governors in Yucatán. These politicians held their own personal agendas for reform, and they usually found themselves at odds with embittered Yucatecos.

The first of these appointed governors, Salvador Alvarado (1915–18), arrived ready to fix what he saw as Yucatán's agrarian ailments: debt peonage, inefficient haciendas, and foreign-controlled henequen production.[58] He dipped into the state's ample treasuries—he had caught the last gasps of the henequen boom—to fund his reforms. Alvarado ended debt peonage first. With the oppressive system finally outlawed, one hundred thousand Maya were free to leave the economic bondage of the hacienda. But the haciendas still controlled most of the land, and so many Maya people had to turn right back around to the haciendas to find work. Following the passage of Article 27—the ejido article—in 1917, Alvarado tried to undercut the snares of the hacienda system through modest reforms. The state government distributed several thousand hectares of land to a dozen communities, expecting that the newly landed farmers would better feed Mérida's growing urban population.[59] Even so, Alvarado was not an apologist for Indigenous agriculture. He complained once, "Those (Maya) men want only to sow their miserably small milpas, will eat nothing but corn, and cannot be persuaded to produce anything of worth for society as a whole."[60] Alvarado's appointment in Yucatán ended abruptly when he was summoned for military duty in 1918. Though his efforts were modest and marked by a misunderstanding of Indigenous land relations, he was up against legions of wealthy Yucatecos deeply committed to maintaining the status quo. Meaningful land reform was still distant.

Progress towards implementing the ejido system in Yucatán came under the governorship of Felipe Carrillo Puerto (1922–24). Carrillo Puerto was a native of Yucatán, born in the town of Motul, of Maya and European ancestry. He understood his state in a way his predecessors had not. When his tenure as governor began, the henequen bubble had burst but most lands remained tied up under hacienda ownership. Carrillo Puerto waged a campaign to break up hacienda landholdings and redistribute lands to farming communities. In just a few years he deeded land rights for 438,866 hectares to 22,525 peasants, and soon the lands were brought into collective milpa cultivation.[61] Carrillo Puerto's progressive stance on social and agrarian reform earned him many enemies among the landed Yucateco elites who had made their fortunes in the henequen zone, and he was assassinated in 1924. The Yucateco hostility to land reform was palpable.

A decade later, President Lázaro Cárdenas (1934–40) finally broke the power structures that enabled Yucateco elites to monopolize control over such vast tracts of land. Cárdenas dissolved private landholdings and converted them into communally owned ejidos, and Yucatán at last caught up to the postrevolutionary reforms formalized under Article 27 almost two decades earlier. The plan faced resistance from landowners in the henequen zone, but in the sparsely populated agricultural regions to the south and east, the ejido system took root with less controversy. Cárdenas parceled out seventeen million hectares of land to create ejidos for hundreds of communities.[62] The lands of the Yaxunah ejido at last became the Yaxunah ejido.

ॐ   ॐ   ॐ

The story of Yaxunah's founding is told like this: in the early years of the twentieth century, when a wide slice of central Yucatán was at last cooling from the skirmishes of the Maya Social War, two brothers arrived in these forests.[63] The brothers arrived separately, clandestinely. Neither knew the other was there. The brothers, Rafael and Ignacio Poot, had come from the east. They were part of a massive westward migration of Maya families— refugees, really—looking to make a new life in the depopulated buffer zone as the conflict calmed. Each brother walked through the forest, unaware of the other, moving west, when they each independently found Sacbe 1, the fifteen-hundred-year-old ancient Maya road connecting the city of Yaxuná and the city of Coba. Finding a road through the woods, both brothers chose to follow it west to see where it led.

The road took both brothers through the eastern edge lands of what would become their descendants' ejido. They separately walked past the towering ruin of the Tzacauil Acropolis. They separately passed the deep sink-hole known today as the Joya Rejollada, a lush pocket of moist soils and high-canopy trees. If the brothers had climbed down into the rejollada, they might have seen low stone walls sealing off a rock overhang at the base of the sinkhole. A hundred years later, some Yaxunah ejidatarios say these walls are from the Social War, when Maya people sequestered themselves into the earth for protection, while others say they were used for trapping *jabalí* (peccary). If the wall does belong to the violent days of the war, its tacit emphasis on secrecy in stone helps explain why neither Poot brother knew the other was there, too. This was a time for hiding.

The sacbe took both brothers into the heart of the ancient city of Yaxuná. From there, a short walk further west would have led them to the abandoned colonial town of Yaxunah. Both brothers at first avoided the old town—it was still too dangerous. Ignacio Poot made a home in the ruins of the manor house at Hacienda Cetelac. His brother Rafael made a home in the ruins of one of Yaxuná's acropolis groups. The brothers were refugees living in palaces of the past.

The Poot brothers eventually found each other and were joined by six other families to found a new town on the site of the old town in 1915. Like the old town, their new town would be called Yaxunah. All seven founding families had been displaced from their hometowns—Tinúm, Tixcacalcupul, Chan Kom, Tekom, Muxupip, and Xcopteil—during the war and had migrated west seeking safety and a place to practice milpa farming. Their family names remain some of the most common in Yaxunah today: Poot, Caamal, Canul, Mukul, Ku, Tec, Chan.

Yaxunah elders share the memory of the early twentieth-century town as a dense forest, barely distinguishable from the wild lands outside the street grid. Anthropologists later interviewed Yaxunah elder José Poot, who remembered being a child and living with his family in a vaulted room in the Yaxuná ruins, probably in the North Acropolis. José Poot recalled that later his family relocated to live in the Catholic church in the old town of Yaxunah; the church had been partly destroyed during the war. He remembered that the town plaza was thick with tall trees and inhabited by forest animals. People could hunt right there in the central plaza. Over time, the town was tamed again.

The founding families began farming the forests around Yaxunah even while they had no legal claim to the land. In Mérida, Yucateco landowners and federal officials grappled with agrarian policy reform, but they don't seem to have cared much about lands outside the lucrative henequen zone. Central Yucatán slipped through the land debacle mostly unnoticed. Soon after President Cárdenas formalized the ejido system in Yucatán, the Yaxunah ejido appears on the books of the Registro Agrario Nacional (National Agrarian Registry) in 1934. The federal government endowed Yaxunah with 2,979 hectares of ejido land, to be managed and worked by thirty ejidatarios representing a larger population of ninety-five inhabitants.[64] Now, Yaxunah farmers could practice milpa agriculture without fear that their lands would be taken from them.

Things were pretty stable for the next few decades, though sometimes conflicts bubbled up at the local level. When I was working at Tzacauil with Yaxunah community members, some of the men shared stories about how the forests we were in—the ejido's eastern edge lands—had been won during a land dispute sometime in the 1950s. Back then, the men told me, ejidatarios from Yaxunah and those from a neighboring town both alleged claims to the lands around Tzacauil. The stakes were high: these were good lands for milpa, and they also included the Xauil Cenote, the spring called El Manantial, the soil-rich sinkhole of the Joya Rejollada, and the rights to harvest firewood, honey, forage, timbers, game, medicine, and fruit from the forest.

The two camps took the dispute to county authorities in Yaxcabá. The decision passed down was simple: whichever side could first cut a *brecha*—a clear path through the forest—around the land would be declared its rightful owners. Yaxunah ejidatarios would light up at this point in the story. "*¡Jálale!*" the storytellers would exclaim, remembering the readiness of their fathers and grandfathers. "Let's go!" The Yaxunah ejidatarios charged into the forest on the appointed day, ready with hook-shaped blades hafted on wooden handles, called *coas*. Their descendants, the storytellers, said the ejidatarios carried masa for making pozole—this, I was emphatically told, showed their grit and readiness to stay out chopping brush all day and night, without even returning home to eat, to do whatever it took to secure the edge lands.

The Yaxunah ejidatarios chopped and chopped. The further they got, the more clearly they could hear the sounds of rival *coas* slashing through the forest coming towards them. But the day belonged to Yaxunah: they managed to complete the *brecha* around the contested edge lands first and so won the rights to the forests of Tzacauil.

When Yaxunah ejidatarios would tell this story, they spoke with a mixture of affection and reverence for the men who secured the edge lands we were on. I remember one time when the Yaxunah men stood in a circle, chanting together the names of the deceased heroes who had fought for this ground. "*Difunto* don Canul, *difunto* don Chuc, *difunto* don Tek." And yet, almost every time this memory was shared with me, its telling came alongside frustrated conversations about the same edge lands celebrated in the story. The place was too far from the town. The soil was not so great. The woods were full of coatis who ate crops and spirit guardians who made danger and mischief. I recall the ejidatarios' words, and I hear the germination of a narrative the Plantationocene has propagated for five centuries: that the forests of the edge are unused, empty, *terrenos baldíos*—useless lands.

ॐ   ॐ   ॐ

How did Yaxunah ejidatarios go from fighting for edge lands in one generation to seriously reconsidering their value in the next? The ejido system remained stable—and essentially faithful to its original revolutionary vision for collective land sovereignty—until a crushing economic crisis in 1982.

The years preceding the crisis had been hopeful ones, particularly in the agricultural sector. Mexico embraced the technological advances and policy incentives of the global Green Revolution: agrichemicals, mechanized processing, grain price supports, subsidies, crop insurance. Nationwide, the agricultural changes of the late seventies and first two years of the eighties could even have been said to empower agrarian communities.[65] Many of these innovations bypassed Yucatán as, once again, its thin soils thwarted modern mechanized farming, but some Yucatecan farmers did shift towards industrialization. Farmers living on the thick soils of southern Yucatán, for instance, embraced industrial-scale citrus production. Farmers in Yaxunah and central Yucatán, meanwhile, continued on with the same kind of shifting milpa cultivation they had practiced for years. Even as some subsistence farmers suffered from the changes of the Green Revolution, and even as some regions were left out from the advances entirely, these years were optimistic ones in Mexico as a whole. It felt like the nation could achieve something close to self-sufficiency.[66]

But with the Latin American debt crisis of 1982, Mexico was suddenly bankrupt. State support for the agrarian sector—and especially the ejido system—spun into crisis. Scrambling, the Mexican government worked out a deal with the United States and the International Monetary Fund just to be able to borrow *more* money to service their existing debts. As part of the deal, Mexico had to embrace neoliberal agrarian reform.[67] The implementation of NAFTA in 1994 reduced trade limits and tariffs, inundating Mexican markets with cheap, US-grown corn and flooding shops with industrially manufactured foods. Subsidies and credits that had formerly kept the agricultural sector afloat were slashed. And Article 27—that postrevolutionary pillar of the Mexican Constitution and stalwart protector of the communal ejido—was sent to the chopping block for revisions.

The revisions to Article 27 redefined ejido lands: now, they could be sold. By granting ejidatarios the ability to sell their lands by majority vote, the Mexican government aimed to attract private investors and inject cash into the agricultural sector. In a move that further weakened intergenerational land tenure, the revisions also changed the rules around who got to be an ejidatario. Before, local ejido authorities had the power to add and remove names from the list of official ejidatarios at their discretion; the new system eradicated that right and made it so that ejidatario rights could only be inherited. This meant that a parent with multiple children could only will their rights to a single child, leaving many community members excluded from decision-making and with no open channels to become ejidatarios themselves. That change has contributed to larger shifts in labor patterns in Yucatán and across Mexico, as increasing numbers of people migrate to find cash-earning employment in large cities or in other countries entirely.

In the wake of this reinvention, a familiar problem arose. In most of Yucatán, ejido boundaries were still far too nebulous for the legal purposes of land sales. Ejidatarios interested in the possibility of privatizing their lands must first embark on a lengthy land titling process, and even just starting that process requires a majority vote. State surveyors map out ejido limits, and once boundaries get locked down and lines drawn, ejidatarios can continue the process towards land sales. They first must vote to transfer their lands from *uso común*, common use, to *parcelas*, individual parcels of land titled to individuals. Then, if a majority of ejidatarios vote in favor of privatization, the *parcelas* can be sold. Land titling began in Yucatán in 1994. In the first dozen years, 702 of the state's 786 ejidos initiated the process.[68] While land titling is not the same as privatization, it's the first step.

As I write this, Yaxunah has not privatized its ejido lands. But each summer I've spent there since 2013, there's been talk among the ejidatarios of interested buyers coming around. Sometimes the buyers even make offers. Yaxunah's emergence as a pilgrimage destination for foodies, combined with an ever-encroaching tourist infrastructure—most visibly in the Tren Maya, a vast and wildly expensive government-sponsored rail network that will connect Maya archaeological sites and pass through nearby Chichen Itza—make the likelihood of land sales a concretizing reality.

ô& ô& ô&

Neoliberal agrarian reform is the latest incarnation of a five-hundred-year campaign to dismantle Indigenous Maya land tenure by drawing lines and slashing boundaries. This is the story of the Plantationocene in Yucatán. From the frustrated boundaries of Yucateco reformers, to the uprisings of the Maya Social War, from the henequen boom to the coming of the celebrity chef, the past five centuries have seen shaped by cycles of subordination and resurgence.

The story of Nachi Cocom is a story of lines crossed. Colonial agents, seeking to impose extractive land relations in the Maya forest, wanted desperately to draw lines dividing useful from unused land; perhaps the Spanish chroniclers preserved the Nachi Cocom story because it seemed to confirm the possibility of such lines. But the story implies a warning from Maya to Spaniard. Is it over? Is there still time to retaliate?

Now in the twenty-first century, Nachi Cocom has been taken hostage. His name is better known today as the Nachi Cocom Beach Club and Water Sport Center on Cozumel, an island off the eastern shores of the Yucatán Peninsula where, in 1519, the Maya welcomed Hernán Cortés and replenished the stores of the Spanish caravels with fresh food and water.[69] Every day, 130 cruise ship guests disembark for an all-inclusive dining and drinking beach experience at Nachi Cocom. Guests enjoy Nachi Cocom's swim-up bar, jacuzzi, and seafood restaurant during the daylight hours. At night they board their boats again, leaving the staff of Nachi Cocom to prepare for the next day's 130 guests.[70] But away from the mirage of Nachi Cocom and the other all-inclusive locations, anxieties are mounting on Cozumel.[71] The threat of fraudulent land grabs keeps growing as ejido forests are eyed for profit by private developers, while back on the mainland, just across the narrow waters of the Cozumel Channel, the ruins of Noma Mexico face the rising sea.

SIX

The Ghost of Chaipa Chi

EVER SINCE THEIR FIRST VISIT, abruptly cut short, the two foreigners have been haunted by the work they left unfinished in the ruins of Uxmal. Now they are back. They come riding on horses again into the ruins, returning to the crumbling remains of this great ancient Maya city in the rolling Puuc hills of western Yucatán. Both men, the American writer and the British draftsman, carry their craving to discover something important here; mules and Yucatec Maya porters are left carrying everything else. Both men are ardent, ready to complete the tasks they were forced to abandon the year before. They mean to document the ruins of Uxmal. They mean to introduce their own civilization to the wonders of this lost one. It's 1841.

The American writer and the British draftsman believe themselves discoverers of a lost civilization, and many others back home in their own decidedly not-lost civilization believe that too. They've just published a bestselling illustrated account of their first expedition in Central America, Chiapas, and Yucatán. This second expedition will provide more than enough material for the next installment. The American writer is John Lloyd Stephens; the British draftsman is Frederick Catherwood. They will be remembered as the founders of Maya archaeology. And on this November morning of what is supposed to be their first day back at work in Uxmal, they realize there's a problem. There's no woman to make their breakfast.

Time for mundane tasks—the matter of food, for one—these explorers cannot spare. "We had no servant, and wanted breakfast, and altogether our prospects were not good," Stephens will write of this first morning.[1] Vexed, he'll add: "In fact, except as regards certain obligations they owed, the Indians were their own masters, and, what was worse for us, their own mistresses, for one of our greatest wants was a woman to cook, make tortillas,

166

and perform those numerous domestic offices without which no household can go on well."[2]

Into this domestic distress, a Maya woman appears in the makeshift camp that the American writer, the British draftsman, and their porters have made in the ruins. She is with her grandson. She is there to cook. When the expedition had arrived at the local hacienda the evening before, the hacienda owner had dispatched an official to knock on the doors of all the Maya families who lived as laborers at the hacienda, seeking a woman who would agree to cook for the foreigners. This woman is the only woman who did not refuse, and that only on the condition that she would not have to camp in the ruins with the expedition; she insists that she will return home every evening. Stephens learns of this and is displeased. "This was a great drawback, as we wanted to breakfast early," he will lament later, "but we had no choice, and were glad to get her upon her own terms."[3] This woman, Stephens says, is named Chaipa Chi.

Stephens "immediately install[s] her as chef de cuisine, without assistants" and gives Chaipa Chi her "first essay"—making eggs for breakfast.[4]

Chaipa Chi begins to cook the eggs.

Stephens watches her and becomes still more upset. As he will complain in his next published travelogue,

> She boiled *para beber*, or to drink; that is, by breaking a small hole in the shell, into which a stick is inserted to mix together the white and the yolk; the egg is to be disposed of through this hole in the primitive way in which nature indicates to the new-born babe. . . . This did not suit us, and we wished the process of cooking to be continued a little longer, but Chaipa Chi was impenetrable to hints or signs. We were obliged to stand over her, and, but for the name of the thing, we might as well have cooked them ourselves. This over, we gave up, and left our dinner to the mercies of our chef.[5]

When I read Stephens's travelogue, richly illustrated with prints of Catherwood's intricate engravings in the 1843 two-volume *Incidents of Travel in Yucatán*, my thoughts wander past the tedious lists of temple dimensions and return again and again to Chaipa Chi, a woman viewed only dimly through the filter of Stephens's mind and pen.

After her first appearance for breakfast that November morning in 1841, Chaipa Chi fades in and out of the rest of the chapters on the expedition's work at Uxmal. She appears when Stephens wants to add some color, some drama to his dry reports of architecture—rote recitations of measurements that even he seems to think are stuffy—and she disappears when he's done with her, without explanation. He makes studious scrutiny of her body. He complains about all her cooking except for "the business in which she shone, the making of tortillas."[6] He demotes her to tortilla maker and installs in her stead as head of the camp kitchen a fifteen-year-old boy. The boy, unlike Chaipa Chi, can speak Spanish in addition to Yucatec Maya. Stephens and Catherwood prefer this arrangement because it means they can convey orders for how to cook their eggs.

One of Chaipa Chi's last appearances in the passages of the travelogue comes on Christmas Day, 1841.[7] That morning, Stephens and his team awake in Uxmal and are baffled to discover that the Maya laborers they've been conscripting from the local hacienda have not shown up in the ruins to work. Neither has Chaipa Chi. They've all taken Christmas off.

Stephens is again vexed: a whole day of work in the ruins, lost. But he is a resourceful man. He decides to salvage the day.

So he walks over to the hacienda under the pretext of checking on one of his horses, which is recovering in the stables from an injury. This errand done, Stephens starts to look around. He will recall this morning later, writing, "The hacienda was deserted, but the sound of violins led me to the place where the Indians were congregated." Following the music of strings, Stephens finds a Christmas scene unfolding: "Preparations were making on a large scale for the evening feast. The place looked like a butcher's shambles, for they had cut up what had once composed eight turkeys, two hogs, and I do not know how many fowls." Stephens takes a moment to notice Chaipa Chi, happy at the heart of the merry activity, the "lady-patroness, and up to her elbows in tortillas."[8]

He stares for a few moments longer, then drifts away from the violins and the laughter to his real purpose at the hacienda. He slips into the graveyard, trespassing on the consecrated parcel of land where the Maya families of the hacienda have buried their ancestors and their beloved dead. Stephens spends his Christmas digging around in holy ground, looking for skulls to steal.

That day, Stephens will abandon the quest for plundered bones—he starts to feel superstitious, and notices two Maya women watching him through the trees—but no matter. He has already managed to pilfer some human remains from the hills near Uxmal earlier in the expedition. As Stephens lurks in the hacienda graveyard, those bones are waiting, hidden back at the expedition's camp in the ruins. Stephens will later donate them to the collection of his friend back in Philadelphia, a man named S. G. Morton.[9] Morton's studies of stolen crania will one day mark him as one of the fathers of scientific racism.[10] But Stephens isn't thinking about that as he skulks for bones in the *campo santo* (burial ground) on Christmas Day. He is thinking of the loss of a productive day of work at Uxmal, and he is trying to recoup his loss in the currency of stolen skulls.

ə❧　ə❧　ə❧

Stephens's account of the work at Uxmal is infused with a sense of aspirational productivity, to the point where he must spend Christmas robbing graves just to feel like the day is not wasted. That aspirational productivity was not his alone: it was a driving value of capitalism in the nineteenth century and remains one in the twenty-first. Aspirational productivity is likewise entangled with extractive land relations. The desire to maximize productivity and efficiency drove the transformation of land into plantations and Indigenous people into peons. Subscribers to the doctrines of productivity and efficiency implanted extractive land relations in the Maya forest. They sharply incised the lines defining useless lands. It was in the names of these doctrines that wealthy nineteenth-century Yucatecos were, in everything but name, enslaving Indigenous Maya people to produce cattle and cash crops; Chaipa Chi was among the thousands bound by debt to haciendas.[11]

Stephens did not realize that just a few years after his expedition to Uxmal, Indigenous leaders to the east would ignite the Maya Social War, the most successful Indigenous uprising ever undertaken in the Americas.[12] But I do wonder if he could sense the simmering tensions he was stepping into. Could he feel the bubbling of the coming rebellion manifesting in microcosm in the Uxmal camp kitchen? We can accept Stephens's interpretation of events: Chaipa Chi refused to cook his eggs the way he liked them because she simply did not understand his commands. Or we can read her refusal as an act of resistance.

Those of us alive today were born into a world marked by the extractive land relations of late capitalism. This is a time of fire seasons and rising seas, where seemingly all areas of life are saturated with the doctrine of aspirational productivity. But values based in efficiency are no longer serving most of us, if they ever did; they are the crux of environmental justice conflicts and they drive the ongoing violence of extractive land relations.[13]

I've taken you through the Yaxunah ejido edge lands as I've gotten to know them as part of my attempt to restore history to one particular "useless" patch of forest, within this greater story of mutual and extractive land relations and their meaning for environmental justice. In this final chapter I want to walk the edge lands once more with you, to confront the ways that archaeology is steeped in the logics of extractive land relations. I want us to imagine how archaeology could be aligned with mutual land relations, with anticolonial methodologies, to work actively for Indigenous land sovereignty and environmental justice. This will be a walk shaped by nonarrival: I can promise no solid ground of answers, only the promise of questions and other footpaths to follow.[14] How do we reconcile extractive land relations and their push to maximize short-term gains on the one hand, with mutual land relations and their call for long-term reciprocity, balance, and symbiotic flourishing on the other?[15] How can we conspire to heal land from the damages of profit-driven usefulness? And how can we restore history and relationships with the lands that late capitalism has declared wastelands, used up, useless?

ðŁ   ðŁ   ðŁ

Every archaeological project I've worked on develops its own specific culture of eating. The field season I worked in Belize, lunchtime among the archaeologists felt for me like an unacknowledged but grim competition for food, as the project director kept us on a tight budget; I remember hurrying to skim oil from the bean pot into my plastic container of rice when no one was looking. Lunches during my field seasons in Oaxaca, in welcome contrast, were almost elegant. The archaeologists gathered under a tent, each on a little camp stool, and we ceremonially passed around a spray bottle of hand sanitizer. The smell of the sanitizer mingled with our food, and I can still taste it perfectly as a tang underlying the flavors of my daily sandwich (avocado and tomato on white bread with yellow mustard) that I packed before dawn each morning. In Romania, we picnicked on top of the Bronze Age tell where we were excavating, every day spreading out a blanket with garden-fresh tomatoes, cucumbers, peppers, cheeses, and bread to share together. This lunch always followed a daily morning ritual in which we broke for cookies and coffee poured hot from a huge thermos. I have no memory of ever packing any of this food, which is itself a telling detail.

When it comes to projects that employ local community members, the default for the ones I've been on is that archaeologists and community members eat separately. Archaeological projects in some regions, like Latin America, almost always hire landowners or community members to help with excavations, to clear vegetation, to screen soil, to wash artifacts, and for all the other tasks that go into fieldwork. When it's time to break, there tends to be a divide—the archaeologists eat together, and the locals eat together, at least on most of the projects I joined as a graduate student. There are probably plenty of reasons why this divide happens: language barriers, personality types, friendships, and the desire to eat quickly so you can take a nap all come to mind.

Out at Tzacauil, our meals were different. I think about those meals often, about the daily ritual of eating breakfast in a circle of Yaxunah community members out in the edge lands of the ejido. Under extractive land relations, these are the lands that are defined by their supposed uselessness—aside, that is, from their potential privatization.

It feels important to archive and examine the food that Yaxunah community members and I ate in the forests of the edge lands, partly because that food offers an opening to explore ideas of efficiency (and inefficiency) in the land. It's also because archaeologists don't often honor the mundane logistics of fieldwork in our writing. In leaving those quotidian stories behind, I worry that we archaeologists strip away the context for our learning; we erase the relationships and the stuff of grains, fruits, sugar, and animals that sustained us. We cut out the ways our studies of the past are enmeshed in still-unfolding histories, and we neatly obliterate any acknowledgment that our own presence in these stories is entangled with a global fixation on efficiency, use, and productivity—entangled, in other words, with extractive land relations. Chaipa Chi is made to vanish again. I want to counter that erasure.

$$\partial\!\!\!\partial \quad \partial\!\!\!\partial \quad \partial\!\!\!\partial$$

There can be a certain vulnerability around eating during fieldwork—especially, I think, for archaeologists working in places with pronounced cultural (and culinary) differences from what they're used to. I recognize echoes of this vulnerability in Stephens's impatient interactions with Chaipa Chi. I see it in his desperate attempt to communicate how he wants his eggs, and in his apparent disgust with the "butcher's shambles" of the Christmas feast. I sense that for Stephens, food is a necessary nuisance, a stubborn prerequisite for the more important work of, well, work. Food is fuel. Eat quickly and get back to work.

That attitude, I think, is alive and well on many archaeological projects (and of course in many other kinds of workplaces). I know I internalized that attitude sometime early in graduate school, having worked on a handful of archaeological projects and seen how much efficiency was valued. I brought that attitude with me to my first seasons working in the Yaxunah ejido, when I assisted with ongoing excavations in the Yaxuná archaeological site, just down the road from town.

Like other archaeological projects in Mexico, ours coordinated with local authorities to employ men from the community to do the physically demanding labor of excavation. Sometimes the archaeologists would dig too, but typically we fell into the role of managing the paperwork, artifact tags, and technical drawings of excavation units. How each archaeologist navigated our roles in fieldwork depended in large part on our positionality, especially gender.[16] We'd break for a meal in the early part of the day. Usually the Yaxunah men would eat together, sometimes scattering into small groups, and, separately, the archaeologists would eat together. We archaeologists often numbered around two to six in each subproject, and we were mostly graduate and undergraduate students from Mexico and the United States. The Yaxunah community members working with us might range from six men to a couple dozen, depending on the scale of the excavation.

We archaeologists packed our lunches in camp every morning with groceries bought on the weekends from supermarkets in Mérida or Valladolid. In my early years working in Yaxunah, my lunch was almost always two Nature Valley Sweet and Salty peanut granola bars, bought in bulk by our project coordinator from the Costco in Mérida.[17] I ate them quickly so that I could use the rest of the lunch break to catch up on notes and drawings. I remember, some days, feeling a sort of pride in not eating anything at all in the field. There was something intoxicating about feeling too productive to eat.

By my third field season in the Yaxunah ejido, I had started directing my own excavations, and it was a lot harder than I had expected. For one, as I explained in the introduction, I devoted about two months to excavating a couple of ancient house mounds in Yaxuná before finding out I wasn't going to be able to use them for my doctoral thesis because they were from the "wrong" period. That setback prompted an abrupt mid-season switch to excavate, instead, at Tzacauil out in the ejido edge lands. Looking back, I don't think my efficiency mindset was equipped to deal with the productivity loss of those two months; I think it had an existential crisis, died, and was buried right there in the backfill of my abandoned excavations.

I started work at Tzacauil calmer and slower. Little by little, I learned to focus on the process of fieldwork rather than the anticipated products (data, publications, recognition). And as I relaxed, I began spending more time each day talking with the Yaxunah excavators rather than worrying about their efficiency and my own. We told stories. We theorized about the things coming out of the excavations. We listened to *cumbia* and talked about our favorite accordion players. There were more inside jokes and more laughter. We ate together. And mealtimes got longer—sometimes a lot longer.

We were on the edge of the ejido, about an hour's walk from town or a thirty-minute ride in my rented pickup. Other excavations associated with our project clustered in the Yaxuná archaeological site, and on those excavations community members could easily dash home or to the store to grab a cold Coke or have one of their kids bike a bag of sandwiches out to them. An archaeologist could easily drive back to camp for more Gatorade or granola bars.

Out in the edge lands, we couldn't really do that. So the Yaxunah community members working on the Tzacauil excavations started to coordinate with each other and with the women of their families to organize a sort of daily potluck. Each day of the week a few men would bring food, usually cooked early that morning by their wives, to share with the rest. I stayed loyal to my Sweet and Saltys for only a couple days; early on, and with some gentle teasing about my melted granola bars, the community members invited me to partake in these shared breakfasts.[18]

So started our daily ritual of mealtime at Tzacauil, and so it continued for the rest of the 2015 season and through the final weeks of fieldwork in September 2017. We would halt excavations for *desayuno* at 9:30 a.m. If there was a nice flat boulder around we'd use that for a table, but an empty feedsack or black plastic garbage bag spread on the ground worked just as well. The day's dishes were laid out, the lids of plastic tubs peeled back, and we perched on flipped buckets to gather and eat and talk, sometimes for well over the scheduled hour. At some point I began documenting our daily meals with my phone camera, taking photos of each day's spread (figs. 21 and 22). Before long, a few of the younger locals—my fellow millennials—made a tradition of taking photos too. Over the months these photos created a visual archive of the food we shared out in the forests of the edge lands. I'm glad I have them. They preserve memories of meals I'm sure I would have otherwise forgotten.

Here is some of what we ate together. *Vaporcitos*, small tamales steamed in neatly tied banana leaf packages. *Poc chuc*, thin slices of pork marinated in citrus and grilled over charcoal. Drinkable yogurt in tiny plastic bottles. Guaya fruits, eaten by biting into a taut green peel to release tangy orange pulp with a burst. Cold *panuchos*, tortillas stuffed with refried beans, fried

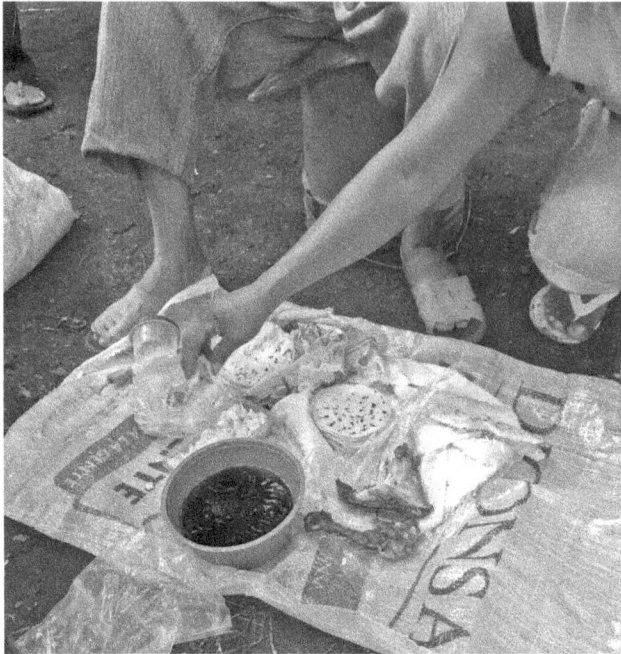

FIGURE 21. One of many breakfasts shared at the Tzacauil excavations: fresh tortillas, chicken, scrambled eggs, salt, chile, and Coke. Photo by the author.

and topped with pickled red onions, tomato, avocado, cabbage, and shredded chicken. Sacks of potato chips, flayed open like animals with shiny metallic hides. Scrambled eggs glistening with *manteca* (pork lard), the hero of Yucatecan cuisine. *Polcanes*, cornmeal dumplings stuffed with white beans and molded into the shape of snake heads, fried and topped with shredded cabbage. Tortillas with cream cheese. Watermelon, both brilliant yellow and jewel red. Pound cake, impossibly golden-colored and vacuum-sealed in plastic. Ham and cheese sandwiches on melt-in-your-mouth white slices of Pan Bimbo, Mexico's equivalent of Wonder Bread. *Tortas de cochinita*, pit-cooked pork on a roll. Fresh ears of new maize. Roasted tomatoes folded into handmade tortillas. Empanadas, beans, *tamales colados*, roast chicken, and cheese omelets. We ate stacks of handmade tortillas and drank from brightly colored plastic bowls, brimming with cold Coke and passed around the circle.

On some mornings we ate only pozole, the traditional field-food eaten by Maya milpa farmers when they're away from their hearths and kitchens. Pozole is made by breaking down a ball of corn *masa* in a bowl of water,

FIGURE 22. Sharing an elaborate end-of-week meal together at Tzacauil. Photo by the author.

squeezing the dough between your fingers and mixing it with the water until it forms a gruel-like beverage. The Yaxunah men trained me how to drink it correctly. When the bowl was passed to me, I'd take a pinch of salt from a small pile in the center of our circle, slip the salt onto the tip of my tongue and then take a long drink from the bowl. I'd finish the draught by biting off a small piece of a shared habanero chile, delicately using only my teeth to spare my lips from burning, and then pass the bowl to the next person. This was a long way from scarfing down a granola bar alone while frantically catching up on paperwork.

It was during these slow meals that I first learned about the changing perspectives on ejido lands in Yaxunah. Because we were in the forests at the edge of the ejido, conversation landed often in talk about how those lands were being used and not used. Our grandfathers farmed here; it's too risky to farm here now. Our grandfathers collected palm fronds from this kind of tree for their roofs; now we buy the leaves from other towns because you can't find them here anymore. Our grandfathers used to keep stingless native bees by that cenote; now foreign bees have wiped out the stingless hives. Back-in-my-day stories are one thing, but in these tellings I heard something bigger lurking just below the surface—the entanglements of extractive land relations, the harbingers of a useless land.

ਡੇ   ਡੇ   ਡੇ

The word *Calorie* first appeared in dictionaries in 1840, just one year before Chaipa Chi tacitly refused to cook Stephens's eggs the way he liked them. A French scientist had developed this capital-*C* Calorie to measure the fuel efficiency of steam engines: one Calorie equals the amount of heat it takes to increase the temperature of a kilogram of water by one degree centigrade.[19] Today we more often use calorie to talk about food, not about power, but even so, the kernel at the core of the calorie remains the same. It's a measure of energy.

NAFTA unleashed cheap corn from the United States into Mexican markets in the early nineties.[20] A lot of it was transgenic; the heirloom varieties of landrace maize that Mexican farmers had developed for thousands of years became endangered in the inundation. Many subsistence farmers couldn't compete with the imported corn's low price point, and many left agriculture for cash-earning jobs in other industries. The corn flood also meant that instead of growing their own food, many rural Mexican communities began to subsist instead on imported grains and their industrially manufactured descendants: white flour, noodles, the syrups of soda and sweetened juice concentrate.[21]

In the logic of capitalism, interchangeability among components—be they people or seeds or calories—is presumed to be not only possible but desirable.[22] It's the same logic at the core of plantations and the extractive land relations that drive them. NAFTA and its neoliberal reforms increased the number of calories available per person in Mexico, so by that logic, the trade pact solved the problem of hunger. But that logic neglects the reality that not all calories are equally nourishing. NAFTA's homogenizing agrarian reforms steamroll over the messy entanglements of food justice. How food is produced, and where, and by whom, and by whose decision-making power—

these things all matter a great deal in creating equitable food systems. As the anthropologist Alyshia Gálvez has put it, by making sheer calorie counts the central focus, NAFTA supplanted food sovereignty with food security.[23]

Calorie-dense (and caffeinated) foods like Coke are more "useful" as fuel, as sources of potential energy, from a standpoint that prioritizes efficiency alone. This logic directs eaters to consume in terms of calories, to treat food as fuel, to eat efficiently, to eat so as to continue working. It's about crushing meal replacement shakes—or Nature's Valley granola bars—to intake fuel as efficiently as possible, to maximize productivity. This aspirational productivity is made to be addictive, as all the while it slashes a boundary between useful and useless, prizing efficiency above all else.

The reforms legalizing the privatization of ejido lands operate under this same aspirational productivity. All that forested land, the archives of evolving mutual land relations, gets rendered useless in the reckoning of aspirational productivity. When the law changed to enable privatization, that useless land suddenly opened up for more efficient ventures. It could be made useful. Just as calories were cast as interchangeable, so too did the sweep of neoliberalism make land and cash interchangeable. This is a logic that contends that private developers will do a better job extracting value and use out of a forest than the farming communities who have lived in mutual relationship with that forest for generations can.

Social and ecological consequences follow the decision to sell ejido lands, but I don't believe that ejidatarios who choose to privatize their landholdings are to blame. All the factors that enter into the decision to sell or hold onto land are something that I, as an outsider, will never fully comprehend. Many communities get locked into desperate situations from converging pressures: failed harvests, out-migration, hurricanes, pandemic. The option to sell land, in many cases, must feel like an opportunity for communities to rescue themselves. Under duress, short-term solutions are often the only choice—even if they come attached with long-term damages.

But I do hold accountable the systems and structures that force those decisions in the first place, as well as the corporate executives and politicians hiding behind those systems and structures. Not only have these entities placed rural communities in impossible positions, but they do so in ways that enable private developers to mislead communities and to seize ejido lands by dubious or downright illegal means. These actors cultivate the useless land narrative in edge lands like the forests of Tzacauil. By striving to convince ejidatarios that their landholdings are useless, private developers begin the work of dismantling Indigenous Maya land tenure long before any contract is signed.

᠃᠃ ᠃᠃ ᠃᠃

Calorie-dense, industrially manufactured foods—Coke and white bread and feedlot pork—materialize the power of extractive land relations to transform plants and animals into commodities. That late capitalist alchemy happens in the ground, too: call it calorie-dense, industrially manufactured land. The kernel at the core of a calorie is a measure of potential energy. The logic of the plantation, close kin of extractive land relations, promises that the more energy we can extract from a hectare of ground, the more valuable it becomes.

Enraptured by this promise, privatization projects across Yucatán are buying up (or stealing) ejidos, taking control of the useless and unused parcels of the edge lands and transforming them into concentrated generators of energy.[24] The land is made useful. Factory farms churn out calories in the bodies of animals. Monocropped fields covenant to produce inexhaustible yields of biofuels. Glittering plantations of silicon-skinned panels capture an endless flow of tropical sunlight. In nearly every form that use takes, the forest is clear-cut, wiped neatly away to make room for efficiency and productivity. For cheap meat and for green energy.

I go down rabbit holes tracing out tangled stories of land grabs online. There are dozens of news articles reporting on the audacious rackets run by developers to manipulate and disenfranchise Maya communities of their ejido lands. The news is full of frauds exposed in outrage by community organizers and networks of Indigenous resistance; I imagine there must be so many more that have not yet been detected or made public. There are stories about ejido lands broken up, stitched back together under new titles and transformed: from forest to feedlot, from forest to dinosaur theme park, from forest to Nachi Cocom Beach Club and Water Sport Center.

But the stories about forests transformed into green energy projects are the ones I can't stop thinking about. These stories center on a set of ventures that, if you weren't really paying attention, would seem unquestionably sustainable and "good for the environment." Green energy projects—developments for generating solar power, wind power, and biodiesel made from seeds—look good from far away. Get closer and you find that many of these same green energy projects let multinational corporations "go carbon neutral" just by purchasing offsets, not by meaningfully changing any of their ongoing practices. Look on the ground in places like Yucatán where land grabs and green energy go hand in hand, and you see that Indigenous communities are the ones often left to pay the long-term costs of corporate sustainability claims.

Sun, wind, seeds. These are three collaborators with Maya farmers in the practice of mutual land relations with the forest, three resources promised to supply renewable energy to alleviate the climate crisis. Extractive land relations marginalize the Maya partnership with sun, wind, and seeds as useless. Green energy projects are proposed instead to optimize the use of sun, wind, and seeds. These tensions between use and useless are grinding down forests and eroding Indigenous land sovereignty across Yucatán. But perhaps I'm being too general—specific histories and particular relationships matter. Here are three stories of sun, wind, and seeds, torn between the mutual and extractive land relations competing for the edges. Let's walk closer.

k'iin—sol—sun

Sunrise in Yucatec Maya is há'atskab, *or strike-earth.*[25] *For the milpa farmer, the tactile contact between sun and ground changes through the seasons. The farmer follows these changes closely. The sun grows hottest in May. In the dry, choking weeks right before the rains begin, the sun becomes* yáax k'iin, *great sun, and the ground becomes* chokow lu'um, *hot earth.*[26] *When the heat peaks, it will be time to burn the dry carcasses of felled vegetation in the milpa. The farmer watches and waits for the signs. The long seed pods of the* Xtakin *tree will explode in the heat. The ground wasps,* xùu-lab, *will swarm in the day, walk the forest floor in the night. The* pú'uhwih *bird will sing. The parched leaves of the* há'abin *tree will rattle in the wind like the tails of snakes.*[27] *And the great sun will be high overhead. It will be time to burn.*[28]

There is a polygon of land earmarked for deforestation in southern Yucatán. The polygon spans more than six hundred hectares and straddles three municipalities, Muna, Sacalum, and Tikul. The plan for this land, as proposed in 2016 but currently on hold as I write, is to clear the forest and then raise up a crop of 1,228,000 solar panels for a photovoltaic park to be known as Ticul A y B. If completed, Ticul A y B will be the biggest photovoltaic park in Latin America. But the land deal has been messy, even violent.[29]

Back at the beginning, the Vega Solar energy company made a deal with a private landowner. The private landowner, who already held the title to 440 hectares of the planned building site for the photovoltaic park, sold those 440 hectares to Vega Solar. Vega Solar's parent company, SunPower Corp., is a mega corporation of solar power based in the United States. After this deal went through, Vega Solar still needed to acquire about three hundred more hectares. Those hectares belong to the forested ejido lands of the town of San José Tipceh. The private landowner approached the community and arranged to lease a portion of the ejido lands, saying it's for citrus orchards. When the San José Tipceh ejidatarios discovered the actual plan, it was too late. They had already signed the contract.

Disputes follow the deal and divide the local community. Some community members fear the solar company has underestimated—perhaps deliberately—the effects that deforestation will have on their livelihoods. They worry that the photovoltaic park will trap heat and exacerbate water shortages, and this at a time when warming weather is already damaging the harvests of milperos and beekeepers. Despite these concerns, the company's communication with the community is delayed and irregular. There are unannounced changes to reports. Technical documents go untranslated, hindering the ability of Yucatec Maya–speaking ejidatarios to fully participate. Consultations are claimed to have happened; they have not.[30]

In 2017, it appears that a majority of ejidatarios endorse a consultation protocol, a critical step in advancing the solar project. But some in San José Tipceh protest the endorsement, saying that the document was fraudulent and padded with the signatures of deceased ejidatarios. With the endorsement suddenly under scrutiny, it looks like community support for the photovoltaic park is eroding.

The energy company looks to rally support for the project. Allegedly the company hires a prominent Indigenous Nahua activist to coax the ejidatarios to buy into the project and to believe in the benefits promised to the community.[31] Many ejidatarios are convinced. Other ejidatarios accuse the activist of being a traitor, of deploying gifts, blackmail, and deception to collect the signatures needed to advance the project. Tensions deepen, then erupt into violence. In July 2018, a local authority is nearly lynched in an attempt to force his support for the project. Two people are attacked with machetes in September.[32]

In a meeting in late November 2018, the ejidatarios of San José Tipceh officially give their consent to build the solar project on ejido land. But can it be considered true consent when the vote is monitored by anti-riot police, delegates from a dozen government agencies, and representatives from the

United Nations Commission for Human Rights? It's hard to say how it all went; reporters were not allowed to attend the meeting. For now, the project has stalled, and the polygon remains forested. Political shifts at the federal level in Mexico have turned the tide back towards fossil fuels, and Indigenous resistance to the project continues in court.[33] The future of the solar park and the tensions it sowed in San José Tipceh remain unresolved.

iik'—viento—wind

> *It's time to burn. The milpa is dry, the sun overhead sears. Much depends on the fire; it needs to burn quickly, but not too hot, to make the right kind of ash. And the fire depends on the wind. The farmer moves from place to place in the dry and desiccated field, setting fire to the felled brush. He sends a prayer to dispatch the* kakal-mozon-ik, *the whirlwind, so that the fire will fan out to consume the entire parcel. A breeze flutters in, too weak. The farmer begins to call the wind: he whistles, inviting and invoking great gusts as air blows from his lips, and he runs, whistling to the wind, lighting the last fires. The flames start to spread. The winds are whipping up.[34]*

Twenty kilometers northeast of Mérida's urban sprawl and a short distance south of the Gulf Coast sits the municipality of Ixil. Ixil is a little town famous for its *cebollitas*, sweet small onions with purple bulbs and long green stalks. In 2014, the ejidatarios of Ixil agree to grant power of attorney to a lawyer named Alejandro Escoffié Gamboa, with the expectation that Escoffié will help Ixil manage their landholding.[35]

Entrusted with the Ixil ejido, the lawyer Escoffié goes behind the community's back and begins breaking up and selling the landholding parcel by parcel in secret.[36] He forges documents and fabricates entire assembly minutes from meetings that never happened, all to make it seem like the Ixil ejidatarios themselves have moved to start privatizing their lands. Escoffié sells more than five thousand hectares of the Ixil ejido without the community knowing anything about it. One of Escoffié's buyers is an energy megaproject, a two-part wind farm named Chicxulub I and II. The wind farm is called Chicxulub after Ixil's neighbor, the coastal town of Chicxulub, slated for development under the same project.

The deception begins to surface in the final days of 2018 and the first days of 2019. Some Ixil community members are confused to see posts on

Facebook about lands being divided and sold. One elderly Ixil man quoted in a newspaper says, "We heard something but about Chicxulub"—not Ixil by name—"so we didn't give it much importance." Then, organizers from a grassroots activist group, the Jo' Resistance and Rebellion Network, come to Ixil. Assuming that the people of Ixil already know about the megaproject, the organizers begin alerting community members about the environmental detriment posed by the wind farms.[37] The Ixil community members have no idea what the activists are talking about—their land, after all, remains communally owned. Around the same time, a corporate official for Chicxulub I and II approaches a local Ixil woman named Peregrina, whose husband is an ejidatario. The corporate official accuses Peregrina of organizing resistance to the wind project. Peregrina will later recount the encounter at an assembly: "Yo no sabía nada de esto. Me enteré cuando un señor llegó a mi casa y me reclamó que yo esté moviendo gente para oponerme al proyecto. ¡Pero de qué proyecto me habla!" (I knew nothing about this. I found out when a man came to my house and accused me of mobilizing people to oppose the project. But what project was he talking about!)[38]

In January 2019, Escoffié decides to catch the community up: Ixil no longer has an ejido, everything is private property, he tells them baldly.[39] The Ixil ejidatarios are outraged. They send a delegation to the National Agrarian Registry, where, unknown to them, Escoffié has filed his fraudulent documentation authorizing the land sales. The registry refuses to give the Ixil ejidatarios any of the documents dealing with the landholding because per their arrangement in 2014, they have ceded all legal authority to Escoffié.

For weeks, the Ixil ejidatarios petition the registry for their documents. Cecilio Cisneros, leader of the Ixil delegation, threatens to chain himself to the front of the registry building if the ejidatarios don't get their documents. At this threat, the registry finally, in April 2019, hands over the documents so that the Ixil ejidatarios can start to secure the status of their lands. Having recovered the documents, the Ixil ejidatarios begin the complicated process of recovering the lands they had almost lost.[40]

But the battle continues. People in Ixil worry that the wind farm company has a different plot of land in their crosshairs, a wooded parcel that in name is federally owned but that has been important to the Ixil community for generations. And now there is a new strategy: the company, some Ixil community members believe, is paying ejidatarios both from Ixil and from the neighboring town of Timul to take over the contested lands on the company's behalf. Timul ejidatarios have been seen cutting down vegetation where the turbines are meant to be built. An Ixil official says that when he asked why they were clearing the land, they gave him a cover story, that they are preparing to launch a tourism project. The Ixil official says, fine, but do it in your own lands, you don't need to come onto our lands. One of the Timul ejidatarios answers him, "Hombre, ¿que no ves que no tenemos tierras, que ya las vendimos todas?" (Man, can't you see that we don't have any land, that we already sold it all?)[41]

i'inaj—semilla—seed

The rains have come to cool the blackened ground. It's time to plant. Four, five, six, seven seeds are placed together in the small hole, dug out by the milpa farmer with the deft movement of his wooden planting stick. He will repeat this fluid motion, sowing each small opening with four, five, six, seven seeds, then filling the hole with earth, all across the milpa. He will not harvest four, five, six, seven plants from each mound, this he knows. The story goes that when seeds were first created, it was the animals that rescued them out of fire. As recompense for the rescue, the animals won the right to eat a share of the plants grown from the seeds. The farmer thanks the animals by planting enough so that they—the raccoons, the coatis, the jabalí, the toh'—will have enough to eat, and the farmer will, too. Seeds create more seeds; generosity creates abundance.[42]

Sucopo is a small village in northeastern Yucatán.[43] In the second half of the twentieth century, ventures in cattle ranching ravaged Sucopo's ejido by replacing the forest with grass. The passing of Article 27 in the early nineties gave the Sucopo ejidatarios an option to monetize their degraded lands. So they sell their ejido almost as soon as it's legal. The buyer doesn't do anything with the lands for a long time. Left alone, thousands of hectares of clear-cut lands begin to recover. Secondary forests regrow, and wild animals return to live among the shrubby young trees. Though the lands are privately owned now, Sucopo people are still permitted to walk and farm the woods. They can hunt, collect firewood, forage for medicinal plants. The abandoned ranches are regenerating into a vibrant forest.

In 2008 a California-based company called Global Clean Energy Holdings purchases 6054 hectares of the rewilding former ejido lands around Sucopo. In the legal documents arranging the sale, the land is described as "abandoned cattle ranches." Nothing is mentioned about the forest recovering on these thousands of hectares, nor the role these lands continue to play in the lives of the Sucopo community. Global Clean Energy Holdings gives a presentation to the Sucopo community. The company announces they are going to plant *Jatropha*, a plant whose oily seeds, their representatives claim, can be cheaply rendered into biodiesel. The company says the plantation will create steady employment for five hundred men and women for the next fifteen to thirty years and will pay better than the wages typical for the area.

For the people of Sucopo, this sounds wonderful. Young men of the community have been migrating out to find employment in construction or tourism, going as far as Cancún just to be able to send money to their families back home. They decide that the prospect of earning reliable wages (for men as well as for women) and being able to live at home outweighs the loss of the young forest. So the jatropha plantation goes ahead.

Three thousand hectares of forest—"abandoned cattle ranches"—are cleared to plant jatropha. The wild animals that had reclaimed homes in the woods are pushed out by the deforestation. Desperate, they go searching for food in the fields of Sucopo farmers, destroying harvests in their hunger. The flowers of the recovering forest are lost, too, and without them the local honeybee populations struggle to survive.

Perhaps all would have been worth it if the company delivered on its promises, but after only three harvests, Global Clean Energy Holdings shuts the plantation down. It turns out that jatropha as a source of biodiesel has been hyped up as a cheap font of green energy without the research to back the claims. The seed yield on plantations, not just in Sucopo but across Yucatán, is quickly discovered to be too low to be profitable.[44] The biodiesel projects are swiftly abandoned, leaving the people of Sucopo without the jobs they had been promised and without the forest that had been reawakening back into life.

಄   ಄   ಄

There is no single version of the useless land narrative. In attending to the granular stories of San José Tipceh, Ixil, Sucopo, and Yaxunah, we push back against the homogenizing forces of extractive land relations. Specific histories and particular relationships matter. These stories are not interchangeable, but in gathering them together, we can recognize the ways that edge lands are deracinated from their history. We can see the useless land narrative more clearly.

Yaxunah has not, as I write this now, accepted the offers of potential buyers interested in purchasing parcels of the ejido. But the forests around

Tzacauil and the other edge lands of the ejido have been attracting developers for years now and probably will keep attracting them for years to come. The low hum of conversation among Yaxunah ejidatarios, the talk that the edge lands might no longer be useful, whispers and warns that the long game of privatization may already be under way.

This hum found its way many times into the circle of our long breakfasts at Tzacauil. The slow hours of our meals together in the edge lands were full of talk about mask carving and Chichen Itza's souvenir market, about offers from private developers. Most of the Yaxunah community members who worked on the investigations at Tzacauil are ejidatarios; the collective agency of these rights-holding men and women will ultimately determine the future of the edge lands. Ejidatarios rarely make the journey out to the eastern forests anymore, but the paying work that the archaeological project brought meant a short injection of cash value to the edge lands. For a moment, for three summers, the edge lands became productive and useful in a capitalistic sense. The project ended, so that use was certainly not sustainable.

During the weeks of Noma Mexico's run, our talk circled repeatedly around the pop-up and its involvement with Yaxunah. Noma was buying vegetables, herbs, and eggs from a few Yaxunah households, and the prices the restaurant was paying were discussed with keen interest. Someone had heard that Noma was paying three pesos per egg, a good price given that most eggs would get only two pesos in the local tiendas. Chaya, a leafy green, was going for forty pesos a kilo. Epazote, a common herb in Yucatecan cooking, was going for fifty a kilo. A kilo of maize was going for twelve pesos.[45]

We pooled news and gossip from the Yaxunah women who had been recruited to Tulum to make tortillas for the Noma diners, quite a few of whom were wives and family members of men working on the excavations. One well-shared story had to do with how hard a time the women were having in their Tulum lodgings trying to sleep in beds rather than hammocks for the first time in their lives. I asked once how much Noma was paying the tortilla makers. No one knew for sure, but the estimate was around two thousand pesos per week. This was double the wage that our project directors and Yaxunah local authorities had agreed to pay the excavation crews that season.[46] While two thousand pesos seemed like a good wage, the Yaxunah community members noted grimly that much of that money went back into the extra expenses the women accumulated from living in Tulum. I plugged in the cost of dinner at Noma Mexico into my phone's calculator and converted it to pesos. We passed my phone around so everyone could see the number: the price came in at more than 11,000 pesos before taxes. It wasn't clear to me if they knew I was serious, and suddenly I felt ashamed for waving this figure around—one I conceivably could have paid, and even might have paid, to eat at Noma Mexico.

The reality of my presence as an outsider was never far away. I ate with the Yaxunah community members on the project, and I laughed with them. I developed genuine friendships with some of them. But archaeology, a field whose origin story in Maya lands traces to those early expeditions by Stephens and Catherwood, is a long way yet from becoming truly anticolonial.[47]

ə̀ ə̀ ə̀

When we ate during fieldwork at Tzacauil, sometimes the food would steer conversations to the land. Some foods, especially wild foods, evoked collective memories among community members of the ways the forest remains deeply valuable to Yaxunah ejidatarios and their families. Sharing those memories of the forest while physically in it seemed to counter the useless land narrative—at least for a moment.

One day an ejidatario brought out a plastic tub at breakfast. Inside was a hunk of venison, tan-pink filaments of well-muscled flesh that no factory farm animal would have possessed. We tucked the meat into handmade tortillas—tacos de Bambi, the joke was—and listened as the giver of the venison recounted how he had harvested the deer with his relatives from the edge land forests the day before, after we finished work (fig. 23).

Another afternoon, as my truck grumbled up and down the choppy dirt road back towards town, the Yaxunah men riding in the back spotted a wasp nest hanging from a tree bough over the road. At their request I stopped the truck so they could try and get the wasp nest down. A few minutes later the men came sprinting back, laughing (but screaming, too) as they vaulted into the pickup, and then we roared away down the road in escape, making it out with no stings. Even as the escape was happening we were already forming the story that we would tell about it the next day as we would eat the delicacy known as *xux ek'*: the wasp larvae that had been recovered from the nest, toasted over a *comal*, blended with sour orange juice, chile, and salt, and spooned up with tortillas. The value of these wild feasts, foraged from the forests of the edge lands and from far beyond the channels of the global commodity chain, cannot be measured in calories.

FIGURE 23. A venison taco, prepared with a handmade tortilla and meat from a deer harvested from the ejido edge lands, eaten in the same ejido edge lands. Photo by the author.

Beekeeping and hunting, harvesting *chaká* trees and collecting firewood: these are the practices that still bring members of the Yaxunah community out to the edge lands of their ejido in the twenty-first century. The foraging of wild foods remains an opening, an escape hatch out of the cash stream of late capitalism and into mutual relations with the forest. True, often the materials harvested from the forest—the smooth cedar of a souvenir mask, a kilo of new honey—will be sold for cash, but in their invitation to reaffirm connections with the land, these living materials offer pathways for reciprocity and resistance.

This is where this walk has been leading: archaeology, practiced collaboratively and intentionally with communities, can recover the deep histories of land while creating opportunities for community members to reaffirm relations with it. Walking the woods, eating from the forest, sharing memories of the land on the land—embedded in these practices may be the antidote to the useless land narrative, the restoration of roots. In this way, archaeology might be able to align with anticolonial methodologies, support Indigenous land sovereignty, and work for environmental justice.

Indigenous Maya communities are already leading the way in this effort, and they have been for the past five centuries. They have been resisting land grabs since the conquest, and their resistance has taken many forms. When I was first drafting this chapter in 2021, ejidatarios from the Yucatec Maya community of Chablekal were occupying the archaeological site of Dzibilchaltun, demanding restitution for the fifty-three hectares of the Chablekal ejido that had been incorporated into the site's official boundaries without any compensation sixty years ago.[48] The Chablekal blockade prevented thousands of tourists from entering the archaeological site, which was a big deal since Dzibilchaltun was one of the only sites in Yucatán that was allowed to open to the public during the pandemic months of summer 2021. A couple of years earlier, protests by Maya water protectors from the Yucatecan village of Homún rallied opposition against a proposed hog feedlot megaproject that would have contaminated the community's groundwater and damage its ecotourism infrastructure.[49] The Homún community continues to battle over the project's future with Grupo Kekén, the industrial meat company behind the proposed feedlot and the second largest meat producer in Mexico.

Resistance has not always been peaceful. In the southern Maya region of the highlands of Chiapas, the Zapatista Army of National Liberation (EZLN) has organized rural Indigenous Maya communities in military and political resistance against the Mexican government since 1994. The Zapatistas launched their offensive in direct response to the land tenure reforms of Article 27—the same amendment that legalized the privatization of ejido lands—and in protest to the neoliberal economic policies of NAFTA. While in recent years the members of EZLN have turned their strategies towards nonviolent civil resistance, they continue to control significant territories in Chiapas and to advocate for Indigenous and rural agrarian rights.[50]

The Zapatista uprisings echo the Maya Social War, the outbreak of which was coming fast during Stephens's visit to Uxmal in 1841. With the onset of that war, Indigenous Maya rebels coordinated the destruction of haciendas across the peninsula. Following these uprisings, Maya people deserted the haciendas for the forests, and some flocked to new communities in the eastern interior of modern Quintana Roo and Belize. The Maya rebel army laid siege to the city of Mérida for a short time before pulling back to the eastern forests, where they continued to maintain sovereignty over lands for decades. Like the Zapatista uprising, the Maya Social War was catalyzed by systemic state efforts to dismantle Indigenous land tenure, to wrest control of the woodlands and make the forests useful under capitalism.[51]

In the long centuries of colonialism leading up the Maya Social War, Indigenous resistance to land reform often went underground.[52] Direct confrontations with landowning Yucatecos too frequently ended in violence, as when a group of Yucatecos made an example of the rebel Jacinto Canek. Canek was an Indigenous leader who encouraged Maya communities to form militias and take down the haciendas in 1761. Canek's rebellion was swiftly and violently suppressed by the better-armed state army, and Canek himself was publicly executed by dismemberment in Mérida's central plaza less than a month after the uprising began. Because of this kind of outright violence, Maya resistance often moved clandestinely through more subversive channels. The historian Nancy Farriss has said that the act of flight—simply leaving settlements and dispersing into the forest—became a critical strategy for collective survival among Indigenous communities in colonial Yucatán.[53] Passive forms of resistance, whether disappearing into the woods, moving slowly while doing forced labor, or even feigning ignorance became powerful ways for Indigenous Maya people to push back against the extractive forces of colonial rule. To the hacienda owners, this lack of enthusiasm for capitalistic enterprise was recognized not as a subversive strategy of Indigenous resistance but as laziness and stupidity, an assumption that prevailed across the colonial world.[54]

I sense this subversive spirit of resistance smirking behind Stephens's back while he provides aggravated recitations of Chaipa Chi's "inability" to cook his eggs the way he wants them. Sure, maybe Chaipa Chi really couldn't understand the American's frantic second-language Spanish or his mimed attempts to convey "fried, please"—but also, maybe she totally did understand. Maybe she was perfectly capable of frying the eggs but just chose not to comply. Stephens can only see her lack of enthusiasm to meet his needs as laziness and ignorance, a generalized malady of "uselessness" that he corrects by subbing in a more malleable cook and demoting Chaipa Chi to tortilla maker. I don't think she cared one bit about her demotion: in her post she was left alone by the foreigners and still got paid to do something that, it seems, she was good at and perhaps actually enjoyed.

We can see Chaipa Chi the way Stephens does, or we can see her as a rebel against the systems of extraction that were installed in Yucatán under colonialism and that are still alive there today under late capitalism. Doctrines of usefulness have, for centuries, been leveraged to erode Indigenous Maya land sovereignty by casting lands as useless, creating a pretext for taking them. Proponents of extractive land relations have plotted to make edge lands more useful for five hundred years, and their plans are usually imposed with aggression. Henequen and cattle ranches were pressed into useless lands in the past; now we have solar panels, hog feedlots, biodiesel plantations, wind turbines, water parks, and dinosaur theme parks installed in useless lands, with or without the consent of the communities who steward those lands.

The mutual land relations of Maya agriculture emerge from the long conversation between farmers and forests, unfolding across generations. The deep histories of those land relations are legible in places like Tzacauil and the edges of the Yaxunah ejido, where farming communities came together and moved apart in rhythms with the forest for thousands of years. Within those deep histories, within those forests of the edges, may be the keys for future Maya land sovereignty and environmental justice. Those keys risk being lost under the threat of privatization and land grabbing.

Maya people possess a deep knowledge of rooting in so-called useless land. For centuries they have worked collaboratively to push back against capitalism's short-sighted useful/useless binary, and to counteract the long-term ecological and social wounds such binaries create. The resistance can look like rebellion. It can look like protest. It can look like blockades. It can look like walking the woods. It can look like not giving a damn about how someone wants his eggs.

ࢡ   ࢡ   ࢡ

One day during excavations, I was laying out a long line of grid squares between the P'aak homesite and the Tzacauil Sacbe to set up a trench excavation in "empty land." Two Yaxunah men, Pedro and Nazario (the former Chichen Itza hot-dog-stand cook) were helping me. It was tedious work. Pedro and Nazario each held the end of a long cloth measuring tape, and I held the spools of both tapes. We were going square by square, hammering in stakes and crouching down with the tapes to check the hypotenuse length so the lines of the trench would be straight.

We were talking easily as we measured. Then one of the guys wondered out loud how people had first gotten to Cuba, and suddenly I was off in a tangle of tangents. I rocked back on my heels and was soon lost in the reverie of my own monologue (in not great Spanish, I'm sure), meandering from human evolution to hominin migration to the Columbian exchange. I remember crouching, clutching the spools and staring down at the ground as I started to get myself whipped into a frenzy, voice rising as I ended my unsolicited speech by exclaiming, "I mean, can we just talk about everything that had to happen to make it so that we're having this conversation in Spanish?" At that I finally snapped my gaze up from the ground. As I did, I realized suddenly that the tapes were completely slack in my hands and that it felt like I had been talking uninterrupted for somewhere between five minutes and five hours. I stopped talking. The sweltering air hung still and heavy in the silence.

I looked at Nazario and saw him swaying slightly, the measuring tape hanging limp and his eyes half-closed. He was literally falling asleep on his feet. He roused himself with what sounded like a snore, blinked at me, and said, "Chels. It's too hot for your stories. Can we get back to work?"

I love this memory. And he's right—it does feel too hot for my stories sometimes. I look back on this walk through the edge lands and I think of Rick Bayless, of René Redzepi, and of Rosalía Chay Chuc. I think of the ruins of Noma Mexico and jatropha plantations, of dinosaur theme parks and wind farms. I think of *aj kiimsaj káax*, the murderer of the woodland, and of heirloom bowls in plastic buckets buried deep underground. I think of fibrous roots finding moisture in rock, and of Nachi Cocom feeding his guests. I think of learning to root in the useless lands of this warming world. It is too hot.

Just one more story, one more walk, and then I'll be still.

ॐ   ॐ   ॐ

The day the American writer John Lloyd Stephens leaves Uxmal, he sees Chaipa Chi one last time.

"As we passed along the edge of the milpa, half-hidden among the cornstalks was the stately figure of Chaipa Chi. She seemed to be regarding us with a mournful gaze. Alas! Poor Chaipa Chi, the white man's friend! Never again will she make tortillas for the *Ingleses* in Uxmal!"[55]

Stephens tries to catch Chaipa Chi's eye. She says nothing and moves not at all; she is still, half-hidden in the milpa.

Stephens wants a clean end to the story before he takes us on with him to the next ruins on the itinerary. So he tells us that a month after he leaves Uxmal, Chaipa Chi dies.

"She was borne to the *campo santo* of the hacienda," Stephens will later write—the same cemetery he plundered on Christmas Day. He imagines the scene: "The sun and rain are beating upon her grave. Her bones will soon bleach on the rude charnel pile." Then he finishes, his pen dripping with a wretched smugness, "and her skull may perhaps one day, by the hands of some unscrupulous traveler, be conveyed to Dr. S.G. Morton of Philadelphia."[56]

I pray Chaipa Chi is at rest.

In the twenty-first century, hundreds of thousands of tourists visit Uxmal each year. It's an easy day trip from Mérida. To get there, most pass through the town of Muna, where conflict over Vega Solar's plan to build a photovoltaic power plant on nearby ejido land recently erupted in machete attacks. None of this tension will be visible to tourists driving through to Uxmal.

Within the boundary of the Uxmal archaeological park, just a few steps from the ticketing area, is a luxury resort with an attached restaurant. The restaurant is named Coole Chepa Chi, meaning Señora Chepa Chi, which is another spelling of the name Stephens recorded as Chaipa Chi in his visit to Uxmal in 1841. The restaurant has a huge, airy palapa and, I'd guess, is probably staffed by people from Muna and other neighboring Yucatec Maya towns.

I have never eaten at Chaipa Chi's namesake restaurant, but one night recently I read the online reviews voraciously.[57] Some reviewers are happy with their experience at Coole Chepa Chi. Most are not.

Angelica from Los Angeles says, "1 star is for location only. Avoid! Pricey, questionable food and weird service." Tori from Syracuse says, "Day old breads, a little over ripe fruits, but I was at least happy with the location. The best things going for this place is the location, the decor and the cerveza! ... I wouldn't go out of my way to go here...." Izabela from Mérida says, "We were the only table when we came for dinner and yet waited 75 minutes for food that never came.... The waiter just kept repeating that he is sorry and the food is almost there." Luke from Virginia says, "Uh, $10 for a bowl of soup? ... Yes it is next to a major tourist place, but they do not have to charge major rip off tourist prices? We drank our overpriced beers and left."

And Stephen from New Jersey says, "We were at the Mayan ruins and decided to stop after a long day. The place is a great location . . . and decor . . . however the food not so much. . . . Not much selection and the food was overcooked and bland looking. Each dish was stewed meat or fish covered in sauce. We avoided the salad . . . and desserts." But Coole Chepa Chi wasn't a total waste of time, Stephen lets us know. "One high point was a lady making fresh tortillas. . . ."

Time Line of Key Events in the History of the Yaxunah Ejido

Note that dates before the colonial period are approximate. The date ranges assigned to precolonial historical periods (e.g., Postclassic, Late Formative, etc.) vary somewhat region to region in the Maya lowlands, but the ranges provided here are consistent with those used for the Yaxunah ejido.

	Yaxunah ejido and beyond	Tzacauil
	MIDDLE FORMATIVE PERIOD (1000–300 BC)	
1000–900 BC	No documented human presence in the Yaxunah ejido.	
900–400 BC	Foragers and transitional forager-farmers camp seasonally at Yaxuná and elsewhere in the ejido for generations.	Foragers and transitional forager-farmers camp seasonally at Tzacauil for generations.
400–300 BC	Construction of earliest public gathering places begins at Yaxuná circa 400 BC.	Foragers and transitional forager-farmers camp seasonally at Tzacauil for generations.
	LATE FORMATIVE PERIOD (300 BC–AD 1)	
	More and larger public architectural complexes built at Yaxuná	Transition to permanent, intensive, homesite-localized small-holder agriculture in Tzacauil
	Households living and farming permanently around Yaxuná's public gathering places	Jach and P'aak Groups founded at Tzacauil
	Population grows rapidly at Yaxuná; Yaxuná becomes a low-density urban settlement.	Tzacauil Acropolis built in its original form; Tzacauil Sacbe likely under construction
	Yaxuná solidifies its role as a powerful political center in central Yucatán.	Farming village at Tzacauil is founded as an offshoot of Yaxuná's low-density urbanism.

TERMINAL FORMATIVE PERIOD (AD 1–250)

Yaxuná maintains its role as the main political and urban center in central Yucatán.

Yaxuná suffers population declines at the end of the period, likely caused in part by drought.

Chamal, Kaan, and Sáastun Groups are founded in the Late to Terminal Formative transition.

Tzacauil Acropolis undergoes significant renovations during the LF-TF transition; Tzacauil Sacbe likely under construction.

Tzacauil is abandoned at the end of the period, likely caused in part by drought.

EARLY CLASSIC PERIOD (250–550)

Some evidence for low population at Yaxuná.

Yaxuná possibly incorporated into Oxkintok territory.

Scant evidence for occupation at Tzacauil.

LATE CLASSIC PERIOD (550–700)

Population increases at Yaxuná.

Yaxuná incorporated into Coba territory.

Mobile milpa farmers settle on the highest bedrock rise at Tzacauil, founding homesites at Pool, Kaan, and Mukul Groups.

Sacbe 1 connects Yaxuná to Coba and passes by Tzacauil.

EARLIER TERMINAL CLASSIC PERIOD (700–850)

Significant monumental construction at Yaxuná.

Jaltun and T'uup Groups, which appear to be temporary field camps used seasonally by milpa farmers, are built around the Late to Terminal Classic transition.

Yaxuná's population peaks.

Pool and Kaan Groups continue to be occupied at least periodically.

Yaxuná incorporated into territory of a western political center.

LATER TERMINAL CLASSIC PERIOD (850–1100)

Signs of increasing military conflict at Yaxuná.

Kaan and T'uup Groups appear unused/unoccupied.

Yaxuná abandoned after invasion and incorporation into Chichen Itza.

Pool and Jaltun Groups show signs of sporadic occupation/use through the end of the period.

1100–1200 — Scant evidence of occupation in Yaxunah ejido; era of Chichen Itza rule.

POSTCLASSIC PERIOD (1200–1500)

Scattered shrines are found at Yaxuná but no clear signs of occupation.

Chichen Itza is abandoned; Mayapan rises to power.

1441 — Unified peninsula under Mayapan breaks apart.

COLONIAL PERIOD (1500–1800)

1511	Initial Spanish landings in Yucatán.
1527	Conquest of Yucatán begins under the Montejos.
1547	Spanish conquest of Yucatán mostly complete.
1549	First colonial tax list in Yucatán.
1600	Brief mention of Cetel-ak in Maya prophecies.
1773	Land sale deeds Hacienda Cetelac to Dámaso Santana.
1784	205 people living at Yaxunah and 8 people living at Hacienda Cetelac

MODERN PERIOD (1800–PRESENT)

1804	25 people living at Hacienda Cetelac.
1817	Catholic church dedicated in Yaxunah
1818	Two individuals authorized by the Hacienda Cetelac landowner to settle a land dispute between himself and Maya living in Yaxunah.
1821	Yaxunah's population reaches 1,121 people; Yucatán incorporated into Mexico.
1825	Terrenos baldíos policies instated in Yucatán.

1828	51 people living at Hacienda Cetelac, 896 in Yaxunah.
1841	Stephens and Catherwood in Uxmal; terrenos baldíos designations standardized to one square league in four cardinal directions from central church; 500 people living at Yaxunah. Yucatán declares independence from Mexico.
1846	620 people living in Yaxunah.
1847	Maya Social War begins; Yaxunah and Hacienda Cetelac abandoned.
1848	Yucatán rejoins Mexico.
1862	Census shows 11 people living in Yaxunah.
1880	Yucatán henequen boom begins.
1910	Mexican Revolution begins.
1915	Modern Yaxunah founded by seven families.
1917	Mexican Revolution ends; ejido system established.
1920	Yucatán henequen boom ends.
1927–1933	Archaeologists from the Carnegie Institution of Washington visit Yaxuná.
1933	Carnegie Institution of Washington team surveys Sacbe 1, possibly visits Tzacauil.
1934	Yaxunah ejido established.
1950s	Yaxunah claims eastern edge lands for their ejido.

1986	First major archaeological project (Selz Project) begins in Yaxunah ejido.	
1992	NAFTA signed; privatization of ejido lands is legalized in Mexico.	
1994	NAFTA in effect; Fundación Cultural Yucatán (FCY) begins sustainable development in Yaxunah.	(approx.) FCY initiates efforts to open ecotourism trail to Tzacauil.
1996	Selz Project ends.	
1997–2000	Instituto Nacional de Antropología e Historia (INAH) project at Yaxuná.	
2005	Lool K'uum collective forms; INAH project at Yaxuná.	
2007	PIPCY begins regional archaeological research based at Yaxuná.	PIPCY archaeologists map Tzacauil.
2013	Lool K'uum collective and FHMM partner.	Excavations at the Chamal Group.
2015	Rick Bayless films in Yaxunah.	
2016	René Redzepi arranges to source maize and hire tortilla makers for Noma Mexico from Yaxunah via FHMM; CIMMYT launches the Sustainable Milpa Project.	Excavations at the Pool, Jaltun, and Jach Groups; first intrasettlement trench excavations; test pit in Tzacauil Acropolis.
2017	Noma Mexico runs for seven weeks; first iteration of Hokol Vuh festival follows and brings celebrity chefs to Yaxunah.	Excavations at the Jach, P'aak, Sáastun, Kaan, Chamal, and T'uup Groups; intrasettlement trench excavations; TEK-based survey.
2020	Netflix's *Chef's Table* features the Yaxunah cook Rosalía Chay Chuc.	

Comparison of Homesites Documented at Tzacauil

House group	Construction history	Associated structures at time of abandonment	Square meters excavated	Total ceramic sherds Count	Middle Formative sherds Mean sherds per m² excav.	Mass (g)	Mean mass (g) per m² excav.	Grinding tools Count	Mass	Metate fragments	Molcajete (mortar) fragments	Handheld grinding stones
Jach	Built in LF; significantly renovated in LF; occupied in TF; abandoned in TF	Basal platform on bedrock outcrop with stone foundations for at least four dwellings	230	498	2.17	5657.4	24.60	117	2134.4	6	–	6
P'aak	Built in LF; occupied in TF; abandoned in TF	Two adjacent basal platforms, one on bedrock outcrop with the stone foundations for one dwelling, one on flat bedrock with stone foundations for one dwelling divided into three rooms	161	118	0.73	1302.8	8.09	24	360.9	3	1	12
Chamal	Built in LF-TF transition; significantly renovated in TF; minor renovations later in TF; abandoned in TF	Basal platform on bedrock outcrop with stone foundations for two or three dwellings, one off-mound ancillary structure/kitchen	262	610	2.33	5177.9	19.76	23	339.1	5	–	14

Sáastun	Built in LF-TF transition; abandoned in TF	Basal platform on bedrock outcrop with stone foundations for two dwellings (one appears unfinished), one off-mound ancillary structure/ kitchen, possible second off-mound ancillary structure (unexcavated)	178	150	0.84	953.7	5.36	24	92.1	8	–	30
Kaan	Built in LF-TF transition; abandoned in TF; reoccupied and renovated in LC; occupied in first part of TC; abandoned by start of second part of TC	Basal platform on bedrock outcrop with stone foundations for one dwelling (LF-TF), during LC renovations foundations for a second dwelling were added and basal platform expanded	121	713	5.89	7185.9	59.39	23	340.3	–	–	16
Pool	Some evidence for LF-TF construction activity; significant construction in LC; signs of occupation in LC, first part of TC, and second part of TC; abandoned in late TC	Cluster of stone foundations for three dwellings built on modified bedrock outcrop	106	999	9.42	10377.8	97.90	11	69.8	1	–	39

(Continued)

House group	Construction history	Associated structures at time of abandonment	Square meters excavated	Total ceramic sherds	Middle Formative sherds				Grinding tools				
				Count	Mean sherds per m² excav.	Mass (g)	Mean mass (g) per m² excav.	Count	Mass	Metate fragments	Molcajete (mortar) fragments	Handheld grinding stones
Jaltun	Built in LC-TC transition, appears in use through second part of TC; abandoned in late TC	Stone foundations for one ancillary structure on flat expanse of bedrock	44.5	43	0.97	219.9	4.94	—	—	—	—	—
T'uup	Built in LC-TC transition, in use through first part of TC; abandoned by second part of TC	Stone foundations for one ancillary structure on flat expanse of bedrock	51	8	0.16	49.1	0.96	—	—	—	—	—
Mukul	Built and occupied in LC (not horizontally excavated; results inconclusive)	Stone foundations for two structures on top of a modified bedrock outcrop	Not horizontally excavated; artifact counts omitted from analysis.									

NOTE: LC = Late Classic; LF = Late Formative; TC = Terminal Classic; TF = Terminal Formative

NOTES

INTRODUCTION

1. Schulte et al., "Chicxulub Asteroid Impact."
2. Bricker, Po'ot Yah, and Dzul de Po'ot, *Dictionary of the Maya Language.*
3. My translation of the politician's speech from the Spanish, as quoted in Cardeña, "De Basurero al Aire Libre."
4. Constructions of Indigenous identity and Maya identity vary widely through history and across Maya homelands, which include southeastern Mexico, Guatemala, Belize, and parts of El Salvador and Honduras. I want to make transparent four decisions I've made about how to address these complex identities, as someone with no claim to them. First, in this text I will use "Indigenous Maya" and "Maya" to refer to the contemporary peoples of Yucatán who descend from the native peoples of those homelands, but with the caveat that this label is not capable of capturing the complexities of how Indigenous identity is claimed and constructed in Yucatán; see Castañeda, "'We Are *Not* Indigenous!'" Second, I use "Yucatec Maya" to refer to the Indigenous Maya language spoken in the Yucatán Peninsula. Third, I capitalize Indigenous following conventions outlined by the editorial team of the public anthropology journal *Sapiens*, who write, "Why capitalize 'Indigenous'? It articulates and identifies a group of political and historical communities, compared to the lowercase 'i,' which can refer to anyone" (Weeber, "Why Capitalize 'Indigenous'?"). And fourth, I use "ancient Maya" to refer to the precolonial Indigenous peoples of Yucatán. While this term is inadequate and homogenizing too, it opens channels of communication between this text and other archaeological literature on the ancient Maya and past societies more broadly.
5. Tzec Valle, "Sendero Jurásico en Progreso."
6. Martínez-Reyes, *Moral Ecology of a Forest.*
7. Gayou Soto, "Habitantes de Ixil."
8. Thank you to the scholars whose texts have grounded and shaped my understanding of land relations, extraction, and mutualism, with particular gratitude for

Kimmerer, *Braiding Sweetgrass*; Liboiron, *Pollution Is Colonialism*; Povinelli, *Geontologies*; Tsing, *Mushroom at the End*.

9. It's important to acknowledge historical experiences of environmental degradation in Indigenous societies, as counter to the persistent myth of the "ecological Indian" as described in Krech, *Ecological Indian*. Mutual land relations, like extractive land relations, are not inborn or genetic—they are learned and transmitted culturally. Past Indigenous societies could and did at times experience environmental degradation. See, as examples, evidence for "collapse" events in the Maya city of Tikal in Lentz et al., "Imperial Resource Management," and of Hohokam irrigated settlements in Hill et al., "'Collapse' of Cooperative Hohokam Irrigation." Anthropogenic impacts of Indigenous societies varied and could include positive and negative impacts, but it's likewise important to emphasize that those negative impacts are vastly outweighed by the destruction caused by ongoing colonial land relations. See Braje et al., "Archaeology, Historical Ecology."

10. For discussions of late capitalism and extractive land relations, see Tsing, *Mushroom at the End*.

11. This invitation towards mutual land relations and restoration is developed beautifully in Kimmerer, *Braiding Sweetgrass*.

12. Whyte, "Indigenous Experience," 2.

13. Whyte, 2.

14. As I'm writing this in 2022, various pop-sci news outlets are circulating coverage of a recent study that links climate change and civil conflict together in the collapse of the ancient Maya city of Mayapan; see Kennett et al., "Drought-Induced Civil Conflict." My favorite of the ominous pop-sci headlines, from *Science Alert*, reads: "What Triggered the Collapse of the Ancient Maya? A New Study Reads Like a Warning."

15. For more on the entanglements of patchy restoration, see Tsing, *Mushroom at the End*, 218–39.

16. For more on the dynamics of neoliberalism and Mexican food systems, see Gálvez, *Eating NAFTA*.

17. Penfield, "Unlikely Impact."

18. McGurty, "From NIMBY to Civil Rights."

19. McGurty.

20. Bullard, *Dumping in Dixie*.

21. Malin and Ryder, "Developing Deeply Intersectional Environmental Justice"; Taylor, "Rise of the Environmental Justice Paradigm."

22. Whyte, "Indigenous Experience"; Whyte, "Is It Colonial Déjà Vu?"

23. Liboiron, *Pollution Is Colonialism*, 96.

24. The examples I give in the next paragraphs are based in the United States, but the connection between colonialism and environmental justice conflicts permeates borders. This is a global phenomenon. See, for example, Amrith, *Crossing the Bay of Bengal*; Ghosh, *Nutmeg's Curse*; Yusoff, *Billion Black Anthropocenes*.

25. Whyte, "Dakota Access Pipeline," 160–61.

26. Flowers, *Waste*.

27. Pilkington, "Activist Catherine Flowers."

28. Farrell et al., "Effects of Land Dispossession"; Margulis, McKeon, and Borras, "Land Grabbing."

29. Borras and Franco, "Global Land Grabbing"; Rulli, Saviori, and D'Odorico, "Global Land and Water Grabbing."

30. Rulli et al., "Global Land and Water Grabbing."

31. Estimates of total global land grabbing vary considerably. In a 2013 paper, Margulis and colleagues suggest a range of 45 million to 227 million hectares but note that counting processes remain unclear. Margulis et al., "Land Grabbing," 2.

32. Fairhead, Leach, and Scoones, "Green Grabbing."

33. These exclusions will be discussed in more detail in chapter 6. See also Martínez-Reyes, *Moral Ecology of a Forest*.

34. Hennessy, *On the Backs of Tortoises*; Neumann, *Imposing Wilderness*; Baka, "Making Space for Energy"; Voyles, *Wastelanding*.

35. Makki, "Development by Dispossession."

36. Tuck and McKenzie, *Place in Research*, 64.

37. Eve Tuck and K. Wayne Yang make clear that decolonization is the rematriation of land to Indigenous people and is not synonymous with anticolonial practices more broadly; see Tuck and Yang, "Decolonization Is Not a Metaphor." For important discussions of the possibilities and pathways for anticolonial research, see Liboiron, *Pollution Is Colonialism*.

38. Lidgard and Love, "Rethinking Living Fossils."

39. My brilliant student Clara Albacete and I are at work on a paper about the ways ancient civilizations are invoked in superfood branding; we call this pattern "ancient greenwashing."

40. For discussion of sustainability branding as a mechanism to absolve consumer guilt, see Lorr, *Secret Life of Groceries*, 210–12.

41. I-Collective, "Home"; Penniman, *Farming while Black*; Twitty, *Cooking Gene*.

42. My thinking on these dynamics has been shaped by environmental humanities scholars of the "Plantationocene." See Davis et al., "Anthropocene, Capitalocene"; Haraway and Tsing, "Reflections on the Plantationocene"; Murphy and Schroering, "Refiguring the Plantationocene"; Wolford, "Plantationocene."

43. Traditional ecological knowledge (TEK) and Indigenous ecological knowledge (IEK) will be described in more detail in chapter 2. For excellent discussions of the integration of dominant science and TEK/IEK, see Kimmerer, *Braiding Sweetgrass*.

44. For examples, see Chase and Scarborough, "Diversity, Resilience, and IHOPE-Maya"; Guttmann-Bond, "Sustainability out of the Past." I have written about this, too, though my thoughts about archaeology's role in sustainability and environmental justice are always changing. This book marks some of those changes, and I'm hopeful more will come. See Fisher, "Archaeology for Sustainable Agriculture."

45. Klassen and Evans, "Top-down and Bottom-up."

46. Chase and Chase, "Path Dependency."

47. See also Lucero, Fletcher, and Coningham, "From 'Collapse' to Urban Diaspora."

48. Rosenzweig and Marston, "Archaeologies of Empire and Environment."

49. Millhauser and Morehart, "Sustainability as a Relative Process."

50. Logan, *Scarcity Slot.*

51. Nelson et al., "Climate Challenges."

52. See, for example, Delmas and Burbano, "Drivers of Greenwashing."

53. Extractive land relations universalize land into interchangeable, homogenized, ahistorical units. Sites for this flattening include the plantation (see McKittrick, "Plantation Futures") and pollution sinks (see Liboiron, *Pollution Is Colonialism*).

54. Many in this constellation of celebrity chefs are connected to Yaxunah via the Noma expanded universe and particularly Hokol Vuh, a culinary festival held in Yucatán, sponsored by American Express, and hosted by Roberto Solís and Noma's René Redzepi. More about Hokol Vuh, and links to the festival's social media accounts, can be found at https://hokolvuh.com/.

55. Alcocer Puerto, "El ecoturismo cultural."

56. The planning of Noma Mexico is covered in detail in Gordinier, *Hungry.* I'll also note here that in January 2023 Redzepi announced his intention to close the flagship Noma restaurant in Copenhagen at the end of 2024 because it had become "unsustainable." He does plan, however, to continue the pop-ups. See Moskin, "Noma."

57. *Landrace* refers to heirloom varieties of plants or animals that develop in relationship with specific communities and in specific places. The term is similar in meaning to how *terroir* is used to describe wines and other foods that are deeply connected to precise lands and ecologies.

58. Redzepi and Sanchez, "Mayan Producers."

59. Domínguez Aké, *Úuchben kool yetel*; Terán and Rasmussen, *La milpa*; Wells and Mihok, "Ancient Maya Perceptions."

60. Ford and Nigh, *Maya Forest Garden.*

61. Domínguez Aké, *Úuchben kool yetel*; Ford and Nigh, *Maya Forest Garden*; Terán and Rasmussen, *La milpa.*

62. The neoliberalization of Mexico's agrarian sector, and its effect on food systems, is outlined brilliantly in Gálvez, *Eating NAFTA.*

63. For discussion of the connection between climate migration and crop loss in Mexico, see Feng, Krueger, and Oppenheimer, "Linkages."

64. Gálvez, *Eating NAFTA.*

65. FHMM-CIMMYT, "Ofrece milpa sustentable."

66. CIMMYT, "Sustainable Agriculture"; Govaerts, "Sustainable Tradition." See also Fisher, "Maize Politics."

67. CIMMYT, "Sustainable Agriculture."

68. Cepeda and Amoroso, *Sustainable Rural Development.*

69. CIMMYT, "Helping Farming Families."

70. Govaerts, "Sustainable Tradition."

71. CIMMYT, "El restaurante Noma."

72. Eisenberg et al., "Out of the Ashes."

73. Ford and Nigh, *Maya Forest Garden*; Nigh and Diemont, "Maya Milpa."

74. An extensive summary of archaeological remains in the Yaxunah ejido is available in Stanton et al., *Archaeological Investigations at Yaxuná*.

75. The directors of this first project, the Selz Foundation Yaxuná Archaeological Project (1986–96), include David Freidel, Tomás Gallareta Negrón Fernando Robles, Rafael Cobos Palma, Maynard Cliff, Charles Suhler, and Traci Ardren. See Stanton et al., *Archaeological Investigations at Yaxuná*.

76. PIPCY stands for Proyecto de Interacción Política del Centro de Yucatán, or the Political Interaction Project of Central Yucatán. PIPCY was a regional project, based at Yaxuná, and over its decade-long run was directed by Travis Stanton, Aline Magnoni, Scott Hutson, and Traci Ardren. I'm grateful to these directors, and to all of PIPCY's members, for their support of my research in the Yaxunah ejido.

77. The earliest archaeological forays at Yaxuná are described in Kidder, "Archaeological Work in Yucatán"; Morley, "Archaeology"; and O'Neill, "Survey of Yaxuná." The first systematic archaeology project there was the Selz Foundation Yaxuná Archaeological Project. The Instituto Nacional de Antropología e Historia (INAH) project at Yaxuná was directed by Lourdes Toscano Hernández; see Toscano Hernández and Ortegón Zapata, "Yaxuná"; Toscano Hernández et al., "Proyecto Yaxuná." Archaeology thesis projects conducted by my fellow PIPCY student members include Collins, "From Sedentism to Sprawl"; Marengo Camacho, "Análisis funcional de cerámica"; Torres Ochoa, "La producción de artefactos de concha."

78. Stanton, "Founding of Yaxuná."

79. Tiesler et al., *Before Kukulcán*.

80. See Tiffany C. Fryer's important discussion of how structures of labor on archaeological projects can reproduce injustice in archaeology. Fryer, "Against the 'Workmen' Model."

81. For just one example of this trend, see La Ruta de la Garnacha, "Cochinita Pibil."

82. I've never met anyone in Yaxunah who calls Tzacauil by that name. "Tzacauil" was registered when archaeologists misheard *Xauil*, the name of the cenote just east of the site, and so that's the name on record with INAH in Mexico. People in Yaxunah call the site *Xnooj múul*, meaning big mound. See Garza and Kurjack, *Atlas arqueológico*.

83. Brown and Bey, *Pathways to Complexity*.

84. Both El Manantial and Xauil are cenotes, sinkholes that reach groundwater. The Xauil cenote is open to the air, with water visible at the bottom of a deep columnar shaft through bedrock. El Manantial is understood by Yaxunah community members as an underground spring; it is mostly closed on the surface, with only a small hole in the bedrock opening to an underground chamber and the water table

below. El Manantial and Xauil are approximately 225 meters southeast and 450 meters northeast of the Tzacauil Acropolis, respectively.

85. I'm grateful to Scott Hutson and the PIPCY members who mapped Tzacauil and began investigating its role as an early farming settlement. See Hutson, Magnoni, and Stanton, "'All that is solid.'"

86. Archaeologists have not been able to figure out why the Tzacauil Sacbe appears incomplete, but even unfinished, the causeway would have opened possibilities for easier walking between the city of Yaxuná and the village of Tzacauil, and maybe for more formalized processions, too. See Fisher, "Walking Rural"; Hutson et al., "'All that is solid.'"

87. Sacbe 1 has been the subject of archaeological investigation for nearly a century. See Stanton et al., "'Structure,' Density, Area"; Villa Rojas, *Yaxuna-Coba Causeway*.

88. Tsing, *Mushroom at the End*, 152.

89. By engaged archaeology, I refer to various movements within archaeology towards collaborative, participatory, and community-based research. For more on engaged archaeology in the Maya region and beyond, see as examples Atalay, *Community-Based Archaeology*; Colwell-Chanthaphonh et al., "Premise and Promise"; McAnany, *Maya Cultural Heritage*, Pyburn, "Engaged Archaeology"; Stahl, "Assembling 'Effective Archaeologies.'"

CHAPTER ONE

1. This description of the Noma Mexico "ruin" is based on Google Maps imagery as of May 2019.

2. As some readers know, though, even the original Noma's days are now numbered: in January 2023, Redzepi announced he would close the restaurant at the end of 2024. See Moskin, "Noma, Rated the World's Best Restaurant, Is Closing Its Doors." For my discussion of Redzepi and the various offshoots of the Noma brand here, I've drawn on journalist Jeff Gordinier's memoir of traveling with Redzepi in Mexico and elsewhere. I've also relied on the Noma blog known as "The Weather Report," as well as the public social media accounts of Redzepi and his collaborators. See Gordinier, *Hungry*; Noma, "The Weather Report."

3. Canavan, Burton, and Sutton, "Noma Named 'World's Best Restaurant'—Again."

4. WCED, *Brundtland Report*.

5. Delmas and Burbano, "Drivers of Greenwashing;" Drew et al., "Ancient Grains and New Markets;" Lorr, *Secret Life of Groceries*.

6. For additional discussion of Redzepi's connections to neoliberal agrarian reform in Mexico, see Gálvez, *Eating NAFTA*.

7. Ayora-Diaz, *Foodscapes, Foodfields, and Identities*, 16.

8. Ayora-Diaz, "Gastronomic Inventions," 64.

9. Ayora-Diaz, *Foodscapes, Foodfields, and Identities*, 2.

10. The term *Yucateco* refers to the primarily European-descended gentry class of Yucatecan society at the time.

11. Ayora-Diaz, *Foodscapes, Foodfields, and Identities.*

12. Ayora-Diaz, "Gastronomic Inventions," 72.

13. Ayora-Diaz, 72.

14. Channick, "Rick Bayless' Frontera Foods Sold to ConAgra; Chef's Brand Staying in Chicago."

15. Pashman, "Other People's Food, part 1."

16. Bayless, *Mexico: One Plate at a Time.*

17. For robust discussions of how NAFTA transformed Mexican food systems, see Fitting, *Struggle for Maize*; Gálvez, *Eating NAFTA.*

18. Gálvez.

19. For more about the history of sustainable development initiatives in Yaxunah, see Alcocer Puerto, "Manejo sustentable"; Alcocer Puerto, "Ecoturismo cultural"; Alcocer Puerto, Bascopé, and Vela Cano, "El turismo en una comunidad maya yucateca"; Ardren, "Now Serving Maya Heritage"; Magnoni, Ardren, and Hutson, "Tourism in the Mundo Maya." For discussion of FCY sustainable development initiatives in Yucatán, see Meyers, *Outside the Hacienda Walls.*

20. Alcocer Puerto et al., "El turismo en una comunidad maya yucateca."

21. Patjane Floriuk, "De la milpa a la producción artesanal."

22. Names of Yaxunah community members have been changed.

23. For my discussion of FHMM's history and its brands Traspatio Maya and Taller Maya, I've relied on FHMM's website, accessible at www.haciendasmundomaya.org/.

24. Ardren, "Now Serving Maya Heritage."

25. Ardren.

26. For further discussions of performativity in Maya heritage tourism, see Magnoni et al., "Tourism in the Mundo Maya."

27. Fitting, *Struggle for Maize.*

28. Henderson, "Celebrity Chefs"; Kong, "Feasting on 'the Other'"; Mapes, "(De)Constructing Distinction."

29. Ardren, "Now Serving Maya Heritage"; Magnoni et al., "Tourism in the Mundo Maya."

30. For more on Noma cuisine, see Noma, "The Weather Report"; Gordinier, *Hungry.*

31. Gordinier, *Hungry.*

32. Gordinier, 167.

33. See, for instance, CIMMYT, "El restaurante Noma"; Redzepi and Sanchez, "Mayan Producers"; Redzepi and Sanchez, "Bar Menu."

34. Gordinier, *Hungry,* 169.

35. Gordinier, 169–70.

36. This use of "Mayan" is telling, I think. The Noma team's use of "Mayan" is consistent with most tourist-focused English-language descriptors of Maya culture. In English-language scholarship, "Mayan" is used only to refer to languages; "Maya"

refers to people, culture, food, and traditions, and "Yucatec Maya" refers to the specific Indigenous language spoken in Yucatán. Among Spanish speakers, *maya* is most used, as in *la cultura maya* (Maya culture). The Noma team's use of "Mayan" places them squarely in the realm of tourist-focused language. It feels off to me.

37. Gordinier, *Hungry*, 187.

38. Gordinier, 188.

39. Redzepi and Sanchez, "Mayan Producers."

40. Gordinier, *Hungry*, 188–89.

41. Maybe? This is the kind of tour guide trivia lots of visitors love because it lets them interact with ruins. I'm skeptical, but I get that this is how guides make their tours more fun.

42. Gordinier, *Hungry*, 189–90.

43. Gordinier, 185.

44. Wells, "Why I'm Not Reviewing."

45. Richler, "At $600 Each."

46. Sintumuang, "Shelling Out $1,500."

47. Sietsema, "A World-Class Chef."

48. Stein, "Behind the Scenes."

49. Wells, "Why I'm Not Reviewing."

50. CIMMYT, "El restaurante Noma."

51. More about Hokol Vuh, and links to related social media accounts, can be found at https://hokolvuh.com/. The festival is also described in Gordinier, *Hungry*.

52. As an example of social media posts showing these chefs participating in Hokol Vuh, see Hokol Vuh, "Izamal recibe con los brazos abiertos."

53. The list of participating celebrity chefs was announced over social media. See Hokol Vuh, "Hoy estamos a unos días."

54. Hokol Vuh, "Nuestra herencia milenaria."

55. For just three examples of these posts, see Hokol Vuh, "El maíz"; Hokol Vuh, "Exposición de Frutas y Verduras"; Hokol Vuh, "Experiencia de bebidas."

56. For more about the food porn phenomenon, see Romm, "What 'Food Porn' Does."

57. Chang, *Ugly Delicious.*

58. The Spanish title *doña* is a term of respect for adult women and is used often in Yaxunah.

59. For discussion of *Chef's Table*, see Genzlinger, "Review: 'Chef's Table'"; Rayner, "Chef's Table."

60. Chandra, "Netflix's Chef's Table."

61. *Chef's Table BBQ*, "Rosalia Chay Chuc."

62. Rosalía Chay Chuc has an Instagram profile, @chefrosaliachay, and a website that proclaims, "This is not a restaurant. This is a culinary experience." Visitors can book their "experience" with Chef Rosalía as well as multiday "Culinary Mayan Journey Discovery" excursions through this website, accessible at https://chefrosaliachay.com/.

63. Mitchell, "Ate the most authentic."

64. Ochoa, "Conocí a Rosalía!"

65. For discussion of cartel violence and the avocado market, see Larmer, "How the Avocado Became the Fruit of Global Trade." For discussion of the globalization of quinoa, see Drew et al., "Ancient Grains and New Markets"; Kerssen, "Food Sovereignty."

66. Lorr, *Secret Life of Groceries*, 189. For excellent anthropological analysis of the on-the-ground realities of fair-trade certifications, see also Besky, *Darjeeling Distinction*.

67. Moskin, "The Island Is Idyllic."

68. Gordinier, *Hungry*, 176.

69. Redzepi and Sanchez, "Bar Menu."

70. Media coverage of the announcement included Burton, "90% of Noma Mexico's Much Cheaper Bar Menu"; Sherman, "Profits from Noma."

71. Moskin, "Noma."

CHAPTER TWO

1. Terán and Rasmussen, *La milpa*, 37.

2. Because the Maya milpa is traditionally associated with men and men's labor, I refer to milperos as men here. See Domínguez Aké, *Úuchben kool yetel*; Terán and Rasmussen.

3. Milpa is one of several similar agricultural practices that developed independently in the tropics and that utilize controlled burns. Other names for this kind of farming are swidden, slash and burn, slash fire, and shifting cultivation. See van Vliet et al., "Swidden Agriculture."

4. For descriptions of traditional Maya milpa agriculture, see Domínguez Aké, *Úuchben kool yetel*; Ford and Nigh, *Maya Forest Garden*; Nigh and Diemont, "Maya Milpa"; Terán and Rasmussen, *La milpa*.

5. For discussions of the role of cosmology, ritual, and religious beliefs in Maya agriculture, see Barrera-Bassols and Toledo, "Ethnoecology of the Yucatec Maya"; Freidel, Schele, and Parker, *Maya Cosmos*; Terán and Rasmussen, *La milpa*; Thompson, *Maya History and Religion*; Wells and Mihok, "Ancient Maya Perceptions."

6. Tedlock, *Popol Vuh*.

7. Tozzer, *Landa's Relación*.

8. Barrera-Bassols and Toledo, "Ethnoecology of the Yucatec Maya," 30.

9. Hanks, *Referential Practice*, 363.

10. Barrera-Bassols and Toledo, "Ethnoecology of the Yucatec Maya," 31.

11. Barrera-Bassols and Toledo.

12. Accounts of late twentieth-century *ch'a-chaak* ceremonies in Yaxunah are reported in Freidel et al., *Maya Cosmos*, 29–33.

13. For more on reciprocal ceremonial traditions in the Maya area, see Vogt, *Tortillas for the Gods*.

14. Freidel et al., *Maya Cosmos*, 130.

15. Hanks, *Referential Practice*, 349.

16. Hanks, 363.

17. For reports of cave offerings found in the Yaxunah ejido, see Slater, "Into the Heart."

18. Excavations of the earliest public complex in Yaxuná, the E-Group Plaza, were directed by Ryan Collins. For discussion of the quincunx etchings found in the Late Formative (ca. 400–300 BC) plaza floor, see Collins, "Incised Lines."

19. Ford and Nigh, *Maya Forest Garden*.

20. For discussions of the sustainability (and potential unsustainability) of the milpa and swidden agriculture more broadly, see Cairns, *Shifting Cultivation and Environmental Change*; Mukul and Herbohn, "Impacts of Shifting Cultivation"; van Vliet et al., "Swidden Agriculture."

21. Kimmerer, *Braiding Sweetgrass*.

22. Kimmerer, 55.

23. For descriptions of Maya agricultural ritual through time see Freidel et al., *Maya Cosmos*; Gabriel, "Ritualidad y Cosmovisión" ; Terán, Rasmussen, and May Cauich, *Las plantas de la milpa entre los mayas*; Thompson, *Maya History and Religion*; Wells and Mihok, "Ancient Maya Perceptions"; Zaro and Lohse, "Agricultural Rhythms and Rituals."

24. For discussion of the role of obligation in Indigenous land relations, see Liboiron, *Pollution Is Colonialism*, 136–38.

25. For more on the power structures inherent in life/nonlife distinctions, see Yusoff, *Billion Black Anthropocenes*.

26. Povinelli, *Geontologies*.

27. Povinelli, 35.

28. Kramm, "When a River Becomes a Person."

29. Tsing, *Mushroom at the End*.

30. Tsing, 22.

31. Tsing, 267.

32. Ortiz Yam, "Formación de Ejidos"; Torres-Mazuera, "Communal and Indigenous Landholding."

33. Gálvez, *Eating NAFTA*.

34. For discussion of the historical role of infield agriculture in the Maya area, see Chase and Chase, "Scale and Intensity"; Fisher, "Role of Infield Agriculture"; Isendahl, "Agro-Urban Landscapes"; Lemonnier and Vannière, "Agrarian Features, Farmsteads, and Homesteads"; Marcus, "Plant World"; Robin, *Chan*.

35. Tzacauil was originally mapped by founding members of the Proyecto de Interacción Política del Centro de Yucatán (PIPCY), which I joined some years later in 2013. Technical details about the mapping can be found in Stanton and Magnoni, "PIPCY tercera temporada de campo." Preliminary interpretations of mapping and surface study at Tzacauil are published in Hutson, Magnoni, and Stanton, "'All that is solid.'"

36. Albuquerque et al., *Methods and Techniques*.

37. Simpson, "Land as Pedagogy," 17–18.

38. Simpson, 21.

39. Wildcat et al., "Learning from the Land," i.

40. Maldonado-Koerdell, "Geohistory and Paleogeography."

41. Gómez Pompa et al., *Lowland Maya Area*.

42. Dine et al., "Famine Foods and Food Security"; Gómez Pompa, Salvador Flores, and Aliphat Fernández, "Sacred Cacao Groves"; Kepecs and Boucher, "Pre-Hispanic Cultivation."

43. Fedick et al., "Adaptation of Maya Homegardens."

44. Brady and Prufer, *In the Maw of the Earth Monster*; Mercer, *Hill-Caves of Yucatan*.

45. Lentz et al., "Forests, Fields, and the Edge"; Puleston, "Role of Ramón"; Robinson and McKillop, "Ancient Maya Wood Selection."

46. Fita et al., "La milpa Comedero-Trampa."

47. Domínguez Aké, *Úuchben kool yetel*.

48. See Ringle, "Settlement Patterns of Komchen." For colonial complaints about soil quality in Yucatán, see Asensio, Pedraza, and Landa, *Relaciones de Yucatán*; Tozzer, *Landa's Relación*.

49. Dunning, "Implication of Folk Soil Taxonomies."

50. Bautista and Zinck, "Construction."

51. For discussion of Amazonian dark earths, see Silva et al., "New Hypothesis." For discussion of similar dark earths formation in the Maya area, see Nigh, "Trees, Fire and Farmers."

52. Bautista and Zinck, "Construction."

53. Gálvez, *Eating NAFTA*; Magnoni, Ardren, and Hutson, "Tourism in the Mundo Maya."

54. Centro Internacional de Mejoramiento de Maíz y Trigo (CIMMYT), "Sustainable Agriculture"; CIMMYT, "Helping Farming Families"; Govaerts, "Sustainable Tradition."

55. CIMMYT, "El restaurante Noma"; CIMMYT, "Helping Farming Families."

56. Names of Yaxunah community members have been changed.

57. Govaerts, "Sustainable Tradition."

58. Bandy, "Energetic Efficiency."

59. For comparative examples of raised field farming traditions in Mesoamerica, see Coe, "Chinampas of Mexico"; Turner and Harrison, *Pulltrouser Swamp*.

60. *Cañihua*, or *Chenopodium pallidicaule*, is a species of goosefoot related to quinoa.

61. Erickson, *Experiments*.

62. Erickson, "Raised Field Agriculture," 14.

63. Kolata, "Agricultural Foundations of the Tiwanaku State"; Kolata, "Technology and Organization."

64. For more detailed analysis of the raised field rehabilitation initiatives, see Bandy, "Energetic Efficiency"; Swartley, "Inventing Indigenous Knowledge."

65. Erickson, "Raised Field Agriculture," 15.

66. Swartley, "Inventing Indigenous Knowledge," 5.

67. Bandy, "Energetic Efficiency."

68. For debates on the organization of Tiwanaku raised field farming, see Bandy, "Energetic Efficiency"; Janusek and Kolata, "Top-Down or Bottom-Up."

69. Swartley, "Inventing Indigenous Knowledge," 6.

CHAPTER THREE

1. For discussions of caching practices in the Maya lowlands, see for example Coe, "Caches and Offertory Practices"; Kunen, Galindo, and Chase, "Pits and Bones."

2. Pozole is a maize-based beverage, *balche* is a fermented drink made from honey and tree bark, and *caldo* is a savory broth or soup. All three would have been part of pre-Hispanic Maya foodways; for more on Maya food, see Ardren, *Her Cup for Sweet Cacao*.

3. See appendix A for a time line of Tzacauil and the Yaxunah ejido, and see appendix B for quick chronological comparisons of all homesites excavated at Tzacauil. Dating based on changes in ceramic styles is the only source of chronological data available for Tzacauil. This method admittedly has its imperfections, as the chronological periods associated with distinctive ceramic styles are sometimes multiple centuries long. Unfortunately, opportunities for absolute dating methods were not available at Tzacauil because of the scarcity of sealed contexts in household excavations. Because of this, I rely on ceramic typologies for dating. In this chapter, I will distinguish when possible between Late Formative (ca. 250 BC—AD 1) and Terminal Formative (ca. AD 1–250) contexts, though often I will use "Late to Terminal Formative" if there is evidence for both periods in a given context. The Middle Formative (ca. 900–250 BC) will also be discussed in this chapter. When I talk about the Formative settlement at Tzacauil, I am specifically talking about the Late to Terminal Formative settlement of farmers who first founded permanent homesites in this place. More information about dating and methodologies used at Tzacauil more generally is available in Fisher, "Maya Farming Communities."

4. For more on the transition from foraging to farming in the Maya area, see Inomata et al., "Monumental Architecture."

5. Heirloom caching practices of the Maya are described in Joyce, "Heirlooms and Houses"; McAnany, *Living with the Ancestors*.

6. Fisher, "Role of Infield Agriculture"; Isendahl, "Agro-Urban Landscapes"; Lucero, Fletcher, and Coningham, "From 'Collapse' to Urban Diaspora."

7. This central plaza at Yaxuná followed the stylistic conventions of an E Group, an architectural form documented throughout the Maya area. Yaxuná's E-Group plaza would have served as a gathering place where communities of mobile foragers and forager-farmers came together to share ecological knowledge and to participate in collective practices of identity formation. E Groups, found all over the Formative

Maya lowlands, adhered to a shared template: a large rectangular plaza, flanked on one side by a pyramid and on the opposite side by a lower and longer building, called a range structure. E Groups were laid out so their architectural focal points aligned with the sunrise on the solstices and equinoxes. Their astronomical orientation hints that the gatherings in Yaxuná's E-Group plaza centered around observances of key seasonal shifts, presaging the detailed agricultural calendars that developed later in the Maya lowlands. Amid these roles, it also served as a venue for early political actors to experiment with new kinds of leadership and power. See Collins, "Selective Memory"; Collins, "Incised Lines"; Freidel et al., *Maya E Groups*; Stanton, "Founding of Yaxuná."

8. Stanton, "Founding of Yaxuná"; Stanton and Collins, "Role of Middle Preclassic Placemaking."

9. Inomata et al., "Development of Sedentary Communities."

10. Cagnato, "Gathering and Sowing."

11. Piperno and Flannery, "Earliest Archaeological Maize."

12. For excellent discussion of the archaeology and historical ecology of mobile foragers, see Thompson, "Whispers on the Landscape."

13. See appendix B.

14. When I use the term *permanent*, I am talking about multigenerational and continuous relationships between multiple generations of people (often biological kin but not necessarily) and particular places.

15. Cagnato, "Gathering and Sowing"; Flannery, *Maya Subsistence*; Piperno, "Origins of Plant Cultivation."

16. The transition to stone dwellings at Late Formative settlements in the Yaxunah ejido is discussed in Stanton et al., *Archaeological Investigations at Yaxuná*.

17. Brown and Bey, *Pathways to Complexity*; Houk, Arroyo, and Powis, *Approaches to Monumental Landscapes*.

18. Stanton, "Founding of Yaxuná"; Stanton and Ardren, "Middle Formative of Yucatan."

19. For more on the ancient Maya monumental tradition at Yaxuná, see Collins, "Selective Memory"; Stanton, "Founding of Yaxuná"; Stanton and Ardren, "Middle Formative of Yucatan"; Stanton and Freidel, "Placing the Centre"; Stanton et al., *Archaeological Investigations at Yaxuná*.

20. For more on early urbanism in Yaxuná, see Collins, "Incised Lines"; Stanton, "Founding of Yaxuná."

21. See Hutson, Magnoni, and Stanton, "'All that is solid'"; Hutson et al., "Memory and Power."

22. Ceramic data suggest a Late Formative construction date for the Jach and P'aak Groups. They are the two oldest permanent homesites documented at Tzacauil. For more details, see Fisher, "Maya Farming Communities."

23. Ceramic data suggest that the Chamal, Sáastun, and Kaan Groups were built during the transition from the Late Formative to the Terminal Formative, or in the very early Terminal Formative. For more details, see Fisher, "Maya Farming Communities."

24. The open spaces between and around homesites at Tzacauil were investigated through a variety of methods, including what I call intrasettlement trench excavations. For more information about these trenches and what we found, see Fisher, "Maya Farming Communities," 146–48.

25. For more detail on the walkability of Tzacauil, see Fisher, "Walking Rural."

26. See Fisher, "Maya Farming Communities," 288–89.

27. Chase, Chase, and Haviland, "Classic Maya City."

28. For discussion of the "vacant ceremonial center" model of Maya settlement, see Chase et al., "Classic Maya City."

29. Ringle, "Settlement Patterns of Komchen"; Tourtellot, "Ancient Maya Settlements"; Turner and Harrison, *Pulltrouser Swamp*.

30. See, for example, Chase et al., "Airborne LiDAR"; Stanton et al., "'Structure' Density."

31. See, for example, Farahani et al., "Identifying 'Plantscapes'"; Hutson et al., "Beyond the Buildings"; Isendahl, "Agro-Urban Landscapes."

32. For discussion of low-density agrarian-urbanism in the Maya area and elsewhere, see Fletcher, "Low-Density, Agrarian-Based Urbanism"; Isendahl and Smith, "Sustainable Agrarian Urbanism"; Lucero et al., "From 'Collapse' to Urban Diaspora"; Scarborough, Chase, and Chase, "Low-Density Urbanism"; Smith, "Classic Maya Settlement Clusters."

33. Redfield and Villa Rojas, *Chan Kom*; Wauchope, *Modern Maya Houses*.

34. For more information on Maya homegardening and the traditional ecological knowledge involved with homegardening practices, see De Clerck and Negreros-Castillo, "Plant Species"; de la Cerda and Guerra Mukul, "Homegarden Production"; Flores-Delgadillo et al., "Sustainable System"; Rico-Gray et al., "Species Composition."

35. De Clerck and Negreros-Castillo, "Plant Species."

36. Redfield and Villa Rojas, *Chan Kom*, 64.

37. Fisher, "Role of Infield Agriculture"; Killion, "Cultivation Intensity"; Marcus, "Plant World."

38. Roys, Scholes, and Adams, "Census and Inspection."

39. See, for example, Fisher, "Role of Infield Agriculture."

40. For an example, see Manzanilla and Barba, "Study of Activities."

41. Chase and Chase, "Scale and Intensity"; Chase et al., "Airborne LiDAR."

42. Chase and Chase, "Urbanism and Anthropogenic Landscapes."

43. Chase and Chase, "Symbolic Egalitarianism."

44. Chase and Chase, "Path Dependency."

45. Arnauld, Michelet, and Nondédéo, "Living Together"; Lemonnier and Vannière, "Agrarian Features, Farmsteads, and Homesteads."

46. The history of Chan, as I'm drawing on it here, is described in Robin, *Everyday Life Matters*; Robin, *Chan*.

47. Wyatt, *Gardens on Hills*.

48. Robin, *Everyday Life Matters*; Robin, *Chan*.

49. Lentz et al., "Agroforestry and Agricultural Production."

50. I have written more about stone gathering and interpreting pyramids through early farming practices elsewhere; see Fisher, "Monumentality as traditional ecological knowledge."

51. See Fisher, "Maya Farming Communities," 241–44, for more information and images of this small modified reservoir.

52. Archaeologists interested in a more detailed description of the methodology used to excavate trenches in intrasettlement lands can refer to Fisher, "Maya Farming Communities," 146–48.

53. For the breakdown of jar fragment to bowl fragment ratios by period across the Tzacauil ceramic assemblage, see Fisher, "Maya Farming Communities," 201. In general, when looking at just the Middle Formative sherds or looking at the Middle, Late, and Terminal Formative sherds combined, the ratio remains consistent at about two-thirds bowl fragments and one-third jar fragments. By the Classic period, the ceramic assemblage veers more towards jars: the Classic ceramics in the Kaan and Pool Groups included about 70–80 percent jar fragments, with the remainder being bowls. This may suggest changing culinary practices across the site history, though more analysis would be needed to confirm this.

54. For more detailed descriptions of the excavations of these heirloom caches, see Fisher, "Maya Farming Communities," 185, 209.

55. See appendix B for comparisons of ceramic densities across investigated Tzacauil homesites.

56. My sincere thanks to my friend and colleague Dr. Mario Zimmermann for helping me with soil chemistry analysis and ceramic residue analysis through the holiday season of 2017, and thanks to Dr. Lilia Fernández Souza and Dr. Héctor Hernández Álvarez for allowing me to use the UADY lab space. The protocols that Mario and I used and the full results can be found described in Fisher, "Maya Farming Communities," 152–59.

57. See Manzanilla and Barba, "Study of Activities"; Middleton et al., "Study of Archaeological Floors."

58. See Barba and Córdoba, "El potencial de hidrógeno"; Middleton et al., "Study of Archaeological Floors."

59. Glover and Stanton, "Assessing the Role"; Webster et al., "Stalagmite Evidence."

60. My deep thanks to my friend and colleague Harper Dine for all her help at Tzacauil, and for our continuing collaborations in the Yaxunah ejido.

CHAPTER FOUR

1. Dickinson and Whigham, "Competition among Surface Roots"; Gillespie, Bocanegra-Ferguson, and Jiménez Osornio, "Propagation of Ramón."

2. Querejeta et al., "Utilization of Bedrock Water."

3. See appendix A for a time line of Tzacauil and the Yaxunah ejido. Ceramic typologies are the only source of chronological data available for Tzacauil. This can

be frustrating, given that ceramic dating can leave vast windows of multiple centuries. Sealed contexts—candidates for more reliable dating methods—were extremely hard to find at Tzacauil, and so here I'm relying on pottery typologies to estimate dates. Because there is some overlap in the ceramic styles of the Late Classic and Terminal Classic, and because often potsherds from those periods occur together at Tzacauil, assigning dates is challenging. Acknowledging this, I will try to distinguish in this chapter whenever I can between Late (AD 550–700) and Terminal Classic (and between the latter's two subperiods, from AD 700–850 and from AD 850–1100). From time to time, I will also use "Classic" to refer to this period (AD 550–1100) more generally in the ejido's history.

4. Hutson, Magnoni, and Stanton, "'All that is solid.'"

5. Stanton et al., "'Structure' Density."

6. Guenter, "Queen of Cobá."

7. Stanton et al., "'Structure' Density."

8. The Mukul Group is the only homesite at Tzacauil that did not undergo substantial, horizontal excavations. Only a small test pit was dug into the Mukul Group's main platform. This yielded enough ceramic data to estimate its chronology (contemporaneous with the Pool and Kaan Late to Terminal Classic occupations) but not enough to know very much about its construction history. The reason that less work was done at Mukul was because the group had slipped by the site mappers about a decade before my excavations; *mukul* means "hidden" in Yucatec. Because it wasn't on my map, I hadn't factored it into my fieldwork timeline or budget. Fortunately, the neighboring Kaan Group to the south and the Pool Group to the north offer portals into the transformations that took place during this dynamic chapter of edge land history.

9. Ceramic data suggest that the Pool Group was built and primarily occupied in the Late Classic, though the presence of pottery dating to the first and second parts of the Terminal Classic indicate the group continued to be at least periodically occupied for several years longer. See Fisher, "Maya Farming Communities," 284.

10. Seligson et al., "Burnt Lime Production."

11. There is some evidence for earlier Late Formative activity on this bedrock outcrop. Around the time the pit was filled in, a ring of stones had been laid out nearby as the foundation for a round building. Our team excavated this Terminal Formative structure (Structure 6A-sub), but because the Late Classic occupants had recycled some of its stones into their own buildings and planted a new house (Structure 6A) right on top of it, we were left with more questions than answers about its role in the Formative Tzacauil community. However, the size and shape of the buried building resembled small ancillary structures our team documented near the Chamal Group and the Sáastun Group—two of Tzacauil's three homesites founded in the Terminal Formative. No similar ancillary structure had been found associated with the third homesite founded in the Terminal Formative, the Kaan Group, but this small building, buried beneath the later Classic cluster of three structures, is just a short walk away from the Kaan basal platform. Perhaps this buried structure was used by the Terminal Formative Kaan residents as a kitchen,

extra sleeping room, or storage shed associated with intensive cultivation in the soil flat just to the south. While these questions remain open, the pit kiln and small structure buried beneath the Late Classic structures of the Pool Group hint at the important role bedrock played in the Formative Tzacauil community. The Late and Terminal Formative settlers had chosen homesites on isolated bedrock outcrops surrounded by soil, but that preference doesn't mean they completely ignored the bedrock-rich areas near their dwellings. See Fisher, "Maya Farming Communities," 281–83.

12. Let me provide a little more detail about excavations. On top of the newly raised surface, the builders laid the stone foundations for their three small buildings. For the southernmost of the three (Structure 6A), the builders simply superimposed a rectangular foundation on and around the preexisting round foundation (Structure 6A-sub), adding only a thin layer of soil and cobbles as a new floor on top of the old building. See Fisher, "Maya Farming Communities," 281–83.

13. To add more detail to this excavation description: for the second structure in the cluster, the builders mounded up a pile of fist-sized cobbles on top of the filled-in pit kiln, forming an oval (Structure 6C). This amorphous cobble pile, without any formal walls, is a common building type found in the Late and Terminal Classic urban settlement at Yaxuná and would have supported an apsidal wood-and-thatch dwelling. See Fisher, "Maya Farming Communities," 281–83.

14. See appendix B for general artifact comparisons across all Tzacauil homesites, and see Fisher, "Maya Farming Communities," for more detailed descriptions.

15. See appendix B for ceramic density comparisons.

16. Fedick et al., "Adaptation of Maya Homegardens"; Kepecs and Boucher, "Pre-Hispanic Cultivation."

17. Stanton et al., *Archaeological Investigations at Yaxuná.*

18. Ceramic data suggests the later reoccupation of the Kaan Group dated primarily to the Late Classic. Sherds dating to the first part of the Terminal Classic (AD 700–850) were also recovered, but no diagnostic sherds from the second part of the Terminal Classic (AD 850–1100) were found in Kaan Group excavations. See Fisher, "Maya Farming Communities," 280.

19. Hutson et al., "'All that is solid.'"

20. Stanton et al., *Archaeological Investigations at Yaxuná*; Tiesler et al., *Before Kukulcán.*

21. Stanton et al., *Archaeological Investigations at Yaxuná.*

22. Tiesler et al., *Before Kukulcán.*

23. Ardren, "Death Became Her."

24. Tiesler et al., *Before Kukulcán.*

25. McAnany, *Living with the Ancestors.*

26. Nash and Colwell, "NAGPRA at 30."

27. Stanton et al., *Archaeological Investigations at Yaxuná.*

28. For more on the few nonlocal artifacts recovered from Classic contexts in Tzacauil, see Fisher, "Maya Farming Communities," 284–85. See also Torres Ochoa, "La producción de artefactos."

29. See appendix B for artifact counts; see Fisher, "Maya Farming Communities" for more detailed reports on the artifact assemblage recovered from Tzacauil.

30. Fisher, "Walking Rural."

31. *Jaltun* is the Yucatec Maya word for these pan-shaped cavities in bedrock.

32. Hence the name: *t'uup* is the Yucatec Maya word for the lastborn child.

33. The height of the walls before collapse was estimated to be about one to one-and-a-half meters, which is comparable to modern *albarrada* constructions.

34. See appendix B for comparisons of sherd counts and ceramic mass by homesite.

35. Farriss, *Maya Society under Colonial Rule*.

36. Farriss, 210.

37. Restall, *Maya World*, 103.

38. This discussion of the political history of Yaxuná draws primarily from Stanton et al., *Archaeological Investigations at Yaxuná*.

39. From AD 250 to 400, a new royal palace was built at Yaxuná, connected to the Formative-era North Acropolis with a sacbe. Inside the North Acropolis, a king was buried in an elaborate royal tomb. Bioarchaeological analysis of his remains tells us that he was not local but instead perhaps grew in the kingdoms of the southern Maya lowlands. This foreigner's presence in one of the great monumental complexes of Formative Yaxuná hints at a political takeover, a usurper's effort to legitimize a new reign through symbolic connection with the past. See Tiesler et al., *Before Kukulcán*.

40. Ardren, "Politics of Place."

41. Marengo Camacho, "Análisis funcional de cerámica"; Suhler, "Excavations at the North Acropolis."

42. Novelo Rincón, "La arquitectura del grupo Puuc."

43. Stanton et al., *Archaeological Investigations at Yaxuná*.

44. Ambrosino, Ardren, and Stanton, "History of Warfare at Yaxuná."

45. The Classic Maya Collapse is one of the most studied periods in Maya archaeology. For key coverage, see, for example, Aimers, "What Maya Collapse?"; Bazy and Inomata, "Multiple Waves of Political Disintegration"; Douglas et al., "Drought, Agricultural Adaptation"; Dunning, Beach, and Luzzadder-Beach, "Kax and Kol"; Haug et al., "Climate and the Collapse"; Kennett et al., "Drought-Induced CIvil Conflict"; Masson, "Maya Collapse Cycles"; Turner and Sabloff, "Classic Period Collapse."

46. For discussion of unsustainable forestry in the ancient Maya world, see Beach et al., "Stability and Instability"; Lentz and Hockaday, "Tikal Timbers and Temples"; Lentz et al., "Imperial Resource Management." For discussion of long-term forest management in the ancient Maya world, see Ford and Nigh, *Maya Forest Garden*; Lentz et al., "Agroforestry and Agricultural Production."

47. Dunning and Beach, "Farms and Forests"; Kunen, *Ancient Maya Life*.

48. Luzzadder-Beach and Beach, "Arising from the Wetlands"; Luzzadder-Beach, Beach, and Dunning, "Wetland Fields as Mirrors"; Pohl and Bloom, "Prehistoric Maya Farming"; Turner and Harrison, *Pulltrouser Swamp*.

49. Iannone, Prufer, and Chase, "Resilience and Vulnerability"; Robin, *Chan*; Smyth et al., "Perfect Storm."

50. Nelson et al., "Climate Challenges."
51. Lucero, Fletcher, and Coningham, "From 'Collapse' to Urban Diaspora."
52. Nelson et al., "Climate Challenges."
53. Johnson, "Late and Terminal Classic Power Shifts."
54. See also Fisher, "Maize Politics."
55. Fisher.
56. Dine et al., "Famine Foods and Food Security"; Puleston, "Role of Ramón."

CHAPTER FIVE

1. The story of Nachi Cocom and the Xiu-Cocom rivalry is recorded in Diego de Landa's 1566 account *Relaciones de las cosas de Yucatán*, which has been translated and annotated in Tozzer, *Landa's Relación*. Tozzer's volume includes an account of the story by Gaspar Antonio Chi, known as Herrera, which may have been part of Landa's original report. Further analysis is provided in Marcus, "From Centralized Systems to City-States" and Roys, *Book of Chilam Balam*. I thank Professor Andrew Shryock and fellow students in his Winter 2013 hospitality seminar at the University of Michigan for their help in developing my interpretations of this narrative.

2. For a comparative case study of drawing lines and dispossessing the Indigenous of lands in northeastern North America, see Cronon, *Changes in the Land*.

3. For comparison with Spanish divide-and-conquer strategies in the Valley of Mexico, see Gibson, *Aztecs under Spanish Rule*.

4. For accounts of Indigenous subjugation in colonial Yucatán, see Chamberlain, *Conquest and Colonization*; Clendinnen, *Ambivalent Conquests*; Quezada, *Maya Lords and Lordship*.

5. Steffen et al., "Anthropocene."

6. For critiques of the Anthropocene concept, see for example Yusoff, *Billion Black Anthropocenes*.

7. Haraway et al., "Anthropologists Are Talking"; Haraway, *Staying With the Trouble*; Haraway and Tsing, "Reflections on the Plantationocene"; Tsing, *Mushroom at the End*.

8. See, for example, Carney, "Subsistence in the Plantationocene"; Davis et al., "Anthropocene, Capitalocene, . . . Plantationocene?"; Wolford, "Plantationocene."

9. Glissant, *Caribbean Discourse*; McKittrick, "Plantation Futures"; Wynter, "Novel and History."

10. See appendix A for a time line of historical events in the Yaxunah ejido lands.

11. Ardren, *Social Identities*.

12. Roys, *Political Geography*; Roys, *Indian Background of Colonial Yucatan*.

13. Chamberlain, *Conquest and Colonization*; Clendinnen, *Ambivalent Conquests*.

14. Restall, *Maya World*.

15. Fisher, "Maize Politics."

16. Farriss, *Maya Society under Colonial Rule*; Restall, *Maya World*.

17. The colonial town of Yaxunah is located under the modern town of Yaxunah, and the remains of Hacienda Cetelac are in the modern Yaxunah ejido, in the southern part of the ancient city of Yaxuná.

18. Roys, *Book of Chilam Balam*.

19. Farriss, *Maya Society under Colonial Rule*.

20. Restall, *Black Middle*.

21. Bracamonte y Sosa, *Amos y sirvientes*; Machuca Gallegos, *Los hacendados de Yucatán*.

22. Bracamonte y Sosa, *Los mayas y la tierra*.

23. Patch, "Decolonization"; Patch, *Maya and Spaniard*.

24. Patch, *Maya and Spaniard*.

25. Meyers, *Outside the Hacienda Walls*; Wells, *Yucatán's Gilded Age*.

26. Patch, *Maya and Spaniard*; Rugeley, *Yucatán's Maya Peasantry*.

27. Reed, *Caste War of Yucatan*; Rugeley, *Yucatán's Maya Peasantry*.

28. Güémez Pineda, *Mayas, gobierno, y tierras*.

29. Ortiz Yam, "De milperos a henequeneros"; Ortiz Yam, "Formación de Ejidos."

30. Ortiz Yam, "De milperos a henequeneros."

31. Güémez Pineda, *Mayas, gobierno, y tierras*.

32. Ortiz Yam, "Formación de ejidos."

33. Patch, "Decolonization."

34. Patch.

35. Güémez Pineda, *Mayas, gobierno, y tierras*; Ortiz Yam, "De milperos a henequeneros"; Ortiz Yam, "Formación de ejidos."

36. Ortiz Yam, "Formación de ejidos."

37. See appendix A's time line.

38. For coverage of the research conducted to date at Hacienda Cetelac, see Alexander, "Colonial Period Archaeology"; Alexander, "Community Organization"; Alexander, *Yaxcabá*; Alexander, "Maya Settlement Shifts"; Alexander and Hernández Álvarez, "Agropastoralism and Household Ecology."

39. Bascopé, "Household Ecology"; Magnoni, Ardren, and Hutson, "Tourism in the Mundo Maya."

40. Alexander, "Colonial Period Archaeology," 454.

41. Rugeley, *Yucatán's Maya Peasantry*.

42. Rugeley.

43. Rugeley.

44. Patch, "Decolonization."

45. Reed, *Caste War of Yucatan*; Rugeley, *Yucatán's Maya Peasantry*.

46. Reed, *Caste War of Yucatan*; Rugeley, *Yucatán's Maya Peasantry*.

47. Reed, *Caste War of Yucatan*.

48. Alexander, "Colonial Period Archaeology."

49. Gil, *Age of Porfirio Díaz*.

50. Chacón, "Salvador Alvarado," 80.

51. Diggles, "Popular Response."

52. Chacón, "Salvador Alvarado."

53. Wells, *Yucatán's Gilded Age.*

54. Evans, *Bound in Twine*; Wells, *Yucatán's Gilded Age.*

55. Wells, *Yucatán's Gilded Age.*

56. Chacón, "Salvador Alvarado," 182.

57. Gálvez, *Eating NAFTA*; Ortiz Yam, "De milperos a henequeneros"; Torres-Mazuera, "Communal and Indigenous Landholding."

58. Chacón, "Salvador Alvarado"; Joseph, *Revolution from Without.*

59. Chacón, "Salvador Alvarado"; Joseph, *Revolution from Without.*

60. Joseph, *Revolution from Without*, 128.

61. Spenser, "Workers against Socialism?"

62. Beaucage, "Third Wave of Modernization"; Joseph, *Revolution from Without.*

63. The story of Yaxunah's founding after the Caste War was told to me by members of the community. The account has previously been published by other scholars working there. See Hernández Álvarez, "Memoria e identidad"; Hernández Álvarez, "Etnoarqueología de grupos domésticos mayas"; Rejón Patrón, "La comunidad de Yaxuná"; Rosales González and Rejón Patrón, "Las redes que tejen un pueblo."

64. Hernández Álvarez, "Etnoarqueología de grupos domésticos mayas."

65. Gálvez, *Eating NAFTA.*

66. Fox, *Politics of Food.*

67. Gálvez, *Eating NAFTA.*

68. Diggles, "Popular Response."

69. Chamberlain, *Conquest and Colonization.*

70. I gleaned this information about the Nachi Cocom Cozumel Beach Club and Water Sports Center from its website, http://cozumelnachicocom.com.

71. Carvalho Rodrigues, "Expropiación de tierras ejidales."

CHAPTER SIX

1. Stephens, *Incidents of Travel*, 161.

2. Stephens, 161–62.

3. Stephens, 162.

4. Stephens, 163.

5. Stephens, 163.

6. Stephens, 164.

7. Stephens, 295.

8. Stephens, 295.

9. Stephens, 280.

10. Wade, "Ghosts in the Museum."

11. Hernández Álvarez and Zimmermann, *Sendas del henequén*; Wells, *Yucatán's Gilded Age.*

12. Patch, "Decolonization"; Reed, *Caste War of Yucatan*; Rugeley, *Yucatán's Maya Peasantry*.

13. Tsing, *Mushroom at the End*.

14. In August 2022, right before I began my revisions on this manuscript, I had the wonderful experience of participating in the Colby Summer Institute in Environmental Humanities. This workshop infused new insights into this text, and one insight that remains especially salient to me is this idea of embracing infinite nonarrival, as articulated by Dr. Mel Chen. I'm thankful to Mel and the others in the Summer Institute for so generously sharing these and so many other ideas.

15. I'm again grateful for the writings of Robin Wall Kimmerer, who so beautifully helps her readers recognize that "all flourishing is mutual." Kimmerer, *Braiding Sweetgrass*, 20.

16. For more discussions of positionality in Yucatán archaeology, see Fryer, "Reflecting on Positionality"; Hutson et al., "Reflecting."

17. I will be grateful always to those who made the PIPCY camp feel like a home during my seasons there, especially Nelda Issa Marengo Camacho for her exceptional skills as project manager, and Travis Stanton for buying us powdered Gatorade, cashews, soy milk, and all the foods that are not available to projects in the Petén. Thanks also to Aline Magnoni and Traci Ardren.

18. For more reflections on eating on archaeological projects based in Yaxunah, see Fisher and Ardren, "Partaking in Culinary Heritage."

19. Hargrove, "History of the Calorie."

20. Fitting, *Struggle for Maize*; Gálvez, *Eating NAFTA*.

21. Gálvez.

22. For further discussions of interchangeability and plantations, see Tsing, *Mushroom at the End*.

23. This is a central idea Gálvez develops in her excellent book, *Eating NAFTA*.

24. See Lawrence et al., "Linking Changes."

25. Hanks, "Plurality of Temporal Reckoning," 6.

26. Hanks, 8.

27. For a discussion of traditional Maya agriculture auguries, or seasonal signals like these, see Hanks, 8.

28. Hanks, *Referential Practice*, 355.

29. Coverage of the events surrounding this proposed photovoltaic park can be found in "Piden respeto al pueblo"; Reyes Maturano, "Yucatán ante un nuevo horizonte." I also recommend the Environmental Justice Atlas (https://ejatlas.org/) as a starting place for learning about this and other environmental justice conflicts in Yucatán, particularly for its attention to compiling local news coverage of these conflicts.

30. CEMDA, "Consulta indígena."

31. "La UNAM se deslinda."

32. "Machetazos entre ejidatarios."

33. See "Piden respeto al pueblo"; Reyes Maturano, "Yucatán ante un nuevo horizonte."

34. Thompson, *Maya History and Religion*; Villa Rojas, *Maya of East Central Quintana Roo*.

35. Gayou Soto, "Habitantes de Ixil."

36. "Ejidatarios de Ixil."

37. Gayou Soto, "Habitantes de Ixil."

38. "No estoy en contra."

39. Gayou Soto, "Habitantes de Ixil."

40. "Júbilo en Ixil."

41. "Timul le 'invade.'"

42. Terán, Rasmussen, and May Cauich, *Las plantas de la milpa*, 38.

43. Information for this segment was drawn from Victoria, Eastmond, and Sánchez, "From Conquest to Jatropha."

44. For more on jatropha plantations in Yucatán, see Eastmond, Sacramento Rivero, and Sweitz, *Quest for Jatropha*.

45. The average exchange rate for May 2017 was about 18.8 Mexican pesos per 1 US dollar.

46. The question of setting equitable weekly wages for project staff is an area that can use ongoing attention and improvement, and I'm grateful to my colleagues in community-engaged archaeology for discussions on the topic. My thanks in particular go to Tiffany C. Fryer and Sarah Kurnick. On projects in the Yaxunah ejido, weekly wage rates are set through an agreement among project directors, community authorities, and ejidatarios. Consultation with the Mexican National Institute of Anthropology and History, in my understanding, is also important in determining wage rates. I'll note that in the summer 2022 field season at Yaxunah, the weekly wage was raised to two thousand pesos.

47. On a more hopeful note, there are promising developments in anticolonial archaeology thanks to the efforts of leaders in community-engaged and Indigenous archaeology, as well as in organizations like the Society of Black Archaeologists and the Disabled Archaeologists Network. See, for example, Atalay, *Community-Based Archaeology*; Colwell-Chanthaphonh et al., "Premise and Promise of Indigenous Archaeology"; McAnany, *Maya Cultural Heritage*.

48. Cámara, "Zona arqueológico de Dzibilchaltún."

49. Rejón and Rodríguez, "Ejidatarios, contra Kekén."

50. Estrada Saavedra, *La comunidad armada rebelde*.

51. Reed, *Caste War of Yucatan*.

52. Patch, "Decolonization"; Rugeley, *Yucatán's Maya Peasantry*.

53. Farriss, *Maya Society under Colonial Rule*.

54. See Alatas, *Myth of the Lazy Native*.

55. Stephens, *Incidents of Travel*, 327–28.

56. Stephens, 328.

57. The reviews of Coole Chepa Chi I quote here are all public posts on Yelp, accessible as of October 2022 at www.yelp.com/biz/restaurante-coole-chepa-chi-uxmal.

BIBLIOGRAPHY

Aimers, James J. "What Maya Collapse? Terminal Classic Variation in the Maya Lowlands." *Journal of Archaeological Research* 15, no. 4 (2007): 329–77.

Alatas, Syed Hussein. *The Myth of the Lazy Native: A Study of the Image of the Malays, Filipinos and Javanese from the 16th to the 20th Century and Its Function in the Ideology of Colonial Capitalism*. London: Frank Cass, 1977.

Albuquerque, Ulysses Paulino, Luiz Vital Fernandes Cruz da Cunha, Reinaldo Farias Paiva de Lucena, and Rômulo Romeu Nóbrega Alves, eds. *Methods and Techniques in Ethnobiology and Ethnoecology*. New York: Springer, 2014.

Alcocer Puerto, Elias M. "El ecoturismo cultural dentro de una comunidad maya de Yucatán." Master's thesis, Centro de Investigación y Estudios Avanzados, Instituto Politécnico Nacional, Mexico City, 2007.

———. "Manejo sustentable de recursos naturales y culturales por parte de una comunidad maya de Yucatán: El caso de Yaxunah." Licentiate thesis, Universidad Autónoma de Yucatán, Mérida, 2001.

Alcocer Puerto, Elias M., Grace Bascopé, and Nidelvia Vela Cano. "El turismo en una comunidad maya yucateca: Pasado, presente, y un probable futuro." *Teoría y Praxis* 8 (2010): 95–112.

Alexander, Rani T. "Colonial Period Archaeology of the Parroquia de Yaxcaba, Yucatan, Mexico." PhD diss., University of New Mexico, 1993.

———. "Community Organization in the Parroquia de Yaxcaba, Yucatan, Mexico, 1750–1847." *Ancient Mesoamerica* 9, no. 1 (1998): 39–54.

———. "Maya Settlement Shifts and Agrarian Ecology in Yucatán, 1800–2000." *Journal of Anthropological Research* 62, no. 4 (2006): 449–70.

———. *Yaxcabá and the Caste War of Yucatán: An Archaeological Perspective*. Albuquerque: University of New Mexico Press, 2004.

Alexander, Rani T., and Héctor Hernández Álvarez. "Agropastoralism and Household Ecology in Yucatán after the Spanish Invasion." *Environmental Archaeology* 23, no. 1 (2018): 69–79.

Ambrosino, James, Traci Ardren, and Travis W. Stanton. "The History of Warfare at Yaxuná." In *Ancient Mesoamerican Warfare*, edited by M. K. Brown and T. W. Stanton, 109–23. Walnut Creek, CA: AltaMira Press, 2003.

Amrith, Sunil S. *Crossing the Bay of Bengal: The Furies of Nature and the Fortunes of Migrants*. Cambridge, MA: Harvard University Press, 2015.

Ardren, Traci. "Death Became Her: Images of Female Power from Yaxuna Burials." In *Ancient Maya Women*, edited by Traci Ardren, 68–88. Walnut Creek, CA: AltaMira Press, 2002.

———, ed. *Her Cup for Sweet Cacao: Food in Ancient Maya Society*. Austin: University of Texas Press, 2020.

———. "Now Serving Maya Heritage: Culinary Tourism in Yaxunah, Yucatan, Mexico." *Food and Foodways* 26, no. 4 (2018): 290–312.

———. "The Politics of Place: Architecture and Cultural Change at the Xkanha Group, Yaxuna, Yucatan, Mexico." PhD diss., Yale University, 1997.

———. *Social Identities in the Classic Maya Northern Lowlands: Gender, Age, Memory, and Place*. Austin: University of Texas Press, 2015.

Arnauld, M. Charlotte, Dominique Michelet, and Philippe Nondédéo. "Living Together in Río Bec Houses: Coresidence, Rank, and Alliance." *Ancient Mesoamerica* 24 (2013): 469–93.

Asensio, José María, Cristóbal de Pedraza, and Diego de Landa. *Relaciones de Yucatán*: Colección de documentos inéditos relativos al descubrimiento de las antiguas posesiones españolas de ultramar. Madrid: La Real Academia de Historia, 1898.

Atalay, Sonya. *Community-Based Archaeology: Research with, by, and for Indigenous and Local Communities*. Berkeley: University of California Press, 2012.

Ayora-Diaz, Steffan Igor. *Foodscapes, Foodfields, and Identities in Yucatán*. New York: Berghahn Books, 2012.

———. "Gastronomic Inventions and the Aesthetics of Regional Food: The Naturalization of Yucatecan Taste." *Etnofoor* 24, no. 2 (2012): 57–76.

Baka, Jennifer. "Making Space for Energy: Wasteland Development, Enclosures, and Energy Dispossessions." *Antipode* 49, no. 4 (2017): 977–96.

Bandy, Matthew S. "Energetic Efficiency and Political Expediency in Titicaca Basin Raised Field Agriculture." *Journal of Anthropological Archaeology* 24, no. 3 (2005): 271–96.

Barba, Luis, and José Luis Córdoba. "El potencial de hidrógeno en la arqueología." *Antropológicas* 6 (1991): 84–92.

Barrera-Bassols, Narciso, and Victor M. Toledo. "Ethnoecology of the Yucatec Maya: Symbolism, Knowledge and Management of Natural Resources." *Journal of Latin American Geography* 4, no. 1 (2005): 9–41.

Bascopé, Grace. "The Household Ecology of Disease Transmission: Childhood Illness in a Yucatán Maya Community." PhD diss., Southern Methodist University, 2005.

Bautista, Francisco, and J. Alfred Zinck. "Construction of a Yucatec Maya Soil Classification and Comparison with the WRB Framework." *Journal of Ethnobiology and Ethnomedicine* 6, no. 7 (2010): 1–11.

Bayless, Rick. *Mexico: One Plate at a Time.* Season 11, episode 12, "Pit Cooking, Sacred and Smoky." Video, 26:48. Aired December 2, 2016 on PBS. www .rickbayless.com/tv-books/mexico-one-plate-at-a-time-season-11/#1473874602303-b1afd0ae-b423.

Bazy, Damien, and Takeshi Inomata. "Multiple Waves of Political Disintegration in the Classic Maya Collapse: New Insights from the Excavation of Group D, Ceibal, Guatemala." *Journal of Field Archaeology* 42, no. 2 (2017): 82–96.

Beach, Timothy, Sheryl Luzzadder-Beach, Duncan Cook, Samantha Krause, Colin Doyle, Sara Eshleman, Greta Wells et al. "Stability and Instability on Maya Lowlands Tropical Hillslope Soils." *Resilience and Bio-Geomorphic Systems—Proceedings of the 48th Binghamton Geomorphology Symposium* 305 (2018): 185–208.

Beaucage, Pierre. "The Third Wave of Modernization: Liberalism, Salinismo, and Indigenous Peasants in Mexico." In *The Third Wave of Modernization in Latin America: Cultural Perspectives on Neoliberalism*, edited by Lynne Phillips. Delaware: Scholarly Resources, 1998.

Besky, Sarah. *The Darjeeling Distinction: Labor and Justice on Fair-Trade Tea Plantations in India.* Berkeley: University of California Press, 2014.

Borras, Saturnino M., and Jennifer C. Franco. "Global Land Grabbing and Trajectories of Agrarian Change: A Preliminary Analysis." *Journal of Agrarian Change* 12, no. 1 (2012): 34–59.

Bracamonte y Sosa, Pedro. *Amos y sirvientes: Las haciendas de Yucatán, 1789–1860.* Mérida: Universidad Autónoma de Yucatán, 1993.

———. *Los mayas y la tierra: La propiedad indígena en el Yucatán colonial.* Mérida: Centro de Investigación y Estudios Superiores en Antropología Social, 2003.

Brady, James Edward, and Keith M. Prufer. *In the Maw of the Earth Monster: Mesoamerican Ritual Cave Use.* Austin: University of Texas Press, 2005.

Braje, Todd J., Thomas P. Leppard, Scott M. Fitzpatrick, and Jon M. Erlandson. "Archaeology, Historical Ecology and Anthropogenic Island Ecosystems." *Environmental Conservation* 44, no. 3 (2017): 286–97.

Bricker, Victoria, Eleuterio Po'ot Yah, and Ofelia Dzul de Po'ot. *A Dictionary of the Maya Language: As Spoken in Hocabá, Yucatán.* Salt Lake City: University of Utah Press, 1998.

Brown, M. Kathryn, and George J. Bey III, eds. *Pathways to Complexity: A View from the Maya Lowlands.* Gainesville: University of Florida Press, 2018.

Bullard, Robert D. *Dumping in Dixie: Race, Class, and Environmental Quality.* Boulder, CO: Westview Press, 2000.

Burton, Monica. "90% of Noma Mexico's Much Cheaper Bar Menu Will Go to Charity." *Eater*, May 1, 2017. www.eater.com/2017/5/1/15501746/90-of-noma-mexicos-much-cheaper-bar-menu-will-go-to-charity.

Cagnato, Clarissa. "Gathering and Sowing across the Central Maya Lowlands: A Review of Plant Use by Preceramic Peoples and the Early to Middle Preclassic Maya." *Ancient Mesoamerica* 32, no. 3 (2021): 486–501.

Cairns, Malcolm F., ed. *Shifting Cultivation and Environmental Change: Indigenous People, Agriculture, and Forest Conservation.* New York: Routledge, 2015.

Cámara, Jesús. "Zona arqueológica de Dzibilchaltún perdió más de 4 mil visitas por huelga ejidal." *¡Por Esto!*, September 4, 2021. www.poresto.net/yucatan/2021/9/4/zona-arqueologica-de-dzibilchaltun-perdio-mas-de-mil-visitas-por-huelga-ejidal-280745.html.

Canavan, Hillary Dixler, Monica Burton, and Ryan Sutton. "Noma Named 'World's Best Restaurant'—Again." *Eater*, October 5, 2021. www.eater.com/22710694/worlds-50-best-restaurants-number-ones.

Cardeña, Estefanía. "De basurero al aire libre a Sendero Jurásico, parque y espacio para divulgar ciencia." *La Jornada Maya*, May 31, 2022. www.lajornadamaya.mx/yucatan/196695/de-basurero-al-aire-libre-a-sendero-jurasico-parque-y-espacio-para-divulgar-ciencia.

Carney, Judith A. "Subsistence in the Plantationocene: Dooryard Gardens, Agrobiodiversity, and the Subaltern Economies of Slavery." *Journal of Peasant Studies* 48, no. 5 (2021): 1075–99.

Carvalho Rodrigues, Lea. "Expropiación de tierras ejidales como estrategia gubernamental para el desarrollo del turismo de masas en la isla de Cozumel, México." In *Sin tierras no hay paraíso: Turismo, organizaciones agrarias y apropiación territorial en México*, PASOS Revista de Turismo y Patrimonio Cultural 15, edited by Gustavo Marín Guardado, 155–81. El Sauzal, Tenerife, Canary Islands, Spain: PASOS, 2015.

Castañeda, Quetzil E. "'We Are *Not* Indigenous!': The Maya Identity of Yucatan; An Introduction." *Journal of Latin American Anthropology* 9, no. 1 (2004): 36–63.

Centro Internacional de Mejoramiento de Maíz y Trigo (CIMMYT). "El restaurante Noma llega a Tulum y utilizará maíces sustentables de Yaxunah." CIMMYT, April 19, 2017. www.cimmyt.org/es/uncategorized/el-restaurante-noma-llega-a-tulum-y-utilizara-maices-sustentables-de-yaxunah/.

———. "Helping Farming Families Thrive while Fighting Climate Change in Mexico." CIMMYT, November 9, 2017. www.cimmyt.org/news/helping-farming-families-thrive-while-fighting-climate-change-in-mexico/.

———. "Sustainable Agriculture Poised to Save Mayan Rainforests from Deforestation." CIMMYT, November 21, 2016. www.cimmyt.org/news/sustainable-agriculture-poised-to-save-mayan-rainforests-from-deforestation/.

Centro Mexicano de Derecho Ambiental (CEMDA). "Consulta indígena para mega parque solar en Muna, Yucatán, incumple estándares internacionales." CEMDA, November 5, 2019. www.cemda.org.mx/consulta-indigena-para-mega-parque-solar-en-muna-yucatan-incumple-estandares-internacionales/.

Cepeda, Carolina, and Ariel Amoroso. *Experiences on Sustainable Rural Development and Biodiversity Conservation in the Yucatán Peninsula.* Mexico: The Nature Conservancy, 2016.

Chacón, Ramón D. "Salvador Alvarado and Agrarian Reform in Yucatán: Federal Obstruction of Regional Social Change." In *Land, Labor, and Capital in Modern Yucatán: Essays in Regional History and Political Economy*, edited by Jeffrey T. Brannon and Gilbert M. Joseph. Tuscaloosa: University of Alabama Press, 1991.

Chamberlain, Robert Stoner. *The Conquest and Colonization of Yucatan, 1517–1550*. New York: Octagon Books, 1966.

Chandra, Gowri. "Netflix's Chef's Table Is Unappetizing—As It Should Be." *Forbes*, March 28, 2019. www.forbes.com/sites/gowrichandra/2019/03/28 /netflixs-chefs-table-is-unappetizing-as-it-should-be/.

Chang, David, prod. *Ugly Delicious*. Season 1, episode 2, "Tacos." Netflix, February 23, 2018, 53:45. www.netflix.com/title/80170368.

Channick, "Robert. Rick Bayless' Frontera Foods sold to ConAgra; chef's brand staying in Chicago." *Chicago Tribune*, September 26, 2016. www.chicagotribune .com/business/ct-conagra-acquires-frontera-0927-biz-20160926-story.html.

Chase, Arlen F., and Diane Z. Chase. "Scale and Intensity in Classic Period Maya Agriculture: Terracing and Settlement at the 'Garden City' of Caracol, Belize." *Culture & Agriculture* 20 (1998): 60–77.

———. "Symbolic Egalitarianism and Homogenized Distributions in the Archaeological Record at Caracol, Belize: Method, Theory, and Complexity." *Research Reports in Belizean Archaeology* 6 (2009): 15–24.

———. "Urbanism and Anthropogenic Landscapes." *Annual Review of Anthropology* 45 (2016): 361–76.

Chase, Arlen F., Diane Z. Chase, John F. Weishampel, Jason B. Drake, Ramesh L. Shrestha, K. Clint Slatton, Jaime J. Awe, and William E. Carter. "Airborne LiDAR, Archaeology, and the Ancient Maya Landscape at Caracol, Belize." *Journal of Archaeological Science* 38, no. 2 (2011): 387–98.

Chase, Arlen F., and Vernon L. Scarborough. "Diversity, Resilience, and IHOPE-Maya: Using the Past to Inform the Present." *Archeological Papers of the American Anthropological Association* 24, no. 1 (2014): 1–10.

Chase, Diane Z., and Arlen F. Chase. "Path Dependency in the Rise and Denouement of a Classic Maya City: The Case of Caracol, Belize." *Archeological Papers of the American Anthropological Association* 24, no. 1 (2014): 142–54.

Chase, Diane Z., Arlen F. Chase, and William A. Haviland. "The Classic Maya City: Reconsidering the 'Mesoamerican Urban Tradition.'" *American Anthropologist* 92, no. 2 (1990): 499–506.

Chef's Table BBQ. "Rosalia Chay Chuc." Netflix, September 2, 2020, 43:08. www .netflix.com/watch/81147383?trackId=255824129.

Clendinnen, Inga. *Ambivalent Conquests: Maya and Spaniard in Yucatan, 1517–1570*. New York: Cambridge University Press, 1987.

Coe, Michael D. "The Chinampas of Mexico." *Scientific American* 211 (1964): 90–99.

Coe, William R. "Caches and Offertory Practices of the Maya Lowlands." In *Handbook of Middle American Indians*, edited by R. Wauchope and Gordon R. Willey, vol. 2, The Archaeology of Southern Mesoamerica, 462–69. Austin: University of Texas Press, 1965.

Collins, Ryan H. "From Sedentism to Sprawl: Early Urban Process at Yaxuná, Yucatan, Mexico 1000 BCE to 250 CE." PhD diss., Brandeis University, 2018.

———. "Incised Lines: Planning and Design in the Late Formative E Group at Yaxuná, Yucatán, Mexico." *Latin American Antiquity* 33, no. 3 (2022): 648–57.

———. "Selective Memory: Monumental Politics of the Yaxuná E Group in the First Millennium B.C." *Ancient Mesoamerica* 34, no. 1(2021): 140–59.

Colwell-Chanthaphonh, Chip, T.J. Ferguson, Dorothy Lippert, Randall H. McGuire, George P. Nicholas, Joe E. Watkins, and Larry J. Zimmerman. "The Premise and Promise of Indigenous Archaeology." *American Antiquity* 75, no. 2 (2010): 228–38.

Cronon, William. *Changes in the Land: Indians, Colonists, and the Ecology of New England.* New York: Hill and Wang, 1983.

Davis, Janae, Alex A. Moulton, Levi Van Sant, and Brian Williams. "Anthropocene, Capitalocene, . . . Plantationocene?: A Manifesto for Ecological Justice in an Age of Global Crises." *Geography Compass* 13, no. 5 (2019): e12438.

De Clerck, F. A.J., and P. Negreros-Castillo. "Plant Species of Traditional Mayan Homegardens of Mexico as Analogs for Multistrata Agroforests." *Agroforestry Systems* 48 (2000): 303–17.

de la Cerda, H. E., and R. R. Guerra Mukul. "Homegarden Production and Productivity in a Mayan Community of Yucatan." *Human Ecology* 36 (2008): 423–33.

Delmas, Magali A., and Vanessa Cuerel Burbano. "The Drivers of Greenwashing." *California Management Review* 54, no. 1 (2011): 64–87.

Dickinson, M.B., and D.F. Whigham. "Competition among Surface Roots in a Selectively-Logged, Semi-Deciduous Forest in Southeastern Mexico: Effects on Seedlings of Two Species of Contrasting Shade Tolerance." *Caribbean Journal of Science* 47, no. 2–3 (2013): 140–52.

Diggles, Michelle Eileen. "Popular Response to Neoliberal Reform: The Political Configuration of Property Rights in Two Ejidos in Yucatán, Mexico." PhD diss., University of Oregon, Eugene, 2008.

Dine, Harper, Traci Ardren, Grace Bascopé, and Celso Gutiérrez Báez. "Famine Foods and Food Security in the Northern Maya Lowlands: Modern Lessons for Ancient Reconstructions." *Ancient Mesoamerica* 30, no. 3 (2019): 517–34.

Domínguez Aké, Santiago. *Úuchben kool yetel u meyajta'al táankab: u táabal kuxtal yetel tojóolal / La milpa tradicional y el uso del traspatio: Fuente de vida y salud.* Mérida: Secretaría de la Cultura y las Artes, 2015.

Douglas, Peter M.J., Mark Pagani, Marcello A. Canuto, Mark Brenner, David A. Hodell, Timothy I. Eglinton, and Jason H. Curtis. "Drought, Agricultural Adaptation, and Sociopolitical Collapse in the Maya Lowlands." *Proceedings of the National Academy of Sciences* 112, no. 18 (2015): 5607–12.

Douglass, Kristina, and Jago Cooper. "Archaeology, Environmental Justice, and Climate Change on Islands of the Caribbean and Southwestern Indian Ocean." *Proceedings of the National Academy of Sciences* 117, no. 15 (2020): 8254–62.

Drew, John, Aaron Dickinson Sachs, Cecilia Sueiro, and John R. Stepp. "Ancient Grains and New Markets: The Selling of Quinoa as Story and Substance." In

Corporate Social Responsibility and Corporate Governance, vol. 11, 251–74. Developments in Corporate Governance and Responsibility. Bingley, UK: Emerald Publishing, 2017.

Dunning, Nicholas P. "The Implication of Folk Soil Taxonomies for Agricultural Change in Middle America." *Yearbook Conference of Latin Americanist Geographers* 17/18 (1991): 243–47.

Dunning, Nicholas P., and Timothy Beach. "Farms and Forests: Spatial and Temporal Perspectives on Ancient Maya Landscapes." In *Landscapes and Societies: Selected Cases*, edited by I. Peter Martini and Ward Chesworth, 369–89. Dordrecht: Springer Netherlands, 2011.

Dunning, Nicholas P., Timothy P. Beach, and Sheryl Luzzadder-Beach. "Kax and Kol: Collapse and Resilience in Lowland Maya Civilization." *Proceedings of the National Academy of Sciences* 109, no. 10 (2012): 3652–57.

Eastmond, Amarella, Julio C. Sacramento Rivero, and Sam R. Sweitz, eds. *The Quest for Jatropha Biodiesel and Sustainability in Yucatán*. Mérida: Universidad Autónoma de Yucatán, 2018.

Eisenberg, Cristina, Christopher L. Anderson, Adam Collingwood, Robert Sissons, Christopher J. Dunn, Garrett W. Meigs, Dave E. Hibbs et al. "Out of the Ashes: Ecological Resilience to Extreme Wildfire, Prescribed Burns, and Indigenous Burning in Ecosystems." *Frontiers in Ecology and Evolution* 7 (2019): 436.

"Ejidatarios de Ixil anulan una asamblea de hace 4 años y quitan poder a sus abogados." *Maya Politikon*, February 23, 2019. https://mayapolitikon.com/ejidatarios-ixil/.

Erickson, Clark L. *Experiments in Raised Field Agriculture, Huatta, Peru 1981–1982*. Champaign: University of Illinois, 1982.

———. "Raised Field Agriculture in the Lake Titicaca Basin: Putting Ancient Agriculture Back to Work." *Expedition* 30, no. 1 (1988): 8–16.

Estrada Saavedra, Marco. *La comunidad armada rebelde y el EZLN: Un estudio histórico y sociológico sobre las bases de apoyo zapatistas en las cañadas tojolabales de la Selva Lacandona*. Mexico City: El Colegio de México, 2016.

Evans, Sterling. *Bound in Twine: The History and Ecology of the Henequen-Wheat Complex for Mexico and the American and Canadian Plains, 1880–1950*. College Station: Texas A&M University Press, 2007.

Fairhead, James, Melissa Leach, and Ian Scoones. "Green Grabbing: A New Appropriation of Nature?" *Journal of Peasant Studies* 39, no. 2 (2012): 237–61.

Farahani, Alan, Katherine L. Chiou, Anna Harkey, Christine A. Hastorf, David L. Lentz, and Payson Sheets. "Identifying 'Plantscapes' at the Classic Maya Village of Joya de Cerén, El Salvador." *Antiquity* 91, no. 358 (2017): 980–97.

Farrell, Justin, Paul Berne Burow, Kathryn McConnell, Jude Bayham, Kyle Whyte, and Gal Koss. "Effects of Land Dispossession and Forced Migration on Indigenous Peoples in North America." *Science* 374, no. 6567 (2021). https://par.nsf.gov/servlets/purl/10329308.

Farriss, Nancy M. *Maya Society under Colonial Rule: The Collective Enterprise of Survival*. Princeton, NJ: Princeton University Press, 1984.

Fedick, Scott L., Maria de Lourdes Flores-Delgadillo, Sergey Sedov, Elizabeth Sol-leiro-Rebolledo, and Sergio Palacios-Mayorga. "Adaptation of Maya Homegar-dens by 'Container Gardening' in Limestone Bedrock Cavities." *Journal of Eth-nobiology* 28, no. 2 (2008): 290–304.

Feng, Shuaizhang, Alan B. Krueger, and Michael Oppenheimer. "Linkages among Climate Change, Crop Yields and Mexico–US Cross-Border Migration." *Pro-ceedings of the National Academy of Sciences* 107, no. 32 (2010): 14257–62.

Fisher, Chelsea. "Archaeology for Sustainable Agriculture." *Journal of Archaeologi-cal Research* 28, no. 3 (2020): 393–441.

———. "Maize Politics and Maya Farmers' Traditional Ecological Knowledge in Yucatán, 1450–1600." *Human Ecology* 48, no. 1 (2020): 33–45.

———. "Maya Farming Communities and the Long View of Sustainability at Tzacauil." PhD diss., University of Michigan, 2019.

———. "Monumentality as Traditional Ecological Knowledge in the Northern Maya Lowlands." *Antiquity* (2023): 1–17. doi:10.15184/aqy.2023.20.

———. "The Role of Infield Agriculture in Maya Cities." *Journal of Anthropological Archaeology* 36 (2014): 196–210.

———. "Walking Rural in Tzacauil, Yucatán, Mexico." *Ancient Mesoamerica* 33, no. 1 (2022): 148–61.

Fisher, Chelsea, and Traci Ardren. "Partaking in Culinary Heritage at Yaxunah, Yucatán during the 2017 Noma Mexico Pop-Up." *Heritage* 3, no. 2 (2020): 474–92.

Fita, Dídac, Eduardo Naranjo, Eduardo Bello, Erin Estrada-Lugo, Ramón Méndez, and Pedro Macario. "La milpa comedero-trampa como una estrategia de cacería tradicional maya." *Estudios de Cultura Maya* 42 (2013): 87–118.

Fitting, Elizabeth. *The Struggle for Maize: Campesinos, Workers, and Transgenic Corn in the Mexican Countryside*. Durham, NC: Duke University Press, 2010.

Flannery, Kent V., ed. *Maya Subsistence: Studies in Memory of Dennis E. Puleston*. New York: Academic Press, 1982.

Fletcher, Roland. "Low-Density, Agrarian-Based Urbanism: A Comparative View." *Insights* (University of Durham) 2, no. 4 (2009): 2–19.

Flores-Delgadillo, Lourdes, Scott L. Fedick, Elizabeth Solleiro-Rebolledo, Sergio Palacios-Mayorga, Pilar Ortega-Larrocea, Sergey Sedov, and Esteban Osuna-Ceja. "A Sustainable System of a Traditional Precision Agriculture in a Maya Homegar-den: Soil Quality Aspects." *Soil and Tillage Research* 113 (2011): 112–20.

Flowers, Catherine Coleman. *Waste: One Woman's Fight against America's Dirty Secret*. New York: The New Press, 2020.

Ford, Anabel, and Ronald Nigh. *The Maya Forest Garden: Eight Millennia of Sus-tainable Cultivation in the Tropical Wetlands*. Walnut Creek, CA: Left Coast Press, 2015.

Fox, Jonathan. *The Politics of Food in Mexico: State Power and Social Mobilization*. Ithaca, NY: Cornell University Press, 1993.

Freidel, David A., Arlen F. Chase, Anne S. Dowd, and Jerry Murdock, eds. *Maya E Groups: Calendars, Astronomy, and Urbanism in the Early Lowlands*. Gainesville: University Press of Florida, 2017.

Freidel, David A., Linda Schele, and Joy Parker. *Maya Cosmos: Three Thousand Years on the Shaman's Path*. New York: William Morrow, 1993.

Fryer, Tiffany C. "Against the 'Workmen Model' (and Other Mechanisms of Injustice in Archaeology)." Blog, 2020. www.tiffanyfryer.com/post/against-the-workmen-model.

———. "Reflecting on Positionality: Archaeological Heritage Praxis in Quintana Roo, Mexico." *Archeological Papers of the American Anthropological Association* 31, no. 1 (2020): 26–40.

Fundación Haciendas del Mundo Maya and International Maize and Wheat Improvement Center (FHMM-CIMMYT). "Ofrece milpa sustentable más grano y protección del medio ambiente a productores de maíz en Yucatán." CIMMYT, November 25, 2016. https://idp.cimmyt.org/ofrece-milpa-sustentable-mas-grano-y-proteccion-del-medio-ambiente-a-productores-de-maiz-en-yucatan/.

Gabriel, Marianne. "Ritualidad y cosmovisión: Las ceremonias agrarias de los campesinos mayas en Yucatán." In *Estampas Etnográficas de Yucatán*, edited by Francisco Fernández Repetto, 13–41. Mérida: Universidad Autónoma de Yucatán, 2010.

Gálvez, Alyshia. *Eating NAFTA: Trade, Food Policies, and the Destruction of Mexico*. Oakland: University of California Press, 2018.

Garza, Silvia, and Edward B. Kurjack. *Atlas arqueológico del Estado de Yucatán*. Mérida: Instituto Nacional de Antropología e Historia, Centro Regional del Sureste, 1980.

Gayou Soto, Sandra. "Habitantes de Ixil denuncian venta irregular de ejidos." *La Jornada Maya*, January 18, 2019. www.lajornadamaya.mx/yucatan/134970/Habitantes-de-Ixil-denuncian-venta-irregular-de-ejidos.

Genzlinger, Neil. "Review: 'Chef's Table' Profiles Top Culinary Talents." *New York Times*, April 24, 2015. www.nytimes.com/2015/04/25/arts/television/review-chefs-table-profiles-top-culinary-talents.html.

Ghosh, Amitav. *The Nutmeg's Curse: Parables for a Planet in Crisis*. Chicago: University of Chicago Press, 2021.

Gibson, Charles. *The Aztecs under Spanish Rule: A History of the Indians of the Valley of Mexico, 1519–1810*. Stanford, CA: Stanford University Press, 1964.

Gil, Carlos, ed. *The Age of Porfirio Díaz: Selected Readings*. Albuquerque: University of New Mexico Press, 1977.

Gillespie, A. R., D. M. Bocanegra-Ferguson, and J. J. Jiménez Osornio. "The Propagation of Ramón (*Brosimum Alicastrum* Sw.; Moraceae) in Mayan Homegardens of the Yucatan Peninsula of Mexico." *New Forests* 27 (2004): 25–38.

Glissant, Édouard. *Caribbean Discourse: Selected Essays*. Translated by J. Michael Dash. Charlottesville: University Press of Virginia, 1989.

Glover, Jeffrey B., and Travis W. Stanton. "Assessing the Role of Preclassic Traditions in the Formation of Early Classic Yucatec Cultures." *Journal of Field Archaeology* 35 (2010): 58–77.

Gómez Pompa, Arturo, Michael F. Allen, Scott L. Fedick, and Juan J. Jiménez Orsornio, eds. *The Lowland Maya Area: Three Millennia at the Human-Wildland Interface*. Binghamton, NY: Food Products Press, 2003.

Gómez Pompa, Arturo, José Salvador Flores, and Mario Aliphat Fernández. "The Sacred Cacao Groves of the Maya." *Latin American Antiquity* 1, no. 3 (1990): 247–57.

Gordinier, Jeff. *Hungry: Eating, Road-Tripping, and Risking It All with the Greatest Chef in the World*. New York: Penguin Random House, 2019.

Govaerts, Bram. "Sustainable Tradition." CIMMYT blog, June 3, 2019. www .cimmyt.org/blogs/sustainable-tradition/.

Güémez Pineda, Arturo. *Mayas, gobierno, y tierras frente a la acometida liberal en Yucatán, 1812–1847*. Mexico City: El Colegio de Michoacán, 1994.

Guenter, S. P. "The Queen of Cobá: A Reanalysis of the Macanxoc Stelae." In *The Archaeology of Yucatán: New Directions and Data*, edited by T. W. Stanton, 395–421. BAR International Series. Oxford: Archaeopress, 2014.

Guttmann-Bond, Erika. "Sustainability out of the Past: How Archaeology Can Save the Planet." *World Archaeology* 42, no. 3 (2010): 355–66.

Hanks, William F. *Referential Practice: Language and Lived Space among the Maya*. Chicago: University of Chicago Press, 1990.

———. "The Plurality of Temporal Reckoning among the Maya." *Journal de La Société des Américanistes de Paris* 103 (2017): 497–520.

Haraway, Donna, Noboru Ishikawa, Scott F. Gilbert, Kenneth Olwig, Anna L. Tsing, and Nils Bubandt. "Anthropologists Are Talking—About the Anthropocene." *Ethnos* 81, no. 3 (2016): 535–64.

Haraway, Donna, and Anna L. Tsing. "Reflections on the Plantationocene: A Conversation with Donna Haraway and Anna Tsing." *Edge Effects*, 2019. https:// edgeeffects.net/haraway-tsing-plantationocene/.

Haraway, Donna Jeanne. *Staying with the Trouble: Making Kin in the Chthulucene*. Durham, NC: Duke University Press, 2016.

Hargrove, James L. "History of the Calorie in Nutrition." *Journal of Nutrition* 136, no. 12 (2006): 2957–61.

Haug, Gerald H., Detlef Günther, Larry C. Peterson, Daniel M. Sigman, Konrad A. Hughen, and Beat Aeschlimann. "Climate and the Collapse of Maya Civilization." *Science* 299, no. 5613 (2003): 1731–35.

Henderson, Joan C. "Celebrity Chefs: Expanding Empires." *British Food Journal* 113, no. 5 (2011): 613–24.

Hennessy, Elizabeth. *On the Backs of Tortoises: Darwin, the Galapagos, and the Fate of an Evolutionary Eden*. New Haven, CT: Yale University Press, 2019.

Hernández Álvarez, Héctor. "Etnoarqueología de grupos domésticos mayas: Identidad social y espacio residencial de Yaxunah, Yucatán." PhD diss., Universidad Nacional Autónoma de México, 2014.

———. "Memoria e identidad social de los grupos domésticos de Yaxuná, Yucatán." Presentation at the 7th Congreso Internacional de Mayistas, Universidad Nacional Autónoma de México, Mérida, Yucatán, June 24–30, 2007.

Hernández Álvarez, Héctor, and Mario Zimmermann, eds. *Sendas del henequén: Un estudio arqueológico de la Hacienda San Pedro Cholul, Yucatán*. Mérida: Universidad Autónoma de Yucatán, 2016.

Hill, J. Brett, Patrick D. Lyons, Jeffery J. Clark, and William H. Doelle. "The 'Collapse' of Cooperative Hohokam Irrigation in the Lower Salt River Valley." *Journal of the Southwest* 57, no. 4 (2015): 609–74.

Hokol Vuh [@hokol.vuh]. "El maíz es el resultado de un milenario proceso." Instagram, September 5, 2019. www.instagram.com/p/B2ChV3bgfow/?hl=en. Accessed December 22, 2022.

———. "Experiencia de bebidas de maíz en Yaxunah." Instagram, November 20, 2019. www.instagram.com/p/B5GVr46gu3T/?hl=en. Accessed December 22, 2022.

———. "Exposición de Frutas y Verduras." Instagram, November 19, 2019. www.instagram.com/p/B5ECoNlgKOB/?hl=en. Accessed December 22, 2022.

———. "Hoy estamos a unos días de dar la bienvenida." Instagram, November 15, 2019. www.instagram.com/p/B45wUo5ADZA/?hl=en. Accessed December 22, 2022.

———. "Izamal recibe con los brazos abiertos a nuestros invitados." Instagram, June 20, 2017. www.instagram.com/p/BVkSYdRjubJ/?hl=en. Accessed December 22, 2022.

———. "Nuestra herencia milenaria perdura y traspasa fronteras." Instagram, July 7, 2017. www.instagram.com/p/BWRIX7UjUF_/?hl=en. Accessed December 22, 2022.

Houk, Brett A., Barbara Arroyo, and Terry G. Powis, eds. *Approaches to Monumental Landscapes of the Ancient Maya*. Maya Studies. Gainesville: University Press of Florida, 2020.

Hutson, Scott, Céline Lamb, Daniel Vallejo-Cáliz, and Jacob Welch. "Reflecting on PASUC Heritage Initiatives through Time, Positionality, and Place." *Heritage* 3, no. 2 (2020), 228–42.

Hutson, Scott, Aline Magnoni, and Travis Stanton. "'All that is solid . . .': Sacbes, Settlement, and Semiotics at Tzacauil, Yucatan." *Ancient Mesoamerica* 23 (2012): 297–311.

Hutson, Scott R., Aline Magnoni, Travis W. Stanton, Donald A. Slater, and Scott Johnson. "Memory and Power at Joya, Yucatán." In *Power and Identity in Archaeological Theory and Practice: Case Studies from Ancient Mesoamerica*, 39–52. Salt Lake City: University of Utah Press, 2012.

Hutson, Scott R., Travis W. Stanton, Aline Magnoni, Richard Terry, and Jason Craner. "Beyond the Buildings: Formation Processes of Ancient Maya Houselots and Methods for the Study of Non-Architectural Space." *Journal of Anthropological Archaeology* 26 (2007): 442–73.

I-Collective. "Home." 2021. www.icollectiveinc.org.

Iannone, Gyles, Keith Prufer, and Diane Z. Chase. "Resilience and Vulnerability in the Maya Hinterlands." *Archeological Papers of the American Anthropological Association* 24, no. 1 (2014): 155–70.

Inomata, Takeshi, Jessica MacLellan, Daniela Triadan, Jessica Munson, Melissa Burhama, Kazuo Aoyama, Hiroo Nasu, Flory Pinzón, and Hitoshi Yonenobu. "Development of Sedentary Communities in the Maya Lowlands: Coexisting Mobile Groups and Public Ceremonies at Ceibal, Guatemala." *Proceedings of the National Academy of Sciences* 112, no. 14 (2015): 4268–73.

Inomata, Takeshi, Daniela Triadan, Veronica A. Vazquez Lopez, Juan Carlos Fernandez-Diaz, Takayuki Omori, Maria Belen Mendez Bauer, and Melina Garcia Hernandez. "Monumental Architecture at Aguada Fénix and the Rise of Maya Civilization." *Nature* 582, no. 7813 (2020): 530–33.

Isendahl, Christian. "Agro-Urban Landscapes: The Example of Maya Lowland Cities." *Antiquity* 86, no. 334 (2012): 1112–25.

Isendahl, Christian, and Michael E. Smith. "Sustainable Agrarian Urbanism: The Low-Density Cities of the Mayas and Aztecs." *Cities* 31 (2013): 132–43.

Janusek, John Wayne, and Alan L. Kolata. "Top-Down or Bottom-Up: Rural Settlement and Raised Field Agriculture in the Lake Titicaca Basin, Bolivia." *Journal of Anthropological Archaeology* 23, no. 4 (2004): 404–30.

Johnson, Scott A. J. "Late and Terminal Classic Power Shifts in Yucatan: The View from Popola." PhD diss., Tulane University, 2012.

Joseph, Gilbert M. *Revolution from Without: Yucatán, Mexico, and the United States, 1880–1924.* New York: Cambridge University Press, 1982.

Joyce, Rosemary A. "Heirlooms and Houses: Materiality and Social Memory." In *Beyond Kinship: Social and Material Reproduction in House Societies,* edited by Rosemary A. Joyce and Susan D. Gillespie, 189–212. Philadelphia: University of Pennsylvania Press, 2000.

"Júbilo en Ixil: Ejidatarios recuperan sus tierras 'perdidas' hace 5 años." *Maya Politikon,* April 8, 2019. https://mayapolitikon.com/ixil-tierras/.

Kennett, Douglas J., Marilyn Masson, Carlos Peraza Lope, Stanley Serafin, Richard J. George, Tom C. Spencer, Julie A. Hoggarth et al. "Drought-Induced Civil Conflict among the Ancient Maya." *Nature Communications* 13, no. 1 (2022): 3911.

Kepecs, Susan, and Sylvia Boucher. "The Pre-Hispanic Cultivation of Rejolladas and Stone-Lands: New Evidence from Northeast Yucatan." In *The Managed Mosaic: Ancient Maya Agriculture and Resource Use,* edited by Scott L. Fedick, 69–91. Salt Lake City: University of Utah Press, 1996.

Kerssen, Tanya M. "Food Sovereignty and the Quinoa Boom: Challenges to Sustainable Re-Peasantisation in the Southern Altiplano of Bolivia." *Third World Quarterly* 36, no. 3 (2015): 489–507.

Kidder, Alfred V. "Archaeological Work in Yucatán." *Carnegie Institution of Washington Yearbook* 34 (1935): 123–26.

Killion, Thomas W. "Cultivation Intensity and Residential Site Structure: An Ethnoarchaeological Examination of Peasant Agriculture in the Sierra de los Tuxtlas, Veracruz, Mexico." *Latin American Antiquity* 1, no. 3 (1990): 191–215.

Kimmerer, Robin Wall. *Braiding Sweetgrass: Indigenous Wisdom, Scientific Knowledge, and the Teachings of Plants.* Minneapolis, MN: Milkweed Editions, 2013.

Klassen, Sarah, and Damian Evans. "Top-Down and Bottom-Up Water Management: A Diachronic Model of Changing Water Management Strategies at Angkor, Cambodia." *Journal of Anthropological Archaeology* 58 (2020): 101166.

Kolata, Alan L. "The Agricultural Foundations of the Tiwanaku State: A View from the Heartland." *American Antiquity* 51, no. 4 (1986): 748–62.

———. "The Technology and Organization of Agricultural Production in the Tiwanaku State." *Latin American Antiquity* 2, no. 2 (1991): 99–125.

Kong, Jacqui. "Feasting on 'the Other': Performing Authenticity and Commodifying Difference in Celebrity Chefs' Food and Travel Television Programmes." In *Routledge Handbook of Food in Asia*, edited by Cecilia Leong-Salobir, 207–21. New York: Routledge, 2019.

Kramm, Matthias. "When a River Becomes a Person." *Journal of Human Development and Capabilities* 21, no. 4 (2020): 307–19.

Krech, Shepard. *The Ecological Indian: Myth and History*. New York: W. W. Norton, 1999.

Kunen, Julie L. *Ancient Maya Life in the Far West Bajo: Social and Environmental Change in the Wetlands of Belize*. Tucson: University of Arizona Press, 2004.

Kunen, Julie L., Mary Jo Galindo, and Erin Chase. "Pits and Bones: Identifying Maya Ritual Behavior in the Archaeological Record." *Ancient Mesoamerica* 13, no. 2 (2002): 197–211.

La Ruta de la Garnacha. "Cochinita Pibil con la Cocinera Maya Rosalia de Chef's Table de Netflix en Yaxunah." YouTube video, 14:54, November 3, 2021. www.youtube.com/watch?v=VOJ2ii7pFVo.

"La UNAM se deslinda de 'infiltrado' nahua entre los mayas de Yucatán." *Yucatán Ahora!*, August 16, 2018. https://yucatanahora.mx/la-unam-se-deslinda-de-infiltrado-nahua-entre-los-mayas-de-yucatan/.

Larmer, Brook. "How the Avocado Became the Fruit of Global Trade." *New York Times*, March 27, 2018. www.nytimes.com/2018/03/27/magazine/the-fruit-of-global-trade-in-one-fruit-the-avocado.html.

Lawrence, Ted J., Stephen J. Morreale, Richard C. Stedman, and Leo V. Louis. "Linking Changes in Ejido Land Tenure to Changes in Landscape Patterns over 30 Years across Yucatán, México." *Regional Environmental Change* 20, no. 4 (2020): 136.

Lemonnier, Eva, and Boris Vannière. "Agrarian Features, Farmsteads, and Homesteads in the Río Bec Nuclear Zone, Mexico." *Ancient Mesoamerica* 24, no. 2 (2013): 397–413.

Lentz, David L., Nicholas P. Dunning, Vernon L. Scarborough, and Liwy Grazioso. "Imperial Resource Management at the Ancient Maya City of Tikal: A Resilience Model of Sustainability and Collapse." *Journal of Anthropological Archaeology* 52 (2018): 113–22.

Lentz, David L., Nicholas P. Dunning, Vernon L. Scarborough, Kevin S. Magee, Kim M. Thompson, Eric Weaver, Christopher Carr et al. "Forests, Fields, and the Edge of Sustainability at the Ancient Maya City of Tikal." *Proceedings of the National Academy of Sciences* 111, no. 52 (2014): 18513–18.

Lentz, David L., and Brian Hockaday. "Tikal Timbers and Temples: Ancient Maya Agroforestry and the End of Time." *Journal of Archaeological Science* 36, no. 7 (2009): 1342–53.

Lentz, David, Sally Woods, Angela Hood, and Marcus Murph. "Agroforestry and Agricultural Production of the Ancient Maya at Chan." In *Chan: An Ancient*

Maya Farming Community, edited by Cynthia Robin, 89–109. Gainesville: University Press of Florida, 2012.

Liboiron, Max. *Pollution Is Colonialism*. Durham, NC: Duke University Press, 2021.

Lidgard, Scott, and Alan C. Love. "Rethinking Living Fossils." *BioScience* 68, no. 10 (2018): 760–70.

Logan, Amanda L. *The Scarcity Slot: Excavating Histories of Food Security in Ghana*. Oakland: University of California Press, 2020.

Lorr, Benjamin. *The Secret Life of Groceries: The Dark Miracle of the American Supermarket*. New York: Avery, 2020.

Lucero, Lisa J., Roland Fletcher, and Robin Coningham. "From 'Collapse' to Urban Diaspora: The Transformation of Low-Density, Dispersed Agrarian Urbanism." *Antiquity* 89, no. 347 (2015): 1139–54.

Luzzadder-Beach, Sheryl, and Timothy Beach. "Arising from the Wetlands: Mechanisms and Chronology of Landscape Aggradation in the Northern Coastal Plain of Belize." *Annals of the Association of American Geographers* 99, no. 1 (2009): 1–26.

Luzzadder-Beach, Sheryl, Timothy P. Beach, and Nicholas P. Dunning. "Wetland Fields as Mirrors of Drought and the Maya Abandonment." *Proceedings of the National Academy of Sciences* 109, no. 10 (2012): 3646–51.

"Machetazos entre ejidatarios de Muna por conflicto de la planta de energía solar." *Yucatán Ahora!*, September 5, 2018. https://yucatanahora.mx/machetazos-entre-ejidatarios-de-muna-por-conflicto-de-la-planta-de-energia-solar/.

Machuca Gallegos, Laura. *Los hacendados de Yucatán, 1785–1847*. Mérida: Centro de Investigaciones y Estudios Superiores en Antropología Social, 2011.

Magnoni, Aline, Traci Ardren, and Scott Hutson. "Tourism in the Mundo Maya: Inventions and (Mis)Representations of Maya Identities and Heritage." *Archaeologies* 3, no. 3 (2007): 353–83.

Makki, Fouad. "Development by Dispossession: Terra Nullius and the Social-Ecology of New Enclosures in Ethiopia." *Rural Sociology* 79, no. 1 (2014): 79–103.

Maldonado-Koerdell, Manuel. "Geohistory and Paleogeography of Middle America." In *Handbook of Middle American Indians*, edited by R. C. West, vol. 1, 3–32. Austin: University of Texas Press, 1964.

Malin, Stephanie A., and Stacia S. Ryder. "Developing Deeply Intersectional Environmental Justice Scholarship." *Environmental Sociology* 4, no. 1 (2018): 1–7.

Manzanilla, Linda, and Luis Barba. "The Study of Activities in Classic Households: Two Case Studies from Coba and Teotihuacan." *Ancient Mesoamerica* 1 (1990): 41–49.

Mapes, Gwynne. "(De)Constructing Distinction: Class Inequality and Elite Authenticity in Mediatized Food Discourse." *Journal of Sociolinguistics* 22, no. 3 (2018): 265–87.

Marcus, Joyce. "From Centralized Systems to City-States: Possible Models for the Epiclassic." In *Mesoamerica after the Decline of Teotihuacan, A.D. 700–900*, edited by Richard A. Diehl and Janet Catherine Berlo, 201–8. Washington, DC: Dumbarton Oaks Research Library and Collection, 1989.

———. "The Plant World of the Sixteenth- and Seventeenth-Century Lowland Maya." In *Maya Subsistence: Studies in Memory of Dennis E. Puleston*, edited by Kent V. Flannery, 239–73. New York: Academic Press, 1982.

Marengo Camacho, Nelda I. "Análisis funcional de cerámica en un basurero de una acrópolis triádica en Yaxuná, Yucatán." Licenciate thesis, Universidad de las Américas Puebla, Cholula, 2013.

Margulis, Matias E., Nora McKeon, and Saturnino M. Borras. "Land Grabbing and Global Governance: Critical Perspectives." *Globalizations* 10, no. 1 (2013): 1–23.

Martínez-Reyes, José E. *Moral Ecology of a Forest: The Nature Industry and Maya Post-Conservation*. Tucson: University of Arizona Press, 2016.

Masson, Marilyn A. "Maya Collapse Cycles." *Proceedings of the National Academy of Sciences* 109, no. 45 (2012): 18237–38.

McAnany, Patricia A. *Living with the Ancestors: Kinship and Kingship in Ancient Maya Society*. Austin: University of Texas Press, 1995.

———. *Maya Cultural Heritage: How Archaeologists and Indigenous Communities Engage the Past*. Lanham, MD: Rowman & Littlefield, 2016.

McGurty, Eileen Maura. "From NIMBY to Civil Rights: The Origins of the Environmental Justice Movement." *Environmental History* 2, no. 3 (1997): 301–23.

McKittrick, Katherine. "Plantation Futures." *Small Axe* 17, no. 3 (2013): 1–15.

Mercer, Henry C. *The Hill-Caves of Yucatan*. Norman: University of Oklahoma Press, 1975.

Meyers, Allan Dale. *Outside the Hacienda Walls: The Archaeology of Plantation Peonage in Nineteenth-Century Yucatán*. Tucson: University of Arizona Press, 2012.

Middleton, William D., Luis Barba, Alessandra Pecci, James H. Burton, Agustin Ortiz, Laura Salvini, and Roberto Rodriguez Suárez. "The Study of Archaeological Floors: Methodological Proposal for the Analysis of Anthropogenic Residues by Spot Tests, ICP-OES, and GC-MS." *Journal of Archaeological Method and Theory* 17, no. 3 (2010): 183–208.

Millhauser, John K., and Christopher T. Morehart. "Sustainability as a Relative Process: A Long-Term Perspective on Sustainability in the Northern Basin of Mexico." *Archeological Papers of the American Anthropological Association* 29, no. 1 (2018): 134–56.

Mitchell, Zoë Jane [@zoejanemitchell]. "Ate the most authentic Mayan food." Instagram, October 30, 2020. www.instagram.com/p/CG-1q5BHvny/. Accessed December 22, 2022.

Morley, Sylvanus G. "Archaeology." *Carnegie Institution of Washington Yearbook* 26 (1927): 231–40.

Moskin, Julia. "The Island Is Idyllic. As a Workplace, It's Toxic." *New York Times*, April 27, 2021. www.nytimes.com/2021/04/27/dining/blaine-wetzel-willows-inn-lummi-island-abuse.html.

———. "Noma, Rated the World's Best Restaurant, Is Closing Its Doors." *New York Times*, January 9, 2023. www.nytimes.com/2023/01/09/dining/noma-closing-rene-redzepi.html.

Mukul, Sharif A., and John Herbohn. "The Impacts of Shifting Cultivation on Secondary Forests Dynamics in Tropics: A Synthesis of the Key Findings and Spatio Temporal Distribution of Research." *Environmental Science & Policy* 55 (2016): 167–77.

Murphy, Michael Warren, and Caitlin Schroering. "Refiguring the Plantationocene: Racial Capitalism, World-Systems Analysis, and Global Socioecological Transformation." *Journal of World-Systems Research* 26, no. 2 (2020): 400–415.

Nash, Stephen E., and Chip Colwell. "NAGPRA at 30: The Effects of Repatriation." *Annual Review of Anthropology* 49, no. 1 (2020): 225–39.

Nelson, Margaret C., Scott E. Ingram, Andrew J. Dugmore, Richard Streeter, Matthew A. Peeples, Thomas H. McGovern, Michelle Hegmon et al. "Climate Challenges, Vulnerabilities, and Food Security." *Proceedings of the National Academy of Sciences* 113, no. 2 (2016): 298–303.

Neumann, Roderick P. *Imposing Wilderness: Struggles over Livelihood and Nature Preservation in Africa*. Berkeley: University of California Press, 1998.

Nigh, Ronald. "Trees, Fire and Farmers: Making Woods and Soil in the Maya Forest." *Journal of Ethnobiology* 28, no. 2 (2008): 231–43.

Nigh, Ronald, and Stewart A. W. Diemont. "The Maya Milpa: Fire and the Legacy of Living Soil." *Frontiers in Ecology and the Environment* 11, suppl. 1 (2013): e45–54.

"'No estoy en contra de ninguna empresa: Estoy a favor de Ixil.'" *Maya Politikon*, February 27, 2019. https://mayapolitikon.com/no-estoy-en-contra-de-ninguna-empresa-estoy-a-favor-de-ixil/.

Noma. *The Weather Report*. Blog. https://noma.dk/the-weather-report/.

Novelo Rincón, Gustavo A. "La arquitectura del grupo Puuc de Yaxuná." Licentiate thesis, Universidad Autónoma de Yucatán, Mérida, 2012.

Ochoa, Mariana (soymarianaochoa). "Conocí a Rosalía! La famosa chef de Netflix." YouTube video, February 2, 2021, 11:36. www.youtube.com /watch?v=OZHorN6Mh3s.

O'Neill, John P. "Survey of Yaxuná." *Carnegie Institution of Washington Yearbook* 32 (1933): 88–89.

Ortiz Yam, Isaura Inés. "De milperos a henequeneros: Los procesos agrarios en el noroeste de Yucatán, 1870–1937." PhD diss., Centro de Estudios Históricos, El Colegio de México, 2011.

———. "Formación de ejidos en los pueblos de Yucatán, 1870–1909." *Temas Antropológicos: Revista Científica de Investigaciones Regionales* 36 (2014): 17–41.

Pashman, Dan. "Other People's Food, part 1: White Chef, Mexican Food." *The Sporkful*, March 21, 2016. Podcast, MP3 audio. www.sporkful.com/other -peoples-food-part-1-rick-bayless-white-chef-mexican-food/.

Patch, Robert W. "Decolonization, the Agrarian Problem, and the Origins of the Caste War, 1812–1847." In *Land, Labor, and Capital in Modern Yucatán: Essays in Regional History and Political Economy*, edited by Jeffrey T. Brannon and Gilbert M. Joseph. Tuscaloosa: University of Alabama Press, 1991.

———. *Maya and Spaniard in Yucatán, 1648–1812*. Stanford, CA: Stanford University Press, 1993.

Patjane Floriuk, Anuar. "De la milpa a la producción artesanal en serie: implica-ciones socioeconómicas del desarrollo turístico en la región de Chichén Itzá." Licenciate thesis, Universidad de las Américas Puebla, Cholula, 2009.

Penfield, Glen. "Unlikely Impact: The Unexpected Discovery of the Paleogene-Cretaceous Impact Crater." *AAPG* (American Association of Petroleum Geolo-gists) *Explorer*, December 2019. https://explorer.aapg.org/story?articleid=55293.

Penniman, Leah. *Farming while Black: Soul Fire Farm's Practical Guide to Libera-tion on the Land*. White River Junction, VT: Chelsea Green Publishing, 2018.

"Piden respeto al pueblo por unos paneles solares." *Diario de Yucatán*. August 29, 2018. www.yucatan.com.mx/merida/2018/8/29/piden-respeto-al-pueblo-por-unos-paneles-solares-60448.html.

Pilkington, Ed. "Activist Catherine Flowers: The Poor Living amid Sewage Is 'the Final Monument of the Confederacy.'" *The Guardian*, February 11, 2021. www.theguardian.com/us-news/2021/feb/11/catherine-flowers-environmental-justice-sewage-alabama.

Piperno, D. R., and K. V. Flannery. "The Earliest Archaeological Maize (*Zea mays* L.) from Highland Mexico: New Accelerator Mass Spectrometry Dates and Their Impli-cations." *Proceedings of the National Academy of Sciences* 98, no. 4 (2001): 2101–3.

Piperno, Dolores R. "The Origins of Plant Cultivation and Domestication in the New World Tropics." *Current Anthropology* 52, no. S4 (2011): S453–70.

Pohl, Mary, and Paul Bloom. "Prehistoric Maya Farming in the Wetlands of North-ern Belize: More Data from Albion Island and Beyond." In *The Managed Mosaic: Ancient Maya Agriculture and Resource Use*, edited by Scott L. Fedick, 145–64. Salt Lake City: University of Utah Press, 1996.

Povinelli, Elizabeth A. *Geontologies: A Requiem to Late Liberalism*. Durham, NC: Duke University Press, 2016.

Puleston, Dennis E. "The Role of Ramón in Maya Subsistence." In *Maya Subsist-ence: Studies in Memory of Dennis E. Puleston*, edited by Kent V. Flannery, 353–66. New York: Academic Press, 1982.

Pyburn, K. Anne. "Engaged Archaeology: Whose Community? Which Public?" In *New Perspectives in Global Public Archaeology*, edited by Katsuyuki Okamura and Akira Matsuda, 29–41. New York: Springer, 2011.

Querejeta, José Ignacio, Héctor Estrada-Medina, Michael F. Allen, Juan J. Jiménez-Osornio, and Rocío Ruenes. "Utilization of Bedrock Water by *Brosimum alicas-trum* Trees Growing on Shallow Soil atop Limestone in a Dry Tropical Climate." *Plant Soil* 287 (2006): 187–97.

Quezada, Sergio. *Maya Lords and Lordship: The Formation of Colonial Society in Yucatan, 1350–1600*. Translated by Terry Rugeley. Norman: University of Okla-homa Press, 2014.

Rayner, Jay. "Chef's Table Is Another Slice of 'Cool Culinary' Myth-Making." *The Guardian*, April 22, 2015. www.theguardian.com/tv-and-radio/tvandradioblog/2015/apr/22/chefs-table-cool-culinary-myth-making.

Redfield, Robert, and Alfonso Villa Rojas. *Chan Kom: A Maya Village*. Carnegie Institution of Washington, pub. 448. Washington DC: Carnegie Institution, 1934.

Redzepi, René, and Rosio Sanchez. "A Bar Menu to Support the Mundo Maya Foundation." *Noma: The Weather Report* (blog), May 1, 2017. https://noma.dk /the-weather-report/a-bar-menu-to-support-the-mundo-maya-foundation/.

———. "Mayan Producers." *Noma: The Weather Report* (blog), January 3, 2017. https://noma.dk/the-weather-report/mayan-producers/.

Reed, Nelson. *The Caste War of Yucatan.* Stanford, CA: Stanford University Press, 1964.

Rejón, Katia, and Óscar Rodríguez. "Ejidatarios, contra Kekén en Homún." *La Jornada Maya,* October 5, 2017. www.lajornadamaya.mx/yucatan/142258 /ejidatarios-contra-keken-en-homun.

Rejón Patrón, Lourdes. "La comunidad de Yaxuná." In *Proyecto INAH Yaxuná. Informe de la temporada 1998–1999.* Mérida: Archivo de la Sección de Arqueología, Instituto Nacional de Antropología e Historia, Centro Regional Yucatán, 1999.

Restall, Matthew. *The Black Middle: Africans, Mayas, and Spaniards in Colonial Yucatán.* Redwood City, CA: Stanford University Press, 2009.

———. *The Maya World: Yucatec Culture and Society, 1550–1850.* Stanford, CA: Stanford University Press, 1997.

Reyes Maturano, Ivet. "Yucatán ante un nuevo horizonte: Urgencia de conocimiento científico en el proceso local de la transición energética." *Desde el Herbario CICY* (Centro de Investigación Científica de Yucatán), A.C. 9 (2017): 118–25.

Richler, Jacob. "At $600 Each, This Meal Was Worth Every Cent." *Toronto Star,* May 18, 2017. www.thestar.com/life/2017/05/17/at-600-each-this-meal-was- worth-every-cent.html.

Rico-Gray, Victor, Jose G. Garcia-Franco, Alexandra Chemas, Armando Puch, and Paulino Sima. "Species Composition, Similarity, and Structure of Mayan Home- gardens in Tixpeual and Tixcacaltuyub, Yucatan, Mexico." *Economic Botany* 44, no. 4 (1990): 470–87.

Ringle, William M. "The Settlement Patterns of Komchen, Yucatan, Mexico." PhD diss., Tulane University, 1985.

Robin, Cynthia., ed. *Chan: An Ancient Maya Farming Community.* Gainesville: University Press of Florida, 2012.

Robin, Cynthia. *Everyday Life Matters: Maya Farmers at Chan.* Gainesville: University Press of Florida, 2013.

Robinson, Mark E., and Heather I. McKillop. "Ancient Maya Wood Selection and Forest Exploitation: A View from the Paynes Creek Salt Works, Belize." *Journal of Archaeological Science* 40, no. 10 (2013): 3584–95.

Romm, Cari. "What 'Food Porn' Does to the Brain." *The Atlantic,* April 20, 2015. www.theatlantic.com/health/archive/2015/04/what-food-porn-does-to-the- brain/390849/.

Rosales González, Margarita and Lourdes Rejón Patrón. "Las redes que tejen un pueblo: familias y parentelas en comunidades mayas del oriente y sur de Yucatán." In *Los mayas de ayer y hoy,* vol. 2, edited by Alfredo Barrera Rubio and Ruth Gubler, 1052–78. Mérida: Cultur, Conaculta-INAH, and Universidad Autónoma de Yucatán, 2006.

Rosenzweig, Melissa S., and John M. Marston. "Archaeologies of Empire and Environment." *Journal of Anthropological Archaeology*, 52 (2018): 87–102.

Roys, Ralph. *The Political Geography of the Yucatan Maya*. Washington DC: Carnegie Institution of Washington, 1957.

Roys, Ralph L. *The Book of Chilam Balam of Chumayel*. Washington, DC: Carnegie Institution of Washington, 1933.

———. *The Indian Background of Colonial Yucatan*. Norman: University of Oklahoma Press, 1972.

Roys, Ralph, France V. Scholes, and Eleanor B. Adams. "Census and Inspection of the Town of Pencuyut, Yucatan, in 1583 by Diego García de Palacio, Oidor of the Audiencia of Guatemala." *Ethnohistory* 6, no. 3 (1959): 195–225.

Rugeley, Terry. *Yucatán's Maya Peasantry and the Origins of the Caste War*. Austin: University of Texas Press, 1996.

Rulli, Maria Cristina, Antonio Saviori, and Paolo D'Odorico. "Global Land and Water Grabbing." *Proceedings of the National Academy of Sciences* 110, no. 3 (2013): 892–97.

Scarborough, Vernon L., Arlen F. Chase, and Diane Z. Chase. "Low-Density Urbanism, Sustainability, and IHOPE-Maya: Can the Past Provide More than History?" *UGEC Viewpoints* (Urbanization and Global Environmental Change international project) 8 (2012): 20–24.

Schulte, Peter, Laia Alegret, Ignacio Arenillas, José A. Arz, Penny J. Barton, Paul R. Bown, Timothy J. Bralower et al. "The Chicxulub Asteroid Impact and Mass Extinction at the Cretaceous-Paleogene Boundary." *Science* 327, no. 5970 (March 5, 2010): 1214–18.

Seligson, Kenneth, Tomás Gallareta Negrón, Rossana May Ciau, and George J. Bey. "Burnt Lime Production and the Pre-Columbian Maya Socio-Economy: A Case Study from the Northern Yucatán." *Journal of Anthropological Archaeology* 48 (2017): 281–94.

Sherman, Elizabeth. "Profits from Noma: Mexico's New Bar Menu Will Go to Charity." *Food & Wine Magazine*, May 24, 2017. www.foodandwine.com/news/profits-noma-mexicos-new-bar-menu-will-go-charity.

Sietsema, Tom. "A World-Class Chef Built a $600 Pop-up in the Mexican Jungle. It Might Be 'the Meal of the Decade.'" *Washington Post*, April 25, 2017. www.washingtonpost.com/lifestyle/food/a-world-class-chef-built-a-600-pop-up-in-the-mexican-jungle-it-might-be-the-meal-of-the-decade/2017/04/25/e3b75244–284e-11e7-a616-d7c8a68c1a66_story.html.

Silva, Lucas C. R., Rodrigo Studart Corrêa, Jamie L. Wright, Barbara Bomfim, Lauren Hendricks, Daniel G. Gavin, Aleksander Westphal Muniz et al. "A New Hypothesis for the Origin of Amazonian Dark Earths." *Nature Communications* 12, no. 1 (2021): 127.

Simpson, Leanne Betasamosake. "Land as Pedagogy: Nishnaabeg Intelligence and Rebellious Transformation." *Decolonization: Indigeneity, Education & Society* 3, no. 3 (2014): 1–25.

Sintumuang, Kevin. "Shelling Out $1,500—Plus Airfare—for the Most Memorable Date Night in Mexico." *Esquire*, May 19, 2017. www.esquire.com/food-drink/a55034 /noma-mexico-dinner-review/.

Slater, Donald A. "Into the Heart of the Turtle: Caves, Ritual, and Power in Ancient Central Yucatan, Mexico." PhD diss., Brandeis University, Waltham, MA, 2014.

Smith, Michael E. "Classic Maya Settlement Clusters as Urban Neighborhoods: A Comparative Perspective on Low-Density Urbanism." *Journal de la Société des Américanistes* 97, no. 1 (2011): 51–73.

Smyth, Michael P., Nicholas P. Dunning, Eric M. Weaver, Philip van Beynen, and David Ortegón Zapata. "The Perfect Storm: Climate Change and Ancient Maya Response in the Puuc Hills Region of Yucatan." *Antiquity* 91, no. 356 (2017): 490–509.

Spenser, Daniela. "Workers against Socialism? Reassessing the Role of Urban Labor in Yucatecan Revolutionary Politics." In *Land, Labor, and Capital in Modern Yucatán: Essays in Regional History and Political Economy*, edited by J. T. Brannon and Gilbert M. Joseph. Tuscaloosa: University of Alabama Press, 1991.

Stahl, A. B. "Assembling 'Effective Archaeologies' toward Equitable Futures." *American Anthropologist* 122, no. 1 (2020): 37–50.

Stanton, Travis W. "The Founding of Yaxuná: Place and Trade in Preclassic Yucatán." In *Early Maya E-Groups, Solar Calendars, and the Role of Astronomy in the Rise of Lowland Maya Urbanism*, edited by David A. Freidel, Arlen F. Chase, A. S. Dowd, and J. Murdock, 450–79. Gainesville: University of Florida Press, 2017.

Stanton, Travis W., and Traci Ardren. "The Middle Formative of Yucatan in Context: The View from Yaxuna." *Ancient Mesoamerica* 16 (2005): 213–28.

Stanton, Travis W., Traci Ardren, Nicolas C. Barth, Juan C. Fernandez-Diaz, Patrick Rohrer, Dominique Meyer, Stephanie J. Miller, Aline Magnoni, and Manuel Pérez. "'Structure' Density, Area, and Volume as Complementary Tools to Understand Maya Settlement: An Analysis of Lidar Data along the Great Road between Coba and Yaxuna." *Journal of Archaeological Science: Reports* 29 (2020): 102178.

Stanton, Travis W., and Ryan Collins. "The Role of Middle Preclassic Placemaking in the Creation of Late Preclassic Yucatecan Cities: The Foundations of Yaxuná." In *Early Mesoamerican Cities: Urbanism and Urbanization in the Formative Period*, edited by Michael Love and Julia Guernsey, 99–120. Cambridge: Cambridge University Press, 2022.

Stanton, Travis W., and David A. Freidel. "Placing the Centre: Centring the Place: The Influence of Formative Sacbeob in Classic Site Design at Yaxuná, Yucatán." *Cambridge Archaeological Journal* 15, no. 2 (2005): 225–49.

Stanton, Travis W., David A. Freidel, Charles K. Suhler, Traci Ardren, James Ambrosino, Justine M. Shaw, and Sharon Bennett. *Archaeological Investigations at Yaxuná, 1986–1996: Results of the Selz Foundation Yaxuná Project*. BAR International Series 2056. Oxford: Archaeopress, 2010.

Stanton, Travis W., Scott R. Hutson, and Aline Magnoni. "PIPCY (Proyecto de Interacción Política del Centro de Yucatán), primera temporada del campo:

Informe técnico anual al Consejo de Arqueología del Instituto Nacional de Antropología e Historia." Cholula: Universidad de las Américas Puebla, 2008.

Stanton, Travis W., and Aline Magnoni. "PIPCY (Proyecto de Interacción Política del Centro de Yucatán), tercera temporada de campo: Informe técnico anual al Consejo de Arqueología del Instituto Nacional de Antropología e Historia." Cholula: Universidad de las Américas Puebla, 2009.

Steffen, Will, Jacques Grinevald, Paul Crutzen, and John McNeill. "The Anthropocene: Conceptual and Historical Perspectives." *Philosophical Transactions of the Royal Society of London. Series A: Mathematical, Physical, and Engineering Sciences* 369, no. 1938 (2011): 842–67.

Stein, Joshua David. "Behind the Scenes at Noma Mexico." *GQ*, May 21, 2017. www.gq.com/story/photos-noma-mexico-behind-the-scenes.

Stephens, John Lloyd. *Incidents of Travel in Yucatán*, vol. 1. New York: Dover Publications, 1868.

Suhler, Charles. "Excavations at the North Acropolis, Yaxuna, Yucatan, Mexico." PhD diss., Southern Methodist University, 1996.

Swartley, L. "Inventing Indigenous Knowledge: Archaeology, Rural Development, and the Raised Field Rehabilitation Project in Bolivia." PhD diss., University of Pittsburgh, 2000.

Taylor, Dorceta E. "The Rise of the Environmental Justice Paradigm: Injustice Framing and the Social Construction of Environmental Discourses." *American Behavioral Scientist* 43, no. 4 (2000): 508–80.

Tedlock, Dennis. *Popol Vuh: The Mayan Book of the Dawn of Life*. New York: Simon & Schuster, 1996.

Terán, Silvia, and Christian Rasmussen. *La milpa de los mayas*. Mexico City: Universidad Nacional Autónoma de México, 2009.

Terán, Silvia, Christian Rasmussen, and Olivio May Cauich. *Las plantas de la milpa entre los mayas: Etnobotánica de las plantas cultivadas por campesinos mayas en las milpas del noreste de Yucatán, México*. Mérida: Fundación Tun Ben Kin, A.C., 1998.

Thompson, J. Eric S. *Maya History and Religion*. Norman: University of Oklahoma Press, 1970.

Thompson, Victor D. "Whispers on the Landscape." In *The Archaeology and Historical Ecology of Small Scale Economies*, edited by Victor D. Thompson and James C. Waggoner, 1–13. Gainesville: University Press of Florida, 2013.

Tiesler, Vera, Andrea Cucina, Travis W. Stanton, David A. Freidel, and Traci Ardren. *Before Kukulkán: Bioarchaeology of Maya Life, Death, and Identity at Classic Period Yaxuná*. Tucson: University of Arizona Press, 2017.

"Timul le 'invade' 1,500 Ha de terrenos al ejido de Ixil." *Diario de Yucatán*, October 7, 2019. www.yucatan.com.mx/yucatan/2019/10/7/timul-le-invade-1500-ha-de-terrenos-al-ejido-de-ixil-142507.html.

Torres-Mazuera, Gabriela. "Communal and Indigenous Landholding in Contemporary Yucatan: Tracing the Changing Property Relations in the Postrevolutionary Ejido." In *Beyond Alterity: Destabilizing the Indigenous Other in Mexico*, edited by Paula López Caballero and Ariadna Acevedo-Rodrigo, 151–70. Tucson: University of Arizona Press, 2018.

Torres Ochoa, César A. "La producción de artefactos de concha durante el formativo en Yaxuná, Yucatán." Licentiate thesis, Universidad de las Américas Puebla, Cholula, 2017.

Toscano Hernández, Lourdes, and David Ortegón Zapata. "Yaxuná: Un centro de acopio del tributo Itzá." *Los Investigadores de la Cultural Maya* (Universidad Autónoma de Campeche) 11 (2003): 438–45.

Toscano Hernández, Lourdes, Diana Trejo Torres, Luis Cabrera Pardes, and Gustavo Novelo Rincón. *Proyecto Yaxuná: Investigación y restauración arquitectónica en el grupo del juego de pelota, informe de la temporada 1997–1998.* Mérida: Instituto Nacional de Antropología e Historia, Centro INAH Yucatán, 1998.

Tourtellot, Gair. "Ancient Maya Settlements at Seibal, Peten, Guatemala: Peripheral Survey and Excavation." PhD diss., Harvard University, 1983.

Tozzer, Alfred M. *Landa's Relación de las cosas de Yucatán.* Papers of the Peabody Museum of American Archaeology and Ethnology, paper 18. Cambridge, MA: Harvard University, 1941.

Tsing, Anna Lowenhaupt. *The Mushroom at the End of the World: On the Possibility of Life in Capitalist Ruins.* Princeton, NJ: Princeton University Press, 2015.

Tuck, Eve, and Marcia McKenzie. *Place in Research: Theory, Methodology, and Methods.* New York: Routledge, 2014.

Tuck, Eve, and K. Wayne Yang. "Decolonization Is Not a Metaphor." *Decolonization: Indigeneity, Education & Society* 1, no. 1 (2012): 1–40.

Turner, B. L., and Peter D. Harrison, eds. *Pulltrouser Swamp: Ancient Maya Habitat, Agriculture, and Settlement in Northern Belize.* Austin: University of Texas Press, 1983.

Turner, B. L., and Jeremy A. Sabloff. "Classic Period Collapse of the Central Maya Lowlands: Insights about Human-Environment Relationships for Sustainability." *Proceedings of the National Academy of Sciences* 109, no. 35 (2012): 13908–14.

Twitty, Michael W. *The Cooking Gene: A Journey through African American Culinary History in the Old South.* New York: HarperCollins, 2017.

Tzec Valle, Gabino. "El Sendero Jurásico en Progreso, ¿un ex basurero?" *Diario de Yucatán*, May 15, 2022. www.yucatan.com.mx/yucatan/2022/5/15/el-sendero-jurasico-en-progreso-un-ex-basurero-320324.html.

Victoria, Jorge, Amarella Eastmond, and Aurelio Sánchez. "From Conquest to Jatropha: The Decline of Traditional Maya Life in the Village of Sucopo, Yucatán." In *The Quest for Jatropha Biodiesel and Sustainability in Yucatán*, edited by Amarella Eastmond, Julio C. Sacramento Rivero, and Sam R. Sweitz, 67–94. Mérida: Universidad Autónoma de Yucatán, 2018.

Villa Rojas, Alfonso. *The Maya of East Central Quintana Roo.* Washington, DC: Carnegie Institution of Washington, 1943.

———. *The Yaxuna-Coba Causeway.* Contributions to American Archaeology no. 9, Carnegie Institution of Washington, pub. 436. Washington, DC: Carnegie Institution of Washington, 1934.

Vliet, Nathalie van, Ole Mertz, Torben Birch-Thomsen, and Brigit Schmook, eds. "Swidden Agriculture." Special issue, *Human Ecology* 41, no. 1 (2013): 1–168.

Vogt, Evon V. *Tortillas for the Gods: A Symbolic Analysis of Zinacanteco Rituals.* Cambridge, MA: Harvard University Press, 1976.

Voyles, Traci Brynne. *Wastelanding: Legacies of Uranium Mining in Navajo Country.* Minneapolis: University of Minnesota Press, 2015.

Wade, Lizzie. "The Ghosts in the Museum." *Science* 373, no. 6551 (July 9, 2021): 148–52.

Wauchope, Robert. *Modern Maya Houses: A Study of Their Archaeological Significance.* Washington, DC: Carnegie Institution of Washington, 1938.

Webster, James W., George A. Brook, L. Bruce Railsback, Hai Cheng, R. Lawrence Edwards, Clark Alexander, and Philip P. Reeder. "Stalagmite Evidence from Belize Indicating Significant Droughts at the Time of Preclassic Abandonment, the Maya Hiatus, and the Classic Maya Collapse." *Palaeogeography, Palaeoclimatology, Palaeoecology* 250, no. 1 (2007): 1–17.

Weeber, Christine. "Why Capitalize 'Indigenous'?" *Sapiens*, May 19, 2020. www.sapiens.org/language/capitalize-indigenous/.

Wells, Allen. *Yucatán's Gilded Age: Haciendas, Henequen and International Harvester, 1860–1915.* Albuquerque: University of New Mexico Press, 1985.

Wells, E. Christian, and Lorena D. Mihok. "Ancient Maya Perceptions of Soil, Land, and Earth." In *Soil and Culture*, edited by Edward R. Landa and Christian Feller, 311–27. Dordrecht: Springer Netherlands, 2009.

Wells, Pete. "Why I'm Not Reviewing Noma Mexico." *New York Times*, May 23, 2017. www.nytimes.com/2017/05/23/dining/noma-tulum-pete-wells-mexico-rene-redzepi.html.

Whyte, Kyle Powys. "The Dakota Access Pipeline, Environmental Injustice, and US Colonialism." *Red Ink: An International Journal of Indigenous Literature, Arts & Humanities* 19, no. 1 (2017): 154–69.

———. "Indigenous Experience, Environmental Justice and Settler Colonialism." In *Nature and Experience: Phenomenology and the Environment*, edited by Bryan E. Bannon, 157–74. New York: Rowman & Littlefield, 2016.

———. "Is It Colonial Déjà Vu? Indigenous Peoples and Climate Injustice." In *Humanities for the Environment: Integrating Knowledges, Forging New Constellations of Practice*, edited by Joni Adamson and Michael Davis, 88–104. New York: Routledge, 2017.

Wildcat, Matthew, Mandee McDonald, Stephanie Irlbacher-Fox, and Glen Coulthard. "Learning from the Land: Indigenous Land Based Pedagogy and Decolonization." *Decolonization: Indigeneity, Education & Society* 3, no. 3 (2014): i–xv.

Wolford, Wendy. "The Plantationocene: A Lusotropical Contribution to the Theory." *Annals of the American Association of Geographers*, 111, no. 6 (2021), 1622–39.

World Commission on Environment and Development (WCED). *Our Common Future (The Brundtland Report).* Oxford: Oxford University Press for the United Nations, 1987.

Wyatt, Andrew R. "Gardens on Hills: Ancient Maya Terracing and Agricultural Production at Chan, Belize." PhD diss., University of Illinois at Chicago, 2008.

Wynter, Sylvia. "Novel and History, Plot and Plantation." *Savacou* 5 (1971): 95–102.

Yusoff, Kathryn. *A Billion Black Anthropocenes or None.* Minneapolis: University of Minnesota Press, 2019.

Zaro, Gregory, and Jon C. Lohse. "Agricultural Rhythms and Rituals: Ancient Maya Solar Observation in Hinterland Blue Creek, Northwestern Belize." *Latin American Antiquity* 16, no. 1 (2005): 81–98.

INDEX

Note: *f* indicates a figure and *m* indicates a map.

climate change, global, 3, 38, 51, 58, 72–73, 142, 208n14
climate change, historic periods of, 11, 24
Coba, 17, 21, 117, 136
Coca-Cola México, 34
cochinita pibil, 33, 42, 48
Cocom, Nachi, 140, 141, 142, 144, 165, 225n1
Cocom lineage, 144
Coke, 34, 62–63, 131, 174, 174f, 177, 178
collapse, societal, 138. See also Maya Collapse
collective management, 98
colonialism: celebrity chefs obscuring history of, 52; disrupting traditional ecological knowledge, 58; as driver of Anthropocene, 142; extraction at the core of, 3–4, 8; land relations of, 7–8; Maya homegardens before, 96; plantations and, 143; resistance to, 189; on Yucatán Peninsula, 141
colonial land reforms: agrarian, 158–59, 161–62, 163–64; impacts on milpa farmers of, 147–48, 150; neoliberal, 165; resistance to, 96, 133; tax lists and tributes, 146
colonization. See colonialism; decolonization
comal, 39, 42, 46, 186
community agency and engagement, 39–40
community need, lack of, 35
consent for projects, 180–81
consumer anxiety, 51. See also sustainability narratives
controlled burns, 14–15, 72, 73. See also burning in milpa agriculture
cooking, ancient, 108–9
cooking, for explorers, 166–67. See also Chi, Chaipa
cooking shows, 26, 39, 48–50. See also celebrity chefs
Coole Chepa Chi restaurant, 192–93. See also Chi, Chaipa
cooperation, community, 98
Copenhagen, Denmark, 26, 40, 41, 45–46, 52
corn, US-grown, 14, 34, 38, 39, 176

corncribs, 80, 81
corn syrup, 34
corporate branding, 3
Cozumel, 165
Cretaceous-Paleogene (K-Pg) mass extinction, 1, 7
culinary anthropology, 28
culinary experiences, 39–40
culinary tourism, 5, 12, 37, 39–40, 44–47, 48–51
cultural appropriation, 32
cultural identities, 29
Cupul province, 147

Dakota Access Pipeline (DAPL), 8
dating techniques, 218n3, 221n3, 222n9. See also ceramics; potsherds
Day of the Dead, 127
death, attitudes about, 127
debt, 149, 163–64
debt peonage, 149, 158, 169
deception, 51–52, 181–82
decolonization, 65, 209n37
deer, 69, 186, 187f
deforestation, 137, 179–80, 184
de Landa, Diego, 55, 225n1
Detroit, Michigan, 23
development initiatives, 36
Díaz, Porfirio, 156–58
diet, vegetarian, 126
dining prices: at Coole Chepa Chi, 192 (See also culinary tourism); at Noma Mexico in dollars, 15, 27, 41, 44, 45, 51, 52; at Noma Mexico in pesos, 185–86
dinosaurs, extinction of, 1
dirt floors, 120–21
diseases, 147
diversification, 138
documentary series, 49–50
doña Laura, 80
doña Noemí, 80
don Crisanto, 80, 81, 82
don José, 80
don Mateo, 80, 81, 82, 92
don Nazario, 124
don Sebastián, 124, 127
don Tomás, 73–74, 80, 82

droughts: adaptations for, 114, 115, 116; moving as a result of, 135–36, 139; rituals for, 55, 59

Dzibilchaltun archaeological site, 188

dzonot, 66

earthen floors, 120–21

eating, cultures of, 170–74, 174f, 175f, 186

ecolodges, 35–36, 113

Ecological Indian (Krech), 208n9

ecological intimacy, 54, 70, 71, 88, 100, 108

ecological knowledge, 100–101

ecological relationships, 13, 57–60, 94–95

ecological restoration, 143

economic crisis, 163

ecotourism, 16, 18, 35–37, 54

edge lands: author's work in, 172–76; as deracinated from history, 184; flexibility of, 138, 144; future determined by ejidatarios, 185; getting to know through walking, 169–70; mobility of, 138–39; securing, 162–63; tension around, 153; Tzacauil in, 117–18, 129–30, 133–35; useless land narratives for, 177–78. *See also* Tzacauil; useless land narrative; Yaxunah ejido

efficiency, 169, 171, 172, 177

E Group, 218n7

ejidatarias, 63

ejidatarios, 62, 158–59, 162, 164, 180, 183–85

ejidos: Chablekal, 188; changing perspectives on, 175–76, 185; defining boundaries of, 150; formation of system, 158–59; introduction of term, 5; at Ixil, 181, 182; near San José Tipceh, 180; selling of, 13–14, 61, 164, 183

ejido system, 158–59, 162, 163, 164

El Manantial water source, 20, 162, 211n84

Energy Transfer Partners, 8

environmental anxiety, 51

environmental change, 142–43

environmental degradation, 208n9

environmental education, 38

environmental justice: archaeology working toward, 170; conflicts, 4–5, 9, 58, 59, 169; food security as, 34; movement, 7; Plantationocene and, 143

environmental racism, 7, 8

Erickson, Clark, 75–76

Escoffié Gamboa, Alejandro, 181, 182

ethnography of Chan Kom house, 104–5

excavations: author experiences with, 172–73, 190–91; of Chamal Group, 101–3, 104f; descriptions of, 223n12, 223n13; of graves, 124–26; between homesites, 220n24; at Jaltun Group, 130–31; of pottery, 82–83, 87, 88, 108, 121, 132, 221n3, 221n53; trench, 105–6; of Tzacauil homesites, 108, 174f, 175f

exclusion from decision-making, 9

experiments on 60x trees, 114–15

experiments on raised fields, 75–76

extinction events, 1, 7

extraction. *See* land relations, extractive

Facebook, 182. *See also* social media

factory farms, 143, 178. *See also under* agriculture, industrial

family routes, 149–50

farmer-forest relationships, 19–21, 39, 54–61, 65, 66–69, 84–86, 149. *See also* milpa

farmer mobility, 145, 146, 149

farmers as political agents, 139

farming, ancient, 10–11, 75–77

farming, reasons for leaving, 81–82

farming, resilience in, 137

farming, transition to, 89

Farriss, Nancy, 132–33, 189

fiber, 157

field camps: artifacts stored at, 113; food at, 48, 170–74, 174f, 175f, 186; hiring at, 62; at old ecolodge, 35, 36

field huts, 133–35

flexibility, 135, 138

Flowers, Catherine Coleman, 8

food: demand for, 147; porn, 48–49; prices, 8, 185; security, 34, 177; sovereignty, 34, 38, 177; systems, 10, 176–77; television, 48–50

foodies, 47

Food Network, 39

forager-farmers, 84, 86, 87, 218n7

foragers and foraging, 86–88, 109, 112, 187

forests: access to, 139; as active in history, 21; cut for industrial farming, 178–80;

deforestation, 137, 184; foraging from, 187; harvesting from, 162; mimicked in homegardens, 94–95; as a multispecies world, 60–61; in northern Yucatán, 68; as sites of refuge, 147, 149, 156, 160–61; species of, 69; succession, 55, 72; as useless land, 149; walking in, 55. *See also* farmer-forest relationships; useless land narrative

Formative period, 111, 126, 218*n*7

fossils, 9–10, 51

Franciscan friars, 146

frogs, 69

Frontera restaurant, 31

Fundación Cultural Yucatán (FCY), 34

Fundación Haciendas del Mundo Maya (FHMM): celebrity chefs and, 12, 41–42, 46; formation of, 36; partnership with Hokol Vuh festival, 52; partnership with Lool K'uum Collective, 37, 39; Sustainable Milpa Project of, 14, 73

Gálvez, Alyshia, 34, 177

garbage dump, 1–2

García, Fernando Ponce, 34

geological history, 66–68, 107

geontopower, 59

Glissant, Édouard, 143

Global Clean Energy Holdings, 183–84

globalization, 51

global sustainable development, 34

Gordinier, Jeff, 41–43, 52

GQ magazine, 45

grackles, 69

graves, 124–27, 125*f*, 136, 168–69, 192

green energy projects, 178–84

green grabs, 9

Greenland, 138

Green Revolution, 163

green washing, 10–11, 27, 209*n*39

groundwater, 115, 211*n*84

Grupo Kekén, 188

Hacienda Cetelac, 147, 152, 152*f*, 156, 161, 226*n*17

haciendas: Chaipa Chi as worker at, 167; for henequen, 158; Maya enslaved on, 52,

148–49, 151–52; reforms of, 159–60; restoration of, 36

Hanal Pixan, 127

Haraway, Donna, 142–43

heirloom caches, 109, 126

henequen, 4, 52, 148, 157–58, 160

Hernández, Roberto, 36

Hija de Sanchez, 41

Hiša Franko restaurant, 47

history: of agricultural practices, 11; culinary tourism removing, 15–16; of farm-forest land use, 19–20, 54–61, 65, 66–69, 84–86, 149; restoring to land, 25, 54–55, 60, 64–65; of rooting to land, 90, 100–101; of superfoods, 10; of useless lands, 4–5; written of Xiu lineage, 140–41; of Yaxunah, 16

Hokol Vuh festival, 46, 47, 210*n*54

Hol Box, 53

homegardens, 94–96, 95*f*, 100

homesites, 84, 89–91, 95–101, 102*f*, 110, 111–12, 122. *See also* Tzacauil

Homún village, 188

household growth, 103–5

Hungry: Eating, Road-Tripping, and Risking It All with the Greatest Chef in the World (Gordinier), 41–43, 44, 210*n*56

Hurricane Isidore, 36

I-Collective, 10

illegal dumping, 7

Imán, Santiago, 154

imperialism, 8

Inca Empire, 75

Indigenous identity, 207*n*4

Indigenous land tenure. *See* land tenure

Indigenous Maya as laborers, 148

Indigenous Maya communities, 2–3

Indigenous resistance: evidence of, 147, 151; forms of, 188–90; uprising, 154, 155, 169

inequality, social, 108–9, 110, 111, 147, 158

influencer culture, 47, 50–51

infrastructure, centralized, 11

infrastructure, community, 36, 38

inheritance of land, 100

Instagram, 46, 47, 214*n*62

interchangeability of capitalism, 176. *See also* capitalism

International Harvester Corporation, 157
International Maize and Wheat Improvement Center. *See* Centro Internacional de Mejoramiento de Maíz y Trigo (CIMMYT)
International Monetary Fund, 163
internet, 39. *See also* social media
invasions, 136–37
invented indigenous knowledge, 78
Ixil, 181, 182, 183
Ixil ejido, 181, 182
Izamal, 34

Jach Group, 83–84, 86–88, 91, 109, 110, 219*n*22
Jaltun Group, 130–31, 133–34, 135
jatropha, 184
Jo' Resistance and Rebellion Network, 182
Joya Rejollada, 161, 162
Jurassic Trail theme park, 1

Kaan Group: ceramic data for, 223*n*18; changes to homesite of, 123–24; founding of, 122; grave at, 127; homesite excavation of, 118, 125*f*; homesite of, 91–93, 110; nonlocal goods at, 139; as second wave homesite, 134; story of forgetting in homesite of, 123; time period of, 219*n*23; using bedrock outcrop, 120
kancabales, 70*f*, 71, 102*f*, 122, 130
Kancabdzonot, 48
kancab soil, 71, 91, 107. *See also* soils
karst rock, 107
Kimmerer, Robin Wall, 58
Kinch, David, 12
King Charles III of Spain, 148
kitchens, 120–21
Kolata, Alan, 76

labor, forced, 148, 169, 189. *See also* haciendas
laborers, 152
Lady K'awiil Ajaw, 117, 136
laja, 115
Lake Titicaca, 75, 78
land access, 13, 15, 57, 72, 139
land-based pedagogies, 65

land claims, 162
land conversion, 4
land deals, 179–80
land dispossession, 65
land disputes, 153
land grabbing, 8–9, 13, 61, 157, 178, 209*n*31
land grants, 154
landholdings, 100, 150
land narratives, 27–28
land precarity, 13–14
landrace maize, 12, 14, 34, 38–40, 42–43, 46*f*, 210*n*57
land relations: changes in, 139; gaps in understanding between Yucatecos and Maya, 150; green grabs reproducing colonial, 9; of hinterland farmers, 137–38; reconnecting as decolonizing, 65; revealed in tax lists, 146; tensions in, 2–3, 21
land relations, extractive: archaeology with roots in, 59, 170; disenfranchising Maya people, 154; effects of, 210*n*53; efficiency and productivity and, 169; fixed nature of, 149; food cultures and, 171; free trade agreements and, 34; history of land and, 21; industrial food as outcome of, 178; introduction to concept, 3–4; land grabbing as example of, 8; restoration of, 143; as static, 145; sustainable development programs and, 52, 79
land relations, mutual: building through walking the land, 82; as confusing to colonial cartographers, 150; as culturally transmitted, 208*n*9; deep histories of, 190; described in *Braiding Sweetgrass* (Kimmerer), 208*n*11; drawing lines on maps and, 149; flexible, 116; foragers building, 88–89; introduction to concept, 3; milpa agriculture as an example of, 13, 54, 55; misunderstood by Alvarado, 159; as mobile, 145; undermining, 28; uprooting, 142
land sovereignty, 15, 57, 58, 139, 153, 170, 179
land tenure, 100, 147–50, 157, 165, 177–78, 189
language, 58, 71, 213*n*36
Late Classic period, 116, 117–18, 119*f*, 120, 122–23, 222*n*9

Late Formative period: ceramic dating for, 219n22, 219n23; Chamal Group in, 101; evidence for, 222n11; Jach Group in, 84, 86, 88–89; Kaan Group in, 92–93, 123; nature reclaiming after, 116–17; pit kiln dug during, 120; at Tzacauil, 121; Yaxuná in, 129

laws for grave sites, 127

leaf litter, 74

learning about land relations, 3–4. *See also* land relations

legal personhood, 59

Liboiron, Max, 7

libraries, 36

lidar maps, 19*f*, 64, 79–80, 97

Life and Nonlife, 59

limestone, 102

lines on maps as power, 141, 149–51, 165, 169

living fossils, 9–10

Lool K'uum (Squash Blossom) collective, 37, 39, 40, 42–43, 44–45, 47, 48

López Constante, José Tiburcio, 150

Lorr, Benjamin, 51

Lummi Island, 51

luneros, 148

maize, 14, 80, 81, 89, 128–29, 146. *See also* corn, US-grown; landrace maize

maize, landrace. *See* landrace maize

Maní, 141

mano tool, 128, 129

manteca, 174

Māori people, 59

maps, 6*m,* 19*m,* 64, 79–80, 85*m,* 119*m,* 141

marketing, 39

Martínez, Virgilio, 12, 47, 49

masa, 40

Maya archaeological sites, 93–94

Maya army, 154

Maya Collapse, 135–36, 137, 138, 224n45

Maya conquest, 144–45

Maya creation story, 55

Maya history, 144

Maya identity, 207n4

Maya interlocutors, 144

Maya Mundo Foundation, 52, 79

Mayapan, 144, 147

Maya people, 96, 133

Maya prophecies, 147

Maya Social War, 16, 154–56, 157, 160, 169, 188–89

Maya Society under Colonial Rule (Farriss), 132–33

Maya state-level governance, 97

Maya urban agriculture, 93–94

McKenzie, Marcia, 9

McKinsey & Co, 36

McKittrick, Katherine, 143

men, 62

Mérida, Mexico, 2, 12, 23, 41, 153–54, 158, 189

metates, 128–29

Mexican Constitution, 158, 160, 164

Mexican cuisine, 28, 32

Mexican Empire, 153, 155

Mexican Revolution, 61, 156–57, 158

Mexico, 156–57, 163

Mexico: One Plate at a Time (MOPAT), 30, 31, 32–33, 53

Mexico REDD+ Alliance, 14

Michigan, 22

Middle Formative period, 84, 86, 87, 88, 109

milpa: alternative names for, 215n3; associated with men, 215n2; during colonial era, 132–33; emergence of, 135; as flexible and sustainable, 138; introduction to, 13; made at Tzacauil, 130; modern example of, 20*f*; practicing before and during Spanish conquest, 145; practicing on Yaxunah ejido, 162; as relationships, 60; at risk due to land reform, 157; shift to, 116; as sustainable, 57, 58–59; as universe in microcosm, 56–57; viewed as inefficient by Yucateco class, 148

milpa cycle: as an ecological relationship, 13; animal life cycles and, 69; changing familial claims within, 149–50; described, 54–57; field huts for, 133; land clearing and burning in, 54–55, 56*f*, 133; during Maya Social War, 155; misunderstood by Sustainable Milpa Project, 38; misunderstood by Yucatecos, 150–51; read in Tzacauil archaeological site, 133–34

Pisté, 35
pit kilns, 120
Plantationocene, 142–43, 163, 165
plantations, 142–43
plastic pollution, 7
Pleistocene era, 66
pocket gophers, 69
political upheaval, 116, 126, 136–37,
    138, 140
polychlorinated biphenyls (PCBs), 7
Pool Group, 118–20, 121, 128, 129, 134, 139,
    222n9
Poot, Ignacio, 160, 161
Poot, José, 161
Poot, Rafael, 160, 161
Popolá, 138
Popol Vuh, 55
pop-up restaurants, 26–27, 40, 41, 44
Porfiriato, 156, 157
pork, 33, 42, 45f
pork tacos, 45f
potato cropping, 75–76, 77–78
potlucks, 173
potsherds (more), 109, 121, 221n53, 223n18;
    at Jaltun and T'uup sites, 132
pottery excavation, 82–83, 87, 88, 108, 121,
    132, 221n3, 221n53. *See also* ceramics;
    excavations; potsherds
Povinelli, Elizabeth A., 59
pozole, 174–75, 218n2
privatization of land: Article 27 of Mexican
    Constitution and, 164; during Bourbon
    reforms, 148–49; for industrial food
    production, 178; now possible for ejido
    lands, 13–14, 19–20, 54, 60–61, 79, 177;
    during Porfiriato, 157; rejection of, 159;
    requiring lines on maps, 150; in secret,
    181. *See also* land grabbing
productivity, 169, 177
property division, 97, 98
protests, 188
provisional guests, 59
Proyecto de Interacción Política del Centro
    de Yucatán (PIPCY), 211n76, 216n35
public health, 34, 38
Puglisi, Christian Franceso, 12
pumpkin, 44f, 45
Puuc hills region, 136, 166

quail, 69
Quechua language, 77
Quintana Roo, 21, 53, 117, 155, 189

rabbits, 69
racism, 32, 142, 143
raised fields, 75–78
reciprocity in land relations, 3, 13, 56, 58–59,
    187. *See also* land relations, mutual
Redzepi, René, 12, 15, 26, 40–44, 49, 52–53.
    See also celebrity chefs
Registro Agrario Nacional, 162, 182
rejolladas, 66, 67f, 151, 161
relationships, ecological, 13, 57–60, 94–95
research, shifts in, 23, 24
resistance, passive, 189
Restall, Matthew, 145
restaurants: Apoala, 29–30, 31–32; of celeb-
    rity chefs, 47, 52; Coole Chepa Chi,
    192–93; Néctar, 46; Noma, 52–53; Noma
    Mexico, 44–45, 48, 185; owned by Rick
    Bayless, 30, 40–42; pop-up, 26–27
Río Bec, 97–98
rituals, 55–59, 83, 86, 98, 144
Rizzo, Helena, 12
roads, 35, 117–18
roca madre, 66. *See also* bedrock
Rockefeller family, 38
rock piles, 79–81, 105
Romania, 170
rope, 157
Roš, Ana, 12, 47, 49
royal rulers, 126, 136, 138–39, 224n39
rumbo familiar, 149–50

Sáastun Group, 91, 92, 219n23
Sacbe 1, 21, 117–18, 136, 160
sacbes, 21
Sanchez, Rosio, 12, 41, 43, 48
San José Tipceh, 180–81
Santana, Dámaso, 151
sascab, 67–68, 115
sascabera, 113
scrip payment, 149
seeds, 183
seed saving, 38
Selz Foundation Yaxuná Archaeological
    Project, 211n75, 211n77

wild turkeys, 69
Willows Inn, 47, 51
wind farms, 181–82
wind turbines, 2, 2f, 181–82
women, 23, 33, 36–37, 62, 63, 96, 166–67, 185
woodpeckers, 69
worldviews, 58
Wynter, Sylvia, 143

Xauil Cenote, 162, 211n84
Xauil water source, 20
xíimbal k'áax (walking in the woods), 63f,
65, 69, 79, 82, 91, 101, 106–7. *See also*
survey, walking
Xiu lineage, 140, 141, 144, 225n1
Xkanhá, 136
Xunantunich, 98
xux ek', 186

Yam, Ortiz, 149
Yang, K. Wayne, 209n37
Yaxcabá, 162
Yaxuná (ancient settlement): archaeological
site, 17–18, 18f, 20f, 21, 50, 122; connected to Coba by Sacbe 1, 117; differences from Tzacauil site, 127–28, 129–
30; early farming homesites of, 89–90;
living in ruins of, 161; political reach of,
111; as a population center, 136; population peaking, 124–25, 128, 136; royal
palace built at, 224n39; soils of, 71; style
of central plaza, 218n7; takeover and
abandonment of, 136–37; Tzacauil on
edge of, 86; urban abandonment of, 144
Yaxunah (colonial town), 152–53, 156, 161,
226n17
Yaxunah (Indigenous Yucatex Maya community): celebrity chefs in, 5, 12; community members at excavation sites,
104f, 171–72; conversations of farmers,
82; cooks, 33, 42, 46f; edge lands of, 54;
homegarden in, 95f; landrace maize

seed saving in, 38–39; map of, 6m;
members working for archaeologists, 17;
relationship-building in, 23; social
media and, 47; story of founding,
160–63, 227n63; sustainable development project at, 34–35; as a tourist
destination, 37; town hall meetings in,
62–63
Yaxunah ejido: absent from early colonial
records, 146–47; bedrock patterns of,
70f; containing Hacienda Cetelac
remains, 226n17; date of establishment,
61; eastern, 71, 81, 91; edge as start of
milpa, 116, 130; edge lands of, 15–16;
formation of, 160, 162; geology of, 70,
70f; homesites at eastern edge of, 101;
introduction to, 5, 13; map of, 6m;
as part of east-west buffer, 156;
resisting sale of, 184–85; returning
artifacts to, 113; Tzacauil archaeological
site at edge of, 86; walking survey of,
63f
Yucatán Peninsula: as an independent
republic, 28–29, 154; arrival of maize in,
87; cultural identities of, 29; gastronomic festivals in, 46–47; geologic
history of, 1; governors of, 159; political
status of at Spanish colonization, 144–
45; population demographics of, 153–54;
population increases, 147; tourism in, 4;
unified before Spanish colonization,
144; Xiu and Spaniards conquer, 141;
Yaxuná as ancient capital of, 17; as a
young land, 66
Yucatecan cuisine, 28, 29, 32, 185
Yucatec Maya language, 48, 58, 63, 71
Yucateco landowners, 147, 148, 153, 155, 160,
213n10

Zapatista Army of National Liberation
(EZLN), 188
Zea mays, 14. *See also* maize

www.ingramcontent.com/pod-product-compliance
Lightning Source LLC
Chambersburg PA
CBHW020843270326
41928CB00006B/530